The Forex Options Course

The Forex Options Course

*A Self-Study Guide to
Trading Currency Options*

ABE COFNAS

WILEY

John Wiley & Sons, Inc.

Library of Congress Cataloging-in-Publication Data:
Cofnas, Abe, 1950-
    The Forex options course : a self-study guide to trading currency options / Abe Cofnas.
        p. cm. – (Wiley trading series)
    Includes index.
    ISBN 978-0-470-24374-9 (pbk.)
    1. Foreign exchange options.   2. Foreign exchange market. 3. Options (Finance)   I. Title.
    HG3853.C638   2009
    332.4′5–dc22

                                                                2008018570

10   9   8   7   6   5   4   3   2   1

Contents

Preface

This book is designed to help forex traders build upon their knowledge and skills in trading forex and apply it to forex option strategies.

There are important differences between spot forex and options trading. In contrast to the spot forex trader, the options trader puts on trades "anticipating" a move over a longer duration of time. Whereas the spot forex trader concentrates on trades to achieve profits intraday and even intrahour, the option trader is liberated from the slavery of the screen and can set and let fundamental and market forces generate the intended profits. Position trading strategies become an important part of the repertoire of the forex option trader.

Forex option trading also is accompanied by an entirely different mind-set from spot trading. While neither one can claim superiority over the other, there are significant consequences to pursuing a forex option mind-set. The differences between the forex spot and option trading perspectives generate different strategies and goals and also a different need for information. For example, the spot trader often seeks frequent small moves and focuses on intraday and intrahour charts, avoiding the need for constantly absorbing information on fundamentals and the big picture. In contrast, the forex option trader's decision to put on a trade is a result of a more intense evaluative process where the trade fits optimal conditions, since forex option trading is less frequent than spot trading. Forex option trading requires more experience evaluating broad market conditions and top-down analysis, while forex spot trading requires greater focus on trading itself with precision management of moment-to-moment trading.

The presence of high leverage exists in both spot forex and options on forex trading. However, the main difference is that many of the forex option techniques explored in this book provide high leverage without the associated risks of margin calls.

This book is different from the option literature that is available—a great deal on the Internet—because it places the concepts of option trading in a strict forex environment with examples to guide the reader. The book is also designed to prepare the forex trader for new option variations and intermarket choices for shaping and putting on forex options. Those individuals who are familiar with equity option or futures option trading will find the application of basic option principles to be straightforward. But it should be clear that in the coming years forex trading is going to occur in many venues. The rise of exchange-traded funds (ETFs) provides a rich new source of data on forex option price action. Those traders having equity platforms can immediately trade forex options through their equity accounts because of the increasing availability of currency instruments such as those currency options provided at The International Securities Exchange (ISE) and Philadelphia Stock Exchange (PHLX) .

It's also important to note that those forex traders staying in the spot side can use the access through equity accounts to analyze patterns relating to currencies and commodities. The forex option trader will improve the odds of winning by tapping into more than one market for information. The ETFs will certainly become a tool for trading. The futures markets are also improving their forex option product line. The CME's forex product line is expanding and offering new trading opportunities in options. The Chicago Board of Trade's (CBOT's) options on federal fund futures and the more recent binary options on federal funds provides unprecedented opportunities for forex traders to gain market knowledge about the probabilities of Federal Open Market Committee (FOMC) moves—without needing to trade those instruments. But this book is also designed to prepare the forex trader for these and even newer variations in forex options that are coming to the market. Binary options allowing traders to play touch, no-touch, double-touch, and double-no-touch are becoming available worldwide and in the United States. These binary options will revolutionize the ability of people to trade forex with limited risk.

For the serious forex trader, considering forex options and becoming skilled in forex options analysis is advisable because it is increasingly apparent that the world is, more than ever, interconnected. Many of us have heard the phrase, "No man is an island." Today, we can state that no market is isolated. Equity, commodity, and debt markets cannot be totally separated. They all tap into each other and generate a global liquidity market that fuels buying and selling. Today's trader in any of these realizes that currency price movements reflect more than a determination of the value of the dollar versus another pair. The forex market reflects the totality of market psychology versus the prospects of growth versus inflation.

The goal of this book is to provide a "get started" manual for understanding and trading forex options, from the basic plain vanilla calls and puts to the intriguing first-generation exotic binary options. Our goal is to provide the reader access to the right information to make the most well-informed decision. The challenge of trading forex is among the most exciting of all the markets, and this book is designed to help the trader meet those challenges.

Acknowledgments

This book became a reality because of the contribution of many people. Foremost are my students in forex who enabled me to evolve a deeper understanding of forex trading and in particular the potential benefits of understanding forex option trading. In the writing of this book, superderivatives.com deserves special recognition. Their advanced analytics engine was made available to me for the purpose of writing this book and it offered a rare opportunity to present dimensions of analysis that is usually attributable to institutional research. Udi Sela deserves acknowledgement for providing professional forex option trading insight and expertise to ensure that the strategies and tactics described had validity. The strategies and tactics however, reflect the author's judgment only. My student and colleague Reynolds Lee deserves recognition for generating a great deal of the charting in the book. His expertise in visual numerics is world-class.

Lastly my wife, Paula, needs to be acknowledged for providing an environment conducive to the work required to complete the manuscript.

About the Author

A be Cofnas has been the forex trading columnist of *Futures* magazine since 2001 and has written over 10 columns. He has been a leader in designing and delivering forex training courses. He has conducted seminars in the United States, London, and Dubai as well as online training in all time zones. Mr. Cofnas founded www.learn4x.com in 2001 as the desktop forex trading industry started to provide education and training in this field and has been a consultant designing forex education and training material to many firms. He has since developed forex coaching with advanced performance analytics. He is head forex coach at secretsoftraders.com. Recently he founded fxdimensions.com, a forex proprietary trading team, and is the founder of www.currencygames.com, a forex trading game company. He has been in the financial service industry as an equity broker, futures, and forex trader since 1990.

Mr. Cofnas holds two master's degrees, in political science from the Graduate School of Political Science, University of California, and in public policy from the University of California, Graduate School of Public Policy. He currently lives in Longwood, Florida, with his wife, Paula, where he conducts research on artificial intelligence programs using cellular automata and enjoys digital photography. He has a daughter, Paige, and a son, Paul.

The Forex
Options Course

Key Option Elements

The objective of Part One is to provide a knowledge base for learning about the key elements of forex options. This includes a description of plain vanilla options and how option premiums are impacted by volatility. To prepare the forex trader for shaping option trades, Part One also provides a detailed outline on the basic elements of "the Greeks," which are the components that provide insight on how forex option prices change with time and volatility.

CHAPTER 1

The Elements of an Option Trade

PLAIN VANILLA OPTIONS

This chapter provides a review of the key elements that comprise an option trade. The simplest form of option trading is called plain vanilla. Plain vanilla options in all markets include calls and puts and are exactly the same as in forex trading.

PURCHASING AN OPTION

First, let's talk about purchasing an option. Purchasing an option means holding an option. A trader purchases an option by paying a premium for it.

Calls

Once a trader has purchased (gone long) and is holding a call, he has the right but not the obligation to buy the underlying spot forex upon expiration. If it's a European-style option, exercising rights are on expiration and not before. If it's an American-style option, exercising rights are any time up to and including expiration.

   The key concept is that a buyer of a call anticipates an upward move or is bullish. The trader selects a target called a strike price. If the price of the spot forex moves through and beyond the strike price, the position will be in profits. If the spot price is beyond the strike price at the time of expiration, the position is known as "in the money." We can see in the profit payout graph (see Figure 1.1) that a call option becomes profitable once

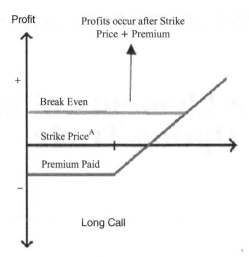

FIGURE 1.1 Currency Call Option Example

the price is beyond the strike price and beyond the cost of the position. This is a generic example for any call.

Let's begin to examine the elements of an option trade by looking at the following example involving the EURUSD.

After scanning the weekly chart of the EURUSD, a trader is anticipating a stronger EUR against the dollar and has selected a 1.47 strike price for a February 14 expiration. The premium charged for this is calculated to be $790 USD. Notice that the EURUSD spot position is at 1.4419. To be clear, the example as shown in Figures 1.2 and 1.3 would mean the trader expects the EURUSD to move to and beyond 1.47 by the expiration date. Actually, to be profitable if held to expiration, the spot position needs to be 79 pips beyond that, or 1.4779 to recover the costs of the premium since each pip is worth $10. But the most that the trader would lose is the premium paid and any associated other fees (source of the premium price example: www.ikongm.com).

Puts

Once a trader has purchased (gone long) and is holding a put, he has the right but not the obligation to buy the underlying spot forex upon expiration. If it's a European-style option, exercising rights are on expiration and not before. If it's an American-style option, exercising rights are any time up to and including expiration.

What is important about purchasing an option is the element of risk control. Once an option is purchased and the premium is paid (along with any other fees), this total cost is the maximum risk facing the trader. No matter what happens to the price action, the *most* the trader can lose is the cost of the premium paid.

The key concept is that a buyer of a put anticipates a downward move or is bearish. The trader selects a target called a strike price. If the price of the spot forex moves

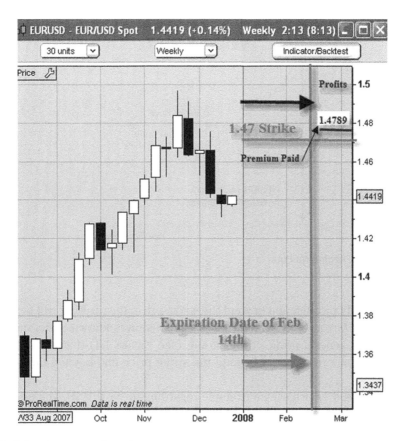

FIGURE 1.2 Placing a Call on the EURUSD
Source: © ProRealTime.com, web-based charting software

Hypothetical Option Chain Data

Call Options			
Strike	Bid	Ask	Delta
1.4300	0.0251	0.0261	0.6090
1.4350	0.0221	0.0231	0.5680
1.4400	0.0192	0.0202	0.5255
1.4450	0.0168	0.0178	0.4823
1.4500	0.0147	0.0157	0.4398
1.4550	0.0127	0.0137	0.3983
1.4600	0.0109	0.0119	0.3584
1.4650	0.0093	0.0103	0.3202
1.4700	0.0079	0.0089	0.2843
1.4750	0.0066	0.0076	0.2507
1.4800	0.0055	0.0065	0.2195
1.4850	0.0046	0.0056	0.1910

Currency Pair: **EUR/USD**

Expiration Date: **2/14/2008**

Market Price: **1.4418**

Option Premium
Ask Price: **$790**

FIGURE 1.3 Trader Expects EURUSD to Move Beyond 1.47

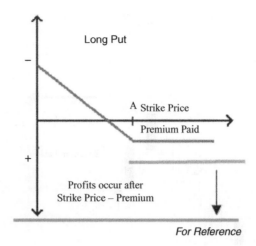

FIGURE 1.4 Profit Region on Puts

toward, and possibly through and beyond the strike price, the position will be in profits. If the spot price is beyond the strike price at the position is known as "in the money." We can see in the generic profit payout graph (see Figure 1.4) that a put option becomes profitable once the price is beyond the strike price and beyond the cost of the position.

In Figures 1.5 and 1.6 we see an example regarding the GBPUSD. The market price is at 1.9816. The strike price selected is at 1.9400. The expiration date is February 14. The cost of a put is $1290. The trader placing this put will pay in pip terms 129 pips if trading a standard lot of 100,000. This means that the break-even point will be 1.9400–0.0129, or 1.9271 if the trade is allowed to go to expiration. It is possible that the premium price could move up in value if volatility in the market increased and the GBPUSD fell quickly and early toward the strike point (source of premium price examples: www.ikongm.com).

The trader needs to always remember that time itself is important. The longer the time to expiration, the greater the risk that the strategy can go wrong and a new event will interfere and change the price direction. However, more time can allow the trade to work out and overcome periods where the price movements go against the trader. Time is a double-edged sword for the forex option trader.

Figure 1.7 shows an example of a put option on the EURUSD. The trader expects a fall in the EURUSD and has selected 1.46 for the strike price. The amount of the premium charged is estimated to be $580. Remember this is 200 pips away from the spot price which is at 1.4829 (see Figure 1.8).

Compare the premium price of this put to the call that was at 150 or 180 pips away, which was at 763. In other words, the market expected the move to be up because the price of an option almost the same distance was much higher for the call.

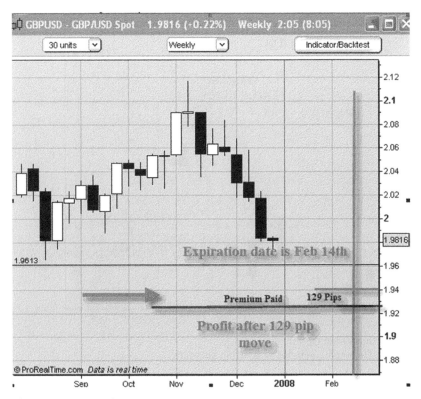

FIGURE 1.5 Profit Range for Put on GBPUSD
Source: © ProRealTime.com, web-based charting software

Hypothetical Option Chain Data

Put Options			
Strike	**Bid**	**Ask**	**Delta**
1.9300	0.0104	0.0114	-0.2451
1.9350	0.0116	0.0126	-0.2670
1.9400	0.0129	0.0139	-0.2901
1.9450	0.0143	0.0153	-0.3143
1.9500	0.0159	0.0169	-0.3396
1.9550	0.0175	0.0185	-0.3658
1.9600	0.0193	0.0203	-0.3930
1.9650	0.0213	0.0223	-0.4209
1.9700	0.0233	0.0243	-0.4496
1.9750	0.0255	0.0265	-0.4788
1.9800	0.0279	0.0289	-0.5083
1.9850	0.0305	0.0315	-0.5379

Currency Pair : **GBP/USD**

Expiration Date : **2/14/2008**

Market Price : **1.9811**

Option Premium
Ask Price : **$1,290**

FIGURE 1.6 Put Option Chain for GBPUSD

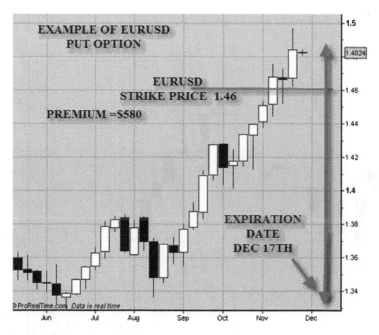

FIGURE 1.7 EURUSD Put Option
Source: © ProRealTime.com, web-based charting software

When there is a difference in the premiums between a call and a put at the same distance from the market, this is an important sentiment indicator that we will discuss in detail.

WRITING AN OPTION—BEGINNERS DON'T

When an option trade is undertaken, there are, of course, two parties to the trade. The trader purchases an option, but from whom? In forex, the other side is the forex firm that makes the market and establishes the premium prices. (In the future it might become direct matching between buyers and writer or options.) The writer originates the option trade and is looking for a buyer. The writer of a call is anticipating that the price of the underlying spot forex position will not get any higher than the strike price at expiration. The writer of the put is anticipating that the underlying spot price will not get any lower.

In the examples earlier, what if the trader wrote the call option? He would have received the premium (minus the spread).

The writer receives the premium from the buyer of the option. That is the most the writer will get! It's always important to ask the question, "Is it worth it?" because there is

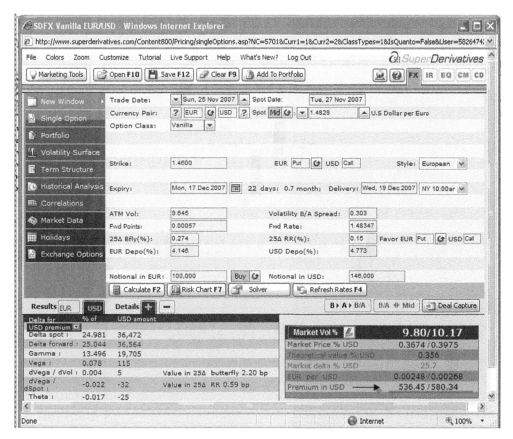

FIGURE 1.8 Premium Prices for EURUSD Put
Source: Reprinted with permission of Super Derivatives, Inc.

substantial risk involved to the writer. If the spot price doesn't behave as anticipated and goes up through and beyond the strike price (in case of a call) or below the strike price (in case of a put), the writer is obligated to pay the difference. The risk is theoretically unlimited if the price of the option goes the other way.

A visualization of the risks of writing a call or put is provided in Figures 1.9 through 1.11. At first, many traders who try writing these options tend to underestimate the risks. The strike prices seem far away, and it appears that the risks for the price to move against the trader are very small. This is a dangerous assumption, particularly in forex markets. Prices move hundreds of pips in hours on unexpected news. Therefore, in writing a call or put, the trader needs to make sure that the strike price gives room for larger-than-expected moves. Figure 1.9 shows a strike price that is below resistance for writing a call. In Figure 1.10 we see a strike price that supports writing a put.

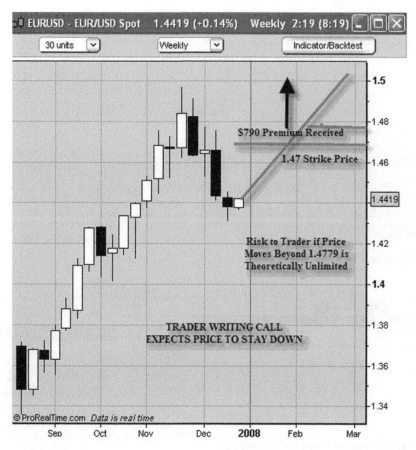

FIGURE 1.9　Risk Zone of Writing a Call
Source: © ProRealTime.com, web-based charting software

ELEMENTS OF AN OPTION TRADE OR TICKET

When putting on an option trade, the forex trader will encounter key terms that are important to know, including the following:

Trade date—the time when the trade is put on.
Spot price—the exact market value of the spot currency at the moment.
Option type—refers to whether the option is a call or put or other variety.
Strike price—the price the trader selects as the barrier, which will determine if the trade becomes profitable.
Valuation date—the date on which the valuation is valid.
Expiration or maturity date—the date when the option expires and the owner of the option no longer has the rights to it.

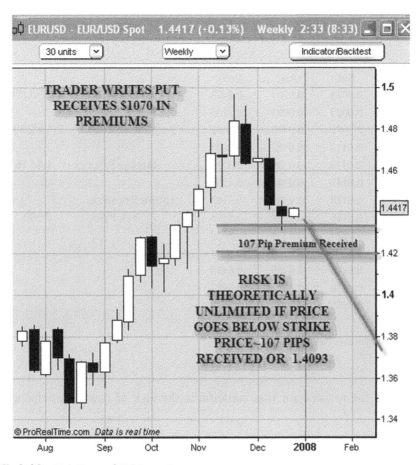

FIGURE 1.10 Risk Zone of Writing a Put
Source: © ProRealTime.com, web-based charting software

Option style—A European option can be exercised only on the exercise date and not before. An American-style option can be exercised before. With European-style options, which are very common in forex, the trader is protected from being exercised against if the trade is not going his way.

Days to expiration—the time until option rights expire.

Notional amount—the amount that a unit of the option (a lot) is controlling (i.e., a standard lot controls 100,000 EURUSD on an option on the EURUSD pair of the underlying spot currency the option is leveraging).

Comparison of Option Premium Pricing among Forex Firms

It is advisable that the forex option trader carefully review option premium pricing among the different firms offering it. There are often great variations in the premiums

Hypothetical Option Chain Data

Put Options					
Strike	Bid	Ask	Delta		
1.4100	0.0071	0.0081	-0.2493	**Currency Pair :**	**EUR/USD**
1.4150	0.0083	0.0093	-0.2815		
1.4200	0.0096	0.0106	-0.3162	**Expiration Date :**	**2/14/2008**
1.4250	0.0112	0.0122	-0.3533		
1.4300	0.0129	0.0139	-0.3926	**Market Price :**	**1.4416**
1.4350	0.0148	0.0158	-0.4337		
1.4400	0.0170	0.0180	-0.4762	**Option Premium**	
1.4450	0.0196	0.0206	-0.5194	**Ask Price :**	**$960**
1.4500	0.0224	0.0234	-0.5619		
1.4550	0.0254	0.0264	-0.6034		
1.4600	0.0285	0.0295	-0.6433		
1.4650	0.0319	0.0329	-0.6813		
1.4700	0.0355	0.0365	-0.7172		

FIGURE 1.11 EURUSD Put Option Chain

offered. One of the reasons for this variation is the lack of many participants in the industry.

In the Money, At the Money, and Out of the Money

In placing an option trade, the center of attention for the forex trader is on where the spot forex price is. The spot price is called the **at-the-money** strike price. Whenever a call or put option is purchased, the strike price is either **in the money (ITM), at the money (ATM),** or **out of the money (OTM).** Options can also be deep in the money and deep out of the money. The term *moneyness* refers to this relationship of the option price to the at-the-money price.

Since there is no "free lunch" in trading, the trader has a range of choices in putting on an option trade regarding increasing the probability of success. The most likely option strategy for success is buying an in-the-money option position. This means that he will get the maximum movement of the option with the spot. Once a position is in the money, it moves on a 1:1 basis with the spot. The advantage of an in-the-money option versus a spot position is that it will cost the trader only the premium and no other risk is associated with it. The disadvantage is that the premium costs a lot more.

The next type of trade relating to moneyness is the at-the-money option. This is when the option strike price is where the spot is. This kind of positioning allows the trader to be close to the action without paying as much as the in-the-money option. ATM options are very common in hedging a position. ATM options move with the spot at 50 percent of the movement. This is called a delta factor and will be discussed in more detail shortly.

The out-of-the-money option trade is the most popular trade. Let's see why: By selecting a strike price that is away from the spot, the trader is anticipating the move. The hope of the forex trader is, of course, that the price will (during the duration of the option trade) move toward the strike price or exceed it. The option trader makes money by being right not only if the spot price actually moves to and beyond the strike price at expiration, but whether along the way it is expected to move in the direction of the price. The objective is trying to use all the tools that are available to increase the probability of being right about the direction of the option trade about market expectations, and about its timing. Time value and the moneyness of an option have a direct relationship, which is shown in Figures 1.12 and 1.13.

Intrinsic Value versus Time Value

The forex option trader is always undertaking a multidimensional bet. Affecting the result is a combination of variables that have to come together in favor of the trader. Of critical importance is the time left to expiration and the risk changes in volatility. Sometimes, if central banks increase interest rates while the trader is holding an option

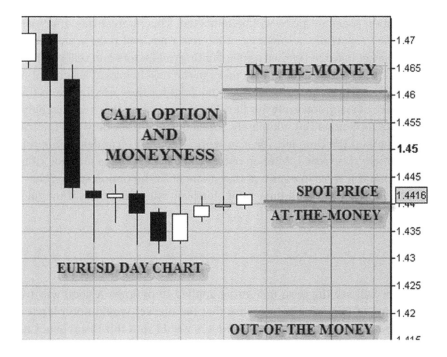

FIGURE 1.12 Moneyness in Option Premiums for Put Options

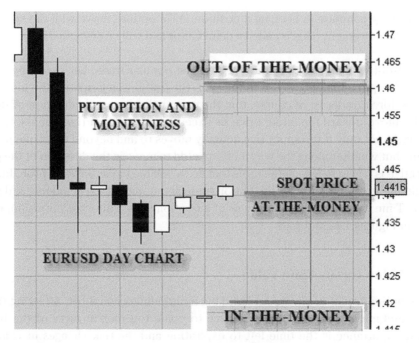

FIGURE 1.13 Moneyness in Option Premiums for Call Options

position, the option premium price will be impacted. This interest rate effect is a small factor (called *rho*). Generally, a lowering of interest rates will reduce the option price. The currency market takes in (known as discounting) all factors and reflects them in the option premium price. This means it also takes in the psychological aspects of fear and greed in the market. Therefore, it would be a mistake for the forex trader to think that the premium price of an option is always fair. The reality is that there is great uncertainty regarding market directions But, ultimately, it is a balancing act between the trade that the trader has on and the time left for it to work. The best term describing this is *intrinsic value versus time value*. After an option trade is put on, the intrinsic value is the value of the option if it were to expire at that moment. If the option strike price has not yet been reached, the value is all time value. Intrinsic value increases if the underlying price exceeds the option strike.

Fair Value

Often, the trader will see the term *fair value* applied to options. A good way to understand the meaning of fair value is to realize that the market would not tolerate for too long an option premium that is mispriced. Traders would spot this discrepancy and take advantage of it through arbitrage. Therefore, fair value is the price where any arbitrage would be impossible.

THE GREEKS

Forex and other options are bets on the future direction of the underlying instrument. The market is always seeking a way to efficiently price an option. If pricing was inefficient or unfair, the thousands of participants in trading the market would seek to find an advantage and be able to significantly profit from that advantage. These are called arbitrage opportunities. A vast body of financial mathematics and expertise has developed to constantly improve the algorithms that generate a fair price of an option. The most famous of all of the mathematics of option pricing has been the Black-Scholes equation. The Nobel Prize was awarded for developing the mathematics behind this equation. It forms the basis for the market to fairly price an option because the equation showed what a fair value would be for a premium on an option. But the equation assumes constant volatility. *Black-Sholes was not developed for forex markets where there is no constant volatility.* The world of forex options is not a Black-Scholes world, and for the average trader, this means he or she must be even more cognizant of the probability that during the option trade period, changes will occur in the market environment that cannot be fairly reflected in the premium prices. The forex option trader has a paramount need during the option trade to allow enough time to be right but not enough time for too many changes in the real-world environment.

More important for the forex trader is monitoring and understanding the Greeks. These are Greek terms that indicate quantifiable parameters that affect the price of the option. Let's look at them briefly. The average retail forex trader does not have to pay too close attention to all of the Greeks. However, they are very important to large hedges and institutional traders who take on big positions. For these traders a small factor in one of the Greeks can make a difference. Among the Greeks, delta is the most important in developing trading strategies. Later on, we will use them in some real trading examples showing the Greeks.

The Popular Greeks in Options

This section provides a review of the most used, or popular, "Greek" terms.

Delta   Delta measures the rate of change of the option premium price to the change in the underlying currency pair. For example, a delta of .50 means that the premium of an option will change half as much as the percentage change in the underlying price.

Vega   Vega displays the amount the price of an option changes when there is a 1 percent change in volatility. The forex trader needs to always observe if vega is expanding or contracting. If vega is expanding, this means volatility is increasing and vice versa.

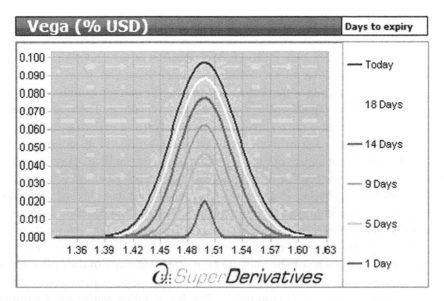

FIGURE 1.14 The Shape of Vega
Source: Reprinted with permission of Super Derivatives, Inc.

dVega/dSpot—Measures a percentage change in vega for a 1 percent change in the spot
   rate based on ATM volatility.
Vega and time—Vega usually expands with time.

Figure 1.14 shows what a vega chart looks like for a recent EURUSD 150 CALL ex-
piring December 17, 2007.

Now if we go out to 53 days, look at what happens to vega (see Figure 1.15). It
expands, showing that volatility will increase over time.

Gamma   Gamma displays the percentage change in the delta for a 1 percent move in
the underlying. High gamma values become important for those who need to hedge their
positions using delta because hedgers need to be constantly rehedging to assure against
changes in the delta. When gamma is very high, it means that the potential profit due to
a change in the underlying price is higher.

Let's look at the gamma chart in Figure 1.16. We see an overlay of hills. All of the hills
are centered and peak at the ATM. This is because gamma is highest at the ATM. This
is what makes ATM options very attractive to traders. The ATM options move the most
quickly when the underlying currency changes prices. Of course, there is a price to pay
for being ATM. The cost of the premium is higher than OTM. This leads to a reason to
avoiding ITM options. They don't move much because they are already close to a gamma
value of 1. Gamma's being highest at the ATM is another reason to avoid ITM options.
ITM options are already close to 1.

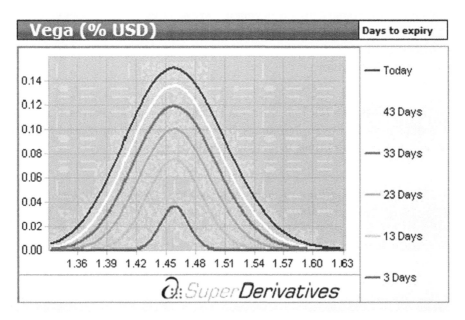

FIGURE 1.15   The Shape of Vega as Time Extends to Expiration
Source: Reprinted with permission of Super Derivatives, Inc.

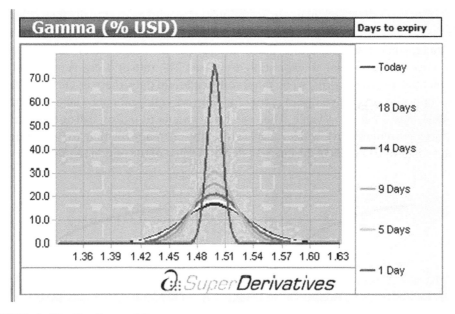

FIGURE 1.16   The Shape of Gamma
Source: Reprinted with permission of Super Derivatives, Inc.

What should the trader look for in gamma? We see that positive gamma means that the delta will move up and, as a result, the option price will also move up. A trader trading a short-term expiration will have a harder time making money if gamma is low. The trader wants a swift move.

Gamma Long Position and the Yen A recent article in Bloomberg serves as an example of how gamma is viewed by professionals. It noted that traders purchased $500 million of dollar call and yen put options to go long gamma. Here is an excerpt:

> *Banks traded $500 million of dollar call–yen put options today that expire this week ... said Takeharu Mmiki, a currency options manager ... All the options traded at an implied volatility of 16 percent, he said. Traders quote implied volatility, a measure of expectations for future currency swings, as part of pricing options.*
>
> *Traders who purchased options today probably did so to increase their exposure to gamma, according to Ryousei Ishida, senior vice president of foreign-exchange options in Tokyo at Mizuho Corporate Bank Ltd.*
>
> —Stanley White, Bloomberg.com (January 7, 2008)

Theta Theta is the rate of change in an option's price with respect to the time to expiry. Theta has a well-known decay curve; the option trader who is a buyer is always worried about theta, while a seller has time decay on his side. However, the focus on theta becomes more intense as time to expiration decreases. The rate of decay is not linear and is exponential. In other words, when purchasing calls and puts, there is a negative theta, and the opposite (a positive theta) is true for shorting calls and puts. Once again at the ATM, theta has the highest value. The trader who wants to put on calls or puts trades when forex currencies have wider ranges, giving the currency the time to move through the range. Figure 1.17 depicts the curve of decay in value of the option as time decreases.

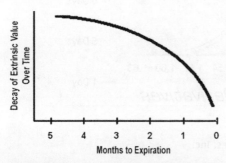
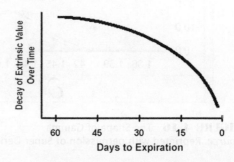

FIGURE 1.17 Extrinsic Value Decay Chart

Rho   Rho is the rate at which the price of an option changes relative to a change in the interest rate. It measures the sensitivity of an option to a 1 percent change in the underlying interest rate. This is one of the least used of the Greeks. But during times when central banks are changing interest rate policies, rho can become a factor to consider. Also, if an option is greater than three months, there is increased interest rate risk: It becomes more expensive to hold. Interestingly, if a currency is in an interest rate–cutting environment, the options on that currency will tend to become less costly (unless volatility increases). For forex traders, rho is more important for longer-term options that go beyond a year. In this longer time frame, rho can affect the price of the option more significantly.

Volatility Quotes at Chicago Mercantile Exchange (CME)

The CME has begun to offer volatility-based quotes on forex options. The CME made this decision because the professional community of traders directly trade volatility. In announcing volatility quoting, the CME Group said: This quoting convention enables "delta-neutral" trading, which eliminates the execution risk inherent to trading in live premium by quoting forex options.

Spot Delta

This Greek term relates to how much the option price changes in response a change in the underlying spot forex prices. It is the most important of the Greeks and there are many delta-related trading strategies the trader can become familiar with, which will be discussed in a later chapter. The trader will primarily look at delta to help identify the ability of the option premium to move. A high delta means that the option premium will track more closely the move of the underlying spot currency. Delta ranges from 0.00 to 1.00. Calls have a positive delta, and puts have a negative delta. An option call or put with a 1.00 delta will move exactly with the underlying spot. When an option is ATM or at the money, the delta is at 0.50. This means that the option premium price will move 50 percent of the movement of the underlying currency pair. Many new beginners, who may have purchased deep-out-of-the money options become surprised when an option trade they took doesn't move as much as the underlying. They were surprised because they didn't look at the deltas, which most likely would have shown deltas below 0.20. While deep-out-of-the-money options may be cheap, they are cheap for reason!

Delta itself is affected by time and by volatility. When an option is ATM, it is the least affected by time and volatility. But if the option is ITM or OTM, it becomes more sensitive to volatility and to changes in time. For example, if a currency option is ITM, its delta may move closer to 1 as it approaches expiration, and deltas of OTM options would approach 0 as expiration came due. Another way to understand the direction of delta is to view it as a probability of becoming profitable. As the chances of being profitable increase, the delta approaches 1, and as it decreases, it approaches 0.

(continued)

Other Delta Measurements

There are also related delta measurements that can be useful if the forex trader wants to be more advanced. There is **dDelta/dVol,** which tracks the change in delta for a 1 percent change in volatility. For those who are technically oriented, there are also forward delta and driftless delta measurements.

Comparing Delta Calls versus Delta Puts—Detecting Market Skew

Traders often compare delta calls with delta puts. When the premiums of calls and puts with the same delta are not equal, the forex trader needs to be alerted to a *skewing* of the market sentiment. This should be taken into consideration on developing trading strategies. In Figure 1.18, for the USDJPY we see a comparison of the deltas along different strike prices and volatility. In the center is the ATM strike price. The 25 delta strike price for the put is 111.05, and for the call it is 113.25. The ATM is 112.24. The volatility for the put is 11.51 percent versus 9.46 percent for the call. At this moment in time, the market shows more volatility for a downward direction but is still pricing calls more than puts, which shows market sentiment favoring the calls. It is important to note that this skew is not a prediction of direction. It is just a reflection of the market sentiment.

Let's look further at this example of the USDJPY and whether there is a market skew. In Figure 1.19, the USDJPY call option (90 days out) shows a premium price of $1115. In Figure 1.20, the USDJPY put option (90 days out) shows a premium price of 1858. Note that both options have the same expiration date of March 28, 2008. The difference in the price of the call option versus the put option may reveal a market sentiment skew.

	5 Δ	10 Δ	15 Δ	20 Δ	25 Δ	30 Δ	ATM	30 Δ	25 Δ	20 Δ	15 Δ	10 Δ	5 Δ
Vol	13.51	12.68	12.19	11.82	11.51	11.16	10.225	9.59	9.46	9.40	9.35	9.34	9.38
Strike	108.86	109.76	110.31	110.72	111.05	111.34	112.24	113.03	113.25	113.49	113.77	114.13	114.68
Vol	14.89	13.70	12.96	12.41	11.96	11.55	10.350	9.56	9.41	9.30	9.20	9.12	9.12
Strike	103.54	105.86	107.26	108.29	109.11	109.81	111.90	113.78	114.28	114.83	115.47	116.29	117.54
Vol	15.22	13.85	12.99	12.36	11.86	11.40	10.100	9.26	9.11	8.99	8.89	8.83	8.89
Strike	100.41	103.55	105.44	106.81	107.90	108.82	111.51	113.93	114.57	115.29	116.12	117.18	118.87
Vol	15.45	13.98	13.02	12.33	11.78	11.29	9.900	9.00	8.83	8.70	8.60	8.55	8.64
Strike	97.88	101.65	103.94	105.58	106.88	107.97	111.11	113.91	114.66	115.49	116.45	117.70	119.70
Vol	15.79	14.09	12.97	12.17	11.54	10.97	9.450	8.47	8.29	8.16	8.07	8.07	8.31
Strike	92.06	97.29	100.47	102.74	104.52	106.00	110.06	113.71	114.70	115.79	117.08	118.79	121.69
Vol	16.17	14.31	13.08	12.20	11.50	10.88	9.250	8.21	8.00	7.87	7.82	7.87	8.23
Strike	87.48	93.83	97.70	100.46	102.61	104.40	109.12	113.40	114.57	115.87	117.43	119.55	123.29
Vol	16.17	14.22	12.96	12.04	11.32	10.66	9.000	7.93	7.72	7.61	7.59	7.70	8.17
Strike	84.03	91.18	95.54	98.65	101.08	103.11	108.28	113.00	114.31	115.79	117.58	120.07	124.59
Vol	15.92	14.02	12.74	11.78	11.02	10.33	8.450	7.28	7.07	6.96	6.94	7.07	7.57
Strike	74.21	82.90	88.40	92.39	95.52	98.13	105.29	111.91	113.53	115.39	117.68	120.94	127.06
	5 Δ	10 Δ	15 Δ	20 Δ	25 Δ	30 Δ	ATM	30 Δ	25 Δ	20 Δ	15 Δ	10 Δ	5 Δ

FIGURE 1.18 Comparing 25 Delta Calls and Puts and Their Premiums
Source: Reprinted with permission of Super Derivatives, Inc.

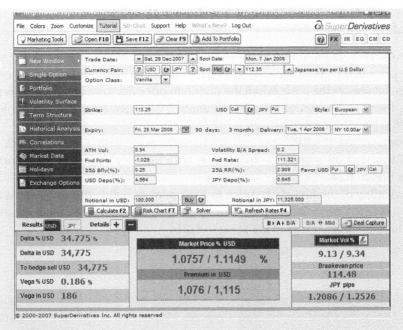

FIGURE 1.19 USDJPY Call Option
Source: Reprinted with permission of Super Derivatives, Inc.

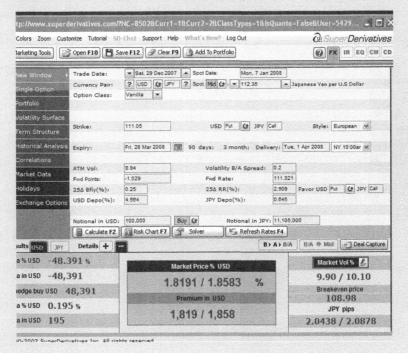

FIGURE 1.20 USDJPY Put Option
Source: Reprinted with permission of Super Derivatives, Inc.

Volatility and Time: The Effect of Volatility's Declining on Premium Prices

When the duration of an option extends over time, more things can go wrong and as a result the price of the premium would go up to reflect this increased level of uncertainty. But that is not always the case. When the premium price does not go up, the forex trader confronts the phenomenon of a decline in implied volatility. Here is an example where the premium price hardly moves up!.

We compare the USDJPY spot call at 110 strike price with a duration of 62 days in Figure 1.21 against the same 110 strike price, with the only change being a duration of 92 days in Figure 1.22.

The volatility of the first strike price is 13.62 percent, while the volatility of the second option is 12.817 percent. The premium price of the first was $1182 but buying another 30 days' duration only increased the price to $1314.

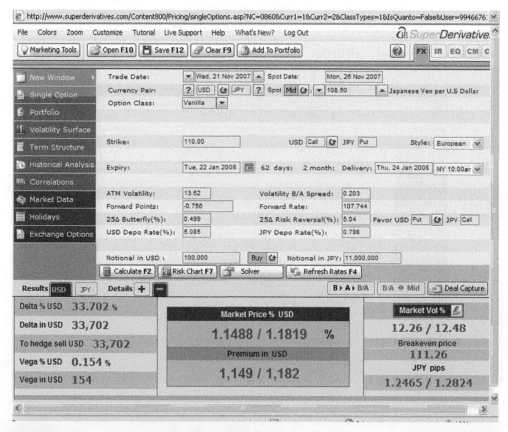

FIGURE 1.21 USDJPY Call Option 62 Days Expiration
Source: Reprinted with permission of Super Derivatives, Inc.

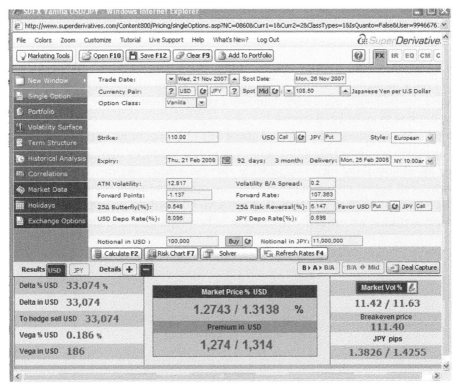

FIGURE 1.22 USDJPY Call Option 92 Days Expiration
Source: Reprinted with permission of Super Derivatives, Inc.

Test Your Knowledge For Finding Market Skew

Find any currency pair and go to a 30-day call option at-the-money strike price; then find the option premium for calls and puts; form an opinion about the future direction of the currency pair; then go to 120 days for the same strike price and find the option premium for calls and puts. What is the difference when expiration is extended? Do the results confirm your opinion? Practice this exercise over and over.

SUMMARY

Risks and Potential of Plain Vanilla Options

- Option buyers have risks limited to the premium paid.
- Option writers (sellers) have theoretically unlimited risks.

- Option buyers have theoretically unlimited potential.
- Option writers have a profit potential limited to the premium received.

In this book, we concentrate only on options strategies that have predetermined and limited risk. This includes writing an option when it is part of a spread or combined with a covered position such as an underlying spot position. However, we are not discussing writing options as an isolated strategy.

In this chapter, the reader learned about key elements of an option trade and how those elements are reflected in the nomenclature of the forex market. The reader also learned about how those elements provide clues to market sentiment. A key concept is comparing call option premium prices with put option premium prices to detect which way the sentiment is skewing. Now that we have covered the essential components of forex option trades, we can move to the task of developing trading ideas.

CHAPTER 2

What Affects Forex Option Prices?

A ll of the elements that come together to shape the forex option premium price are always in a precarious balancing act. But the most important ones are time and volatility.

TIME

Abraham Lincoln is quoted as referring to "the silent artillery of time" as one of the most powerful weapons. In forex option trading, the factor of time is ticking away at the original option trade. Known as *theta*, time can be an enemy or a friend. To buyers of an option it can be an enemy, because the longer it takes to maturity, the more things can go wrong and the option trade can either run out of time and never become profitable or, if it was profitable, can have time to reverse into losses. However, the longer it takes to get to maturity, the more time the trader has to be right in his direction. Often, prices have retracements, try to reverse, but turn around. More time may allow the trade to work out. But to sellers of an option, time is a great friend. The seller or writer knows that as time moves on the probability of a price's reaching a targeted strike price is reduced every day. The writer gets to keep the premium if the price doesn't reach the strike price in time.

In Figures 2.1 and 2.2 we see an example where two option trades are identical except in time. Notice how the premium price changed. The premium price went up from 623 to 1333 as the time to expiration changed from 22 days to 53 days.

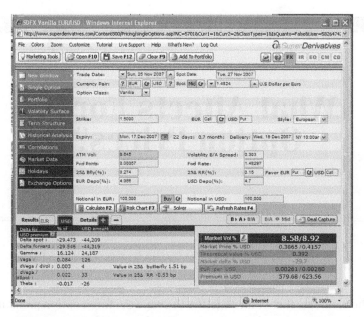

FIGURE 2.1 Premiums at 22 Days
Source: Reprinted with permission of Super Derivatives, Inc.

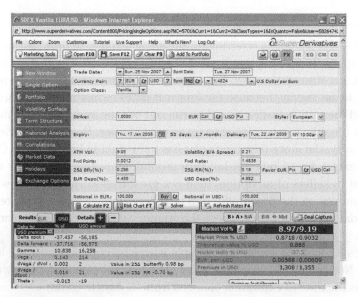

FIGURE 2.2 Premium at 53 days
Source: Reprinted with permission of Super Derivatives, Inc.

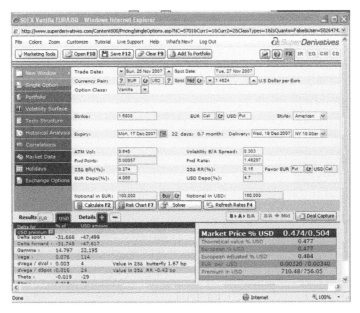

FIGURE 2.3 American-Style Option
Source: Reprinted with permission of Super Derivatives, Inc.

American Style versus European Style: Which Is More Expensive and Which Is More Useful?

American-style options allow for exercise at any time. This increases the uncertainty to the market, and therefore American style options usually are more expensive.

In Figures 2.3 and 2.4 we see a EURUSD strike price of 1.50 with 22 days to expiration, offering a premium of $756 for an American-style option. In contrast, the same option with a European-style expiration has a lower premium of $748.

VOLATILITY

The spot price *is* the horse in the forex race, and the contours of the underlying spot's price movements are the focus of almost all of the attention. Understanding volatility, even for the beginning forex option trader, is essential. Volatility has been called a "crucial input." Most people have a sense about volatility because it is experienced in everyday life. When the weather is volatile, there are storms; when nations conflict with each other, the highest level of volatility is war. In trading, volatility is a mathematical concept that deals with the deviation of prices. The change in prices over time is how volatility is measured. Technically, volatility is the annualized standard deviation of the log-returns. However, we are not concentrating here on the mathematics of volatility but on how it can be used by the forex trader and how it should be understood.

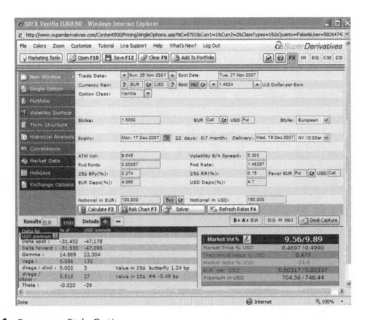

FIGURE 2.4 European-Style Option
Source: Reprinted with permission of Super Derivatives, Inc.

Let's look at the example of an option trade on the EURUSD call option with a strike price of 1.50 and the spot being at 1.4824. The at-the-money (ATM) volatility is 9.645. This volatility is calculated by the firm and is usually available in all option platforms because it's very important. We can see in Figure 2.5 that the premium price for a EURUSD call option calculated at that moment is $748.00. We know that the premium price reflects many variables and that volatility is a key component. It is appropriate to ask, "What happens if the ATM volatility changes?" Usually, when volatility increases, the price of the option premium also increases. This is because the market sees more risk, and therefore the option premium costs more. Notice that this is exactly what happened. A change in volatility from 9.645 (Figure 2.6) to 10.645 (Figure 2.7) increased the premium price to $877. What would happen if volatility decreased? It turned out that a decrease

Market Vol %	9.56/9.89
Market Price % USD	0.4697 / 0.4990
Theoretical value % USD	0.477
Market delta % USD	-31.6
EUR per USD	0.00317 / 0.00337
Premium in USD	704.56 / 748.44

Market Vol %	10.54/10.87
Market Price % USD	0.5555 / 0.5848
Theoretical value % USD	0.565
Market delta % USD	-33.2
EUR per USD	0.00375 / 0.00394
Premium in USD	833.31 / 877.19

OPTION PREMIUM CALL PRICES INCREASE WHEN VOLATILITY INCREASE

FIGURE 2.5 Option Call Premium Prices Increase When Volatility Increases
Source: Reprinted with permission of Super Derivatives, Inc.

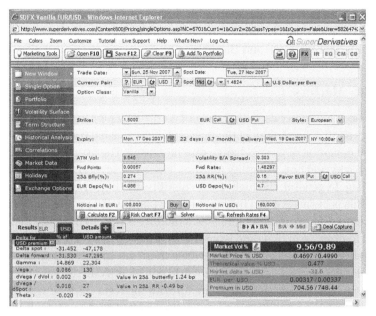

FIGURE 2.6 EURUSD Call Option with 9.645 Percent Volatility
Source: Reprinted with permission of Super Derivatives, Inc.

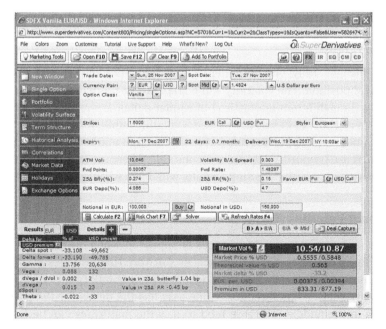

FIGURE 2.7 EURUSD Call Option with 10.645 Percent Volatility
Source: Reprinted with permission of Super Derivatives, Inc.

in volatility to 8.645 percent changed the premium prices down to $623. (Generally in the industry, volatility data is supplied by global financial data firms such as Tullet and Prebon, Superderivatives.com, and Bloomberg).

Why Volatility Matters

If there were no uncertainty as to the price of a currency pair in the future, there would be no volatility at all. Uncertainty in the market leaves a visual track and can be detected if the standard deviation of the exchange rate increases. The average forex option trader needs to know why and how volatility matters. There are several very important features for forex trading. In general, the higher the volatility, the higher the premium the market will require. This is because when there is higher volatility the probability that the option will be in the money at expiration increases. Volatility is easy to measure historically, but it is very hard to observe in real time what the volatility is, and it is even harder to predict whether volatility will increase. This is because there are so many variables that can impact future volatility, and no system in the world can identify all the variables. Therefore, the field of financial mathematics has come up with the term *implied volatility* because it is, in fact, only implied and is an estimate about volatility. The famous Black-Scholes equations assume a constant volatility, which is not the case at all in forex. Financial mathematics professionals are always looking for and developing new ways to project an accurate volatility surface. One of the most useful and famous is known as the *volatility smile*.

The Volatility Smile

In option trading, generally, volatility increases as the option moves away from the spot position or ATM position. The volatility smile graph a 2 or 3 2-dimensional plot of the implied volatility along different maturities but similar deltas. It shows whether the market is favoring puts or calls. In Figure 2.8 we see a volatility smile for the EURJPY that is favoring puts. Smiles can happen for many reasons, such as market fear of a crisis causing volatility to increase proportionally more on one side. There are important option trading implications associated with detecting a smile, which we will explore later on.

3-Dimensional Volatility Surfaces

The ability to understand volatility surfaces is improved when 3D graphics are used. If possible, the forex option trader should access software that provides 3D volatility surfaces. Many third-party software firms are now providing volatility surface visualizations. The 3D volatility surface has three axes; one axis has the deltas for the puts and calls, with the ATM in the middle. The axis next to it is the maturities can be from 1 day to 10 years. The vertical axis displays the volatilities. The trader can see instantly whether the market is favoring puts or calls.

For example, we can see in Figure 2.9 that the chart is "skewed" toward the puts, showing a bias in opinion for a weakening currency. This skew is apparent because the

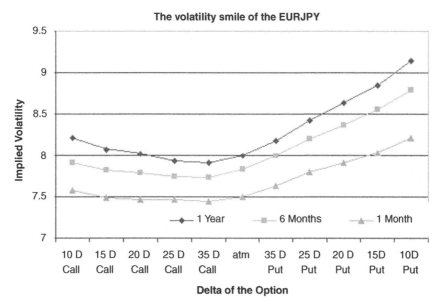

FIGURE 2.8 The Volatility Smile of the EURJPY
Source: Saxo Bank Group at www.saxoeducation.com

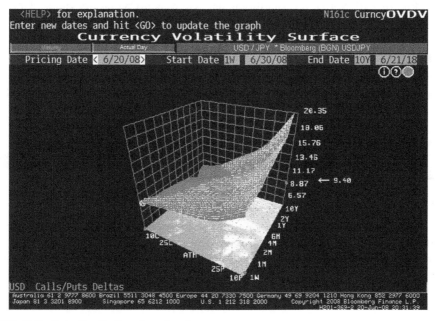

FIGURE 2.9 Volatility Surface Favoring Puts
Source: © 2008 Bloomberg L.P. All rights reserved. Used with permission.

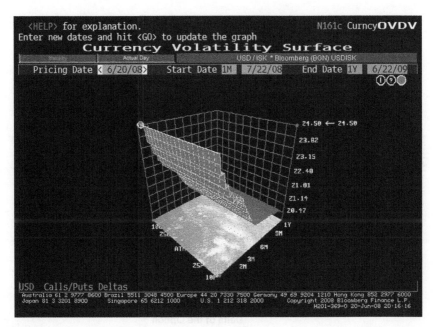

FIGURE 2.10 Iceland Krona Volatility Surface
Source: © 2008 Bloomberg L.P. All rights reserved. Used with permission.

graph slopes up on the put side. Now contrast this with the volatility chart for the Iceland krona in Figure 2.10. Notice its volatility is flat. There is no "volatility smile." Of course, this is to be expected with a nonfloating managed currency such as the Iceland krona.

Trading Tip: When a volatility skew is favoring **calls**, think about a **call ratio spread**. When a volatility skew is favoring **puts**, think about a **put backspread**.

Notice in Figure 2.11 for the Canadian dollar pair the volatility surface matches the well-known description of an almost perfect smile. The market sentiment for calls and puts is nearly the same.

 ASSIGNMENT

Detect a Volatility Smile

For any currency pair, find a call strike position associated with 25 percent delta and then locate the strike price on the puts that also have the 25 percent delta.

Theoretically, the premiums for the calls and puts should be the same. But if the price is greater on one side than the other, the market is said to favor that direction.

Read Emanuel Derman's Article on Volatility Smiles

A helpful article on this topic is Emanuel Derman's "Laughter in the Dark—The Problem of the Volatility Smile" (May 26, 2003). The full text can be found at www.ederman.com/new/docs/euronext-volatility_smile.pdf.

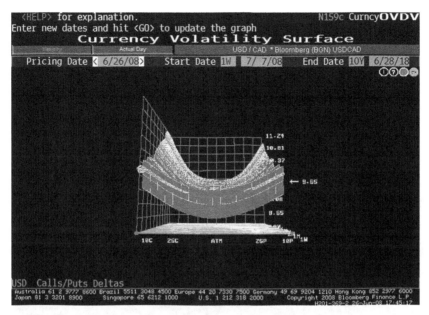

FIGURE 2.11 USDCAD Volatility Surface—A Near "Perfect" Volatility Smile
Source: © 2008 Bloomberg L.P. All rights reserved. Used with permission.

Volatility Smiles and Becoming Cynical

Traders in forex should be a bit cynical about the option prices that are offered by the forex firms, particularly if they are based on the Black-Scholes model. This is because, as noted earlier, the Black-Scholes assumes constant volatility across all strike prices for the same underlying price. The fact is that the market produces a skew in the volatility. This is called a volatility smile. When a trader finds a volatility smile, there is a bias in the market. The trader should realize that the bias reflected in the smile reflects larger forces. Volatility smiles don't go away quickly.

Expect surprises in the underlying volatility, and this will affect probability of profits.

Volatility Smiles at the Beginning of 2008

It will be valuable for students of forex option trading to compare the volatility smiles of the currency pairs over time. Did they change? How long did they last? The purpose of this section is to give the reader a frame of reference for understanding volatility smiles.

 ASSIGNMENT

Volatility Smiles

Scan the volatility smiles that occurred for the currency pairs on January 1, 2008 (see Figures 2.12 through 2.20). Try to answer the following questions: How long did it take for the currency pairs to move in a direction against the volatility smile bias? What was the average time for such a reversal?

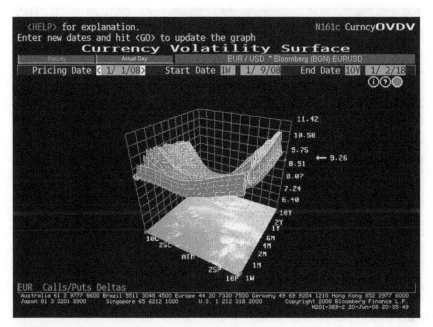

FIGURE 2.12 EURUSD Volatility Surface Jan 1 2008
Source: © 2008 Bloomberg L.P. All rights reserved. Used with permission.

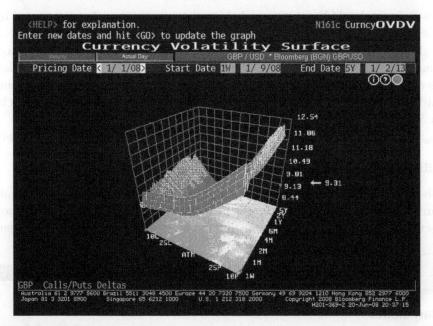

FIGURE 2.13 GBPUSD Volatility Surface Jan 1 2008
Source: © 2008 Bloomberg L.P. All rights reserved. Used with permission.

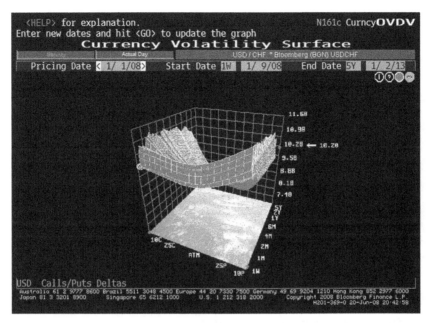

FIGURE 2.14 USDCHF Volatility Surface Jan 1 2008
Source: © 2008 Bloomberg L.P. All rights reserved. Used with permission.

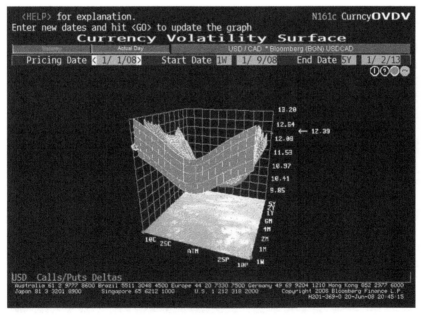

FIGURE 2.15 USD CAD Volatility Surface Jan 1 2008
Source: © 2008 Bloomberg L.P. All rights reserved. Used with permission.

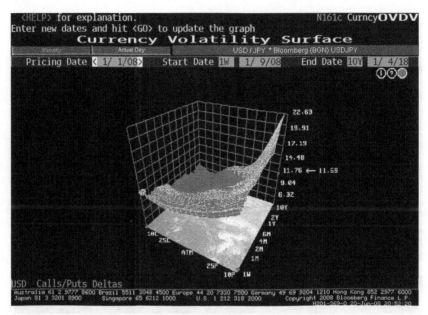

FIGURE 2.16 USDJPY Volatility Surface Jan 1 2008
Source: © 2008 Bloomberg L.P. All rights reserved. Used with permission.

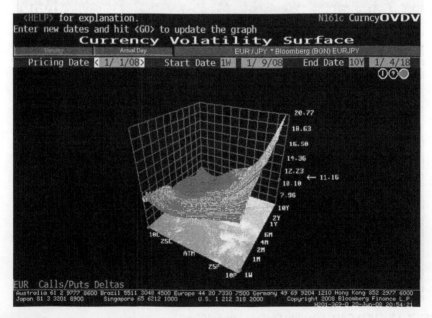

FIGURE 2.17 EURJPY Volatility Surface Jan 1 2008
Source: © 2008 Bloomberg L.P. All rights reserved. Used with permission.

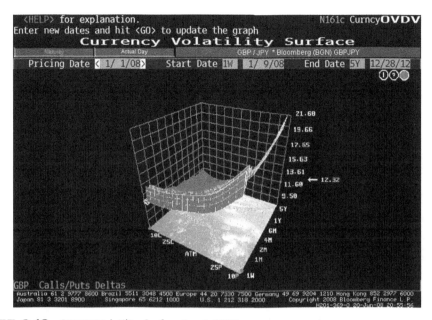

FIGURE 2.18 GBPJPY Volatility Surface Jan 1 2008
Source: © 2008 Bloomberg L.P. All rights reserved. Used with permission.

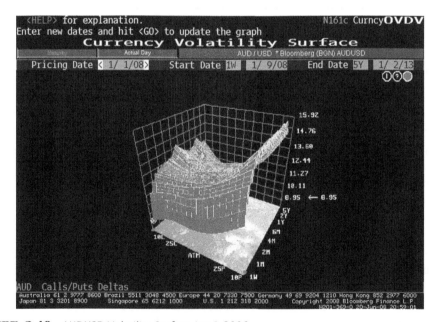

FIGURE 2.19 AUDUSD Volatility Surface Jan 1 2008
Source: © 2008 Bloomberg L.P. All rights reserved. Used with permission.

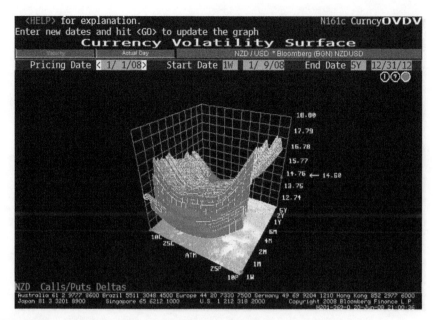

FIGURE 2.20 NZDUSD Volatility Surface Jan 1 2008
Source: © 2008 Bloomberg L.P. All rights reserved. Used with permission.

Historical versus Implied Volatility

The forex trader should constantly be looking for extremes in volatility. When volatility is at an extreme high or low, it contains information about market sentiment and direction. It also is a signal of instability. A good place to begin to answer this question is by comparing historical volatility versus implied volatility. Historical volatility is really statistical volatility measuring the actual variation in prices over time. When the prices widen in their range, the standard deviation rises, and this means that the historic volatility will be higher. Traders use a varying time frame ranging from 1 day to 1 week to 20- and 30-day periods. Twenty days is a common time frame for looking at historical versus implied volatility.

Implied volatility is an expectation of the volatility that the market is anticipating for a particular option during the life of that option. The premium priced for the option reflects market sentiment about many things, and most importantly, the price reflects an implied volatility. *This expectation is not perfect, and the equations generating them are not perfected. But the implied volatility is what the market is assigning at that moment, and it must be respected.*

When comparing historical versus implied volatility, the trader can see if the implied is excessive over the historical. If it is, then an assumption can be made that this excessive period cannot last and there will be what financial mathematics calls a "reversion to the mean." Readers may already have seen in many places the equation:

$$\text{Iv/Hv} = \text{Implied volatility} \div \text{Historical volatility}$$

When comparing historical and implied volatility time frames, one should match time horizons. For example, a 1-month implied volatility chart should be matched with a 1-month historical volatility chart.

Historical versus Implied Volatility on Charts Figures 2.21 and 2.22 show historical volatility versus implied volatility for different periods for the USDCHF pair. Looking at Figure 2.21, we can see that the USDCHF experienced periods where 1-month historical volatility was in sync and close in value to 1-month implied volatility and then entered periods where there was a very wide gap between the historical and implied volatility. In forex option trading, 1-month volatility should not be the only period for evaluation. The common practice is to use a longer time frame such as 3 months. In Figure 2.22 we see a phase where the 3-month historical volatility was contracting. This was in contrast to the 1-month expansion of volatility. According to the theory of reversion to the mean, the trader could conclude that the 1-month gap is exaggerated. It shouldn't stay in the same proportion. Therefore, this leads to trades favoring a contraction of the volatility. For example, if the trader thinks that historical volatility is too low and would increase, a good strategy would be to buy straddles. If the trader thinks that

FIGURE 2.21 USDCHF 1-Month Historical versus Implied Volatility
Source: Reprinted with permission of Super Derivatives, Inc.

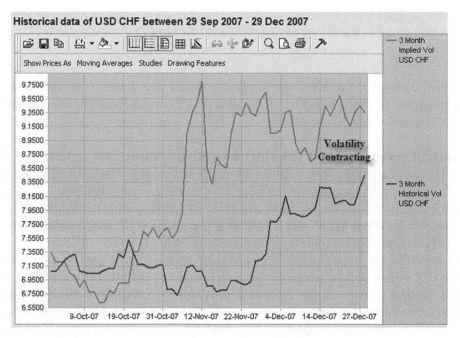

FIGURE 2.22 USDCHF 3-Month Historical versus Implied Volatility
Source: Reprinted with permission of Super Derivatives, Inc.

the historical volatility will remain the same, then selling straddles would be a preferred strategy. *It's important to note that straddles as a strategy is related to playing a breakout of a range or staying in the range.* A good idea is to scan the historical versus the implied volatilities of the currency pairs.

The trader should look for extremes. For example, in such a scan we found that the USDCHF had a scenario where the historical volatility was excessive versus the implied volatility. We can see that this spread was the widest in over a year on the chart below. The trader would correctly anticipate a contraction of volatility.

One month later, the volatility significantly contracted, as seen in Figure 2.22.

The trader observing that the volatility was at an extreme would look to option strategies which benefit from a loss of volatility. One such strategy is the *carry trade.*

Benefiting from a Loss of Volatility   The carry trade is an option strategy that benefits from a loss of volatility.

> *When implied volatility falls, for the USDJPY the carry trade returns.*

> *One month implied volatility for the yen versus the dollar fell to 12.25 percent yesterday, from 12.35 percent on Jan. 8. A decline in volatility encourages carry trades as it makes the profit more predictable.*

"As long as there is some sort of calm besetting the market, carry trades still make the most sense," said Jeff Gladstein, global head of foreign exchange trading at AIG Financial products in Wilton, Connecticut. "If volatility in equities subsides, participants will feel more comfortable to continue putting on carry trades, and the yen may suffer."

—Ye Xie and Bo Nielsen, *Bloomberg*, January 10, 2008)

 ASSIGNMENT

Volatility Scan—Which Is the Best Pair to Trade?

In Figures 2.23 through 2.31 we see a comparison of historical volatility and implied volatility of 1-month time frames. Forex option traders should frequently scan the currency pairs comparing historical versus implied volatility. The key question to ask in reviewing historical versus implied volatility is: Which of these depicted currency pairs would you trade and in what direction? Write down your reasons.

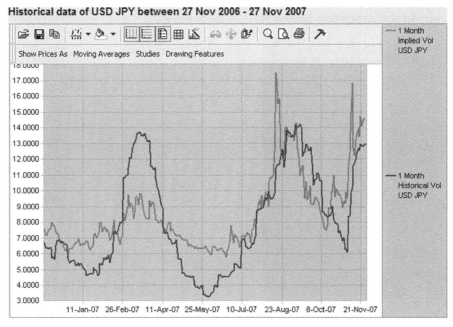

FIGURE 2.23 USDJPY 1-Month Historical versus Implied Volatility
Source: Reprinted with permission of Super Derivatives, Inc.

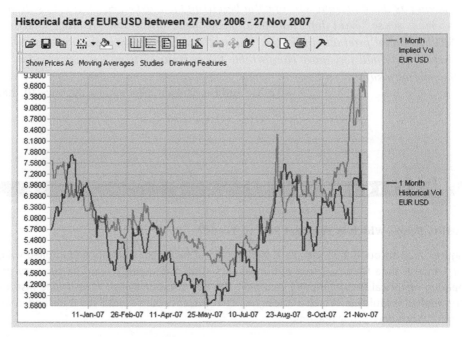

FIGURE 2.24 EURUSD 1-Month Historical versus Implied Volatility
Source: Reprinted with permission of Super Derivatives, Inc.

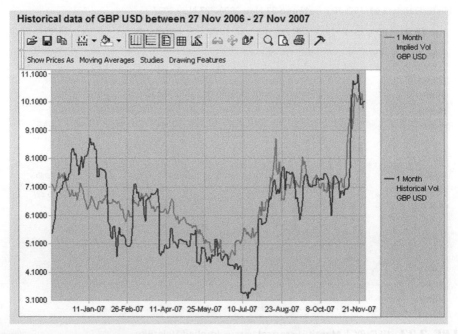

FIGURE 2.25 GBPUSD 1-Month Historical versus Implied Volatility
Source: Reprinted with permission of Super Derivatives, Inc.

FIGURE 2.26 USDCHF 1-Month Historical versus Implied Volatility
Source: Reprinted with permission of Super Derivatives, Inc.

FIGURE 2.27 USDCAD 1-Month Historical versus Implied Volatility
Source: Reprinted with permission of Super Derivatives, Inc.

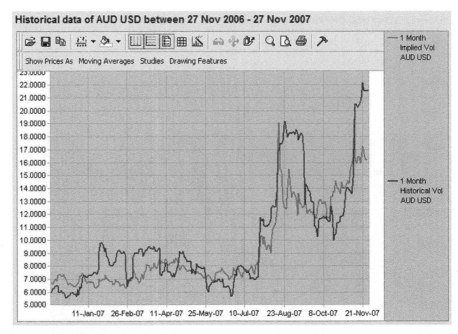

FIGURE 2.28 AUDUSD 1-Month Historical versus Implied Volatility
Source: Reprinted with permission of Super Derivatives, Inc.

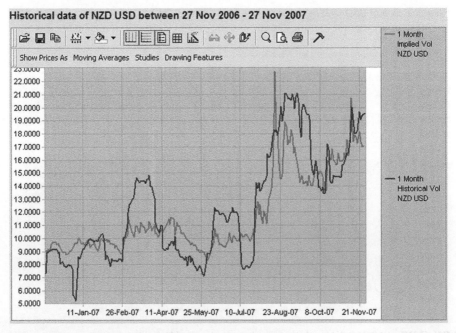

FIGURE 2.29 NZDUSD 1-Month Historical versus Implied Volatility
Source: Reprinted with permission of Super Derivatives, Inc.

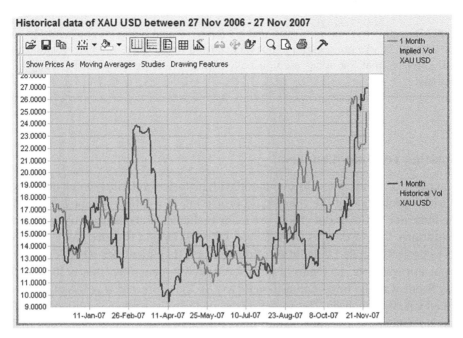

FIGURE 2.30 GOLD SPOT 1-Month Historical versus Implied Volatility
Source: Reprinted with permission of Super Derivatives, Inc.

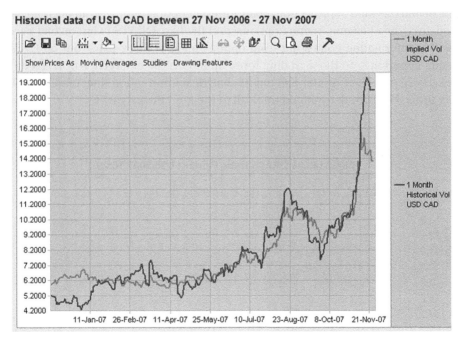

FIGURE 2.31 USDCAD 1 Month Historical versus Implied Volatility
Source: Reprinted with permission of Super Derivatives, Inc.

Answer

The USDCAD has the most extreme relationship between implied volatility and historical volatility. The USDCHF is also quite extreme but was starting to contract. The high volatility of the USDCAD suggests that the prices are unusually high in the underlying, further suggesting a sell strategy.

Forecasting Volatility Changes

While implied volatility is usually compared with historical volatility, it can also be compared with a projection of the volatility. A projection of volatility attempts to provide a leading indicator to the trader. There are many technical analysis firms trying to do this for institutions. One of them is ORATS.com. ORATS (Option Research and Technology Services) projects implied volatilities of options and then identifies what is an extreme situation. For example, in Figure 2.32, a forecast was generated that a 155 EURUSD January 8 put was the best option to sell (write). This forecast was based on the use of implied volatility analysis. This forecast was made on the exchange-traded fund (ETF) FXE on November 26. The idea behind this projection is that the data showed that the implied volatility associated with that strike price was much higher (12.2) compared to the forecast implied volatility or the ORATS program. This was considered very extreme and therefore to have a high probability of returning to a lower volatility level. Once the trader can find this kind of projection, many different option trading strategies can be formulated, including hedging, writing options, and the like. ORATS is interesting because this kind of information comes not from options on spot forex pairs, but on ETFs. Of enormous importance to those trading forex options is the emergence of ETFs on currencies. These provide a greater amount of analytical information than readily available at forex firms. Forex traders should track all of the key currency ETFs.

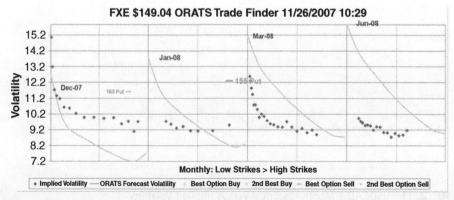

FIGURE 2.32 Identifying Best Option Trade Using ORATS Forecasts of Volatility Slopes
Source: Orats.com

Volatility Slope

If a trader detects a difference between a forecasted volatility slope and the implied one, trading strategies can result. For example, Figure 2.32 also shows that the implied volatility is higher than the forecast volatility in the front month but is lower than forecast volatility in the next three tradable months. This could be used as an indication to put on a long time spread—buy ATM call in January 2008 and sell ATM call in December 2007, for example; comparing the slope of option volatility against a forecasted slope leads to further insights about which option strategies can fit market conditions. Here is what Myron Woods of ORATS, the options analysis firm, says about this:

> *A high forecast slope relative to implied slope indicates that a vertical spread involving selling a lower strike option and buying an upper strike option looks attractive, from the perspective of relative valuation of the implied volatilities of the lower strike versus the upper strike. In other words, the lower strikes (i.e., out-of-the-money puts) are trading at a high implied volatility as compared to the upper strikes (i.e., out-of-the-money calls) and, also, this relationship does not line up with the forecasted relationship that is being generated by ORATS models.*

The Volatility Cheapness Index   The volatility cheapness index at Optima provides another useful way of spotting currencies that are in extreme modes of volatility. The volatility cheapness index measures how implied volatility currently compares to the last five years of history of volatility, ranked on a percentile scale ranging from zero (lowest) to 100 (highest). We can see in Table 2.1 that the yen was ranked at 98.8, which is very high in volatility. The Swiss franc was ranked lower, at 62.9. Knowing this will lead the

TABLE 2.1   Optima Volatility Cheapness Index—Currency Futures

As of: 11/20/07	JYZ07	ECZ07	SFZ97	BPZ07	CDZ07
Implied volatility	14.55s	9.53s	10.94s	10.45s	17.19s
Change	+.32	+.35	+.86	−.24	+.91
Historical volatility					
Max	15.7	16.5	18.4	15.4	14.0
Median	8.3	8.8	9.9	8.3	7.5
Min	2.2	2.9	4.3	3.5	3.1
Volatility cheapness index	98.8	63.3	62.9	86.8	100.0
Change	−.1	+6.3	+11.0	−1.3	Unch
Last 20 sessions					
High	100.0	64.1	62.9	88.1	100.0
Avg	98.8	48.2	45.1	67.8	99.9
Low	67.0	25.6	25.3	37.2	99.0
Last 60 sessions					
High	100.0	64.1	62.9	88.1	100.0
Avg	69.6	29.0	22.1	43.8	91.8
Low	28.7	14.4	4.0	26.8	76.5
Days to expiration	17	17	17	17	17

Source: Optima Investment Research, www.oir.com

trader to consider option trades that take advantage of volatility's being expensive or cheap. We will identify these strategies in Part Two, but generally speaking, if volatility is expected to increase, then the option trader will look to play range-probing or range-breaking price actions.

Volatility and Price Movement—Sigma Boundary Charts

In order to visualize what volatility actually implies for future price movement, it is useful to view a one-standard-deviation projection of price movement out into the future. This is called a sigma boundary chart. In order to do this, we simply take the current level of implied volatility, which is an annualized figure, and reduce it to shorter time frames, projecting the sigma boundary cone ahead from the current date. In a normal data distribution, the price movement will typically remain within plus or minus one standard deviation about two-thirds of the time, within plus or minus two standard deviations 95 percent of the time, and within plus or minus three standard deviations 99 percent of the time. By projecting a one-standard-deviation sigma boundary cone looking ahead, we can get a visual picture of the boundaries for price movement that the market is expecting. Specifically, the options market in the implied volatility figure is forecasting a two-thirds chance that the price movement will remain within the one-standard-deviation boundary in the future.

If a trader believes that the price movement is actually likely to breakout of that envelope, then the trader essentially believes that volatility is cheap and the trader may want to buy volatility. By the same token, if the trader thinks the price movement will remain within the one-standard-deviation envelope, then the trader effectively thinks volatility is expensive and may want to sell volatility.

The trader need not try to calculate the standard deviation of volatilities. This is done for the trader by different analytical services. For example, Optima Investment Research generates standard deviation ranges for five currency futures pairs. This provides a useful source for linking volatility and price movement, and also for identifying resistance and support ranges since the market prices sometimes bounce off the one- and two-standard-deviation price levels (see Table 2.2).

In Figure 2.33 we see the sigma boundary chart for the EURO forex December 2007 option. Seeing this, the trader would look to 1.51 and 1.46 as the probable areas of resistance and support and then would be able to shape option trades using this forecast. There are several strategies. A range trading strategy reflecting this chart would suggest a sell of 1.52 call and a sell of a 1.46 put since these are at the extreme sigmas. A play on a strengthening EURUSD would suggest a 1.49 call, and based on this chart projection, a 1.47 put would be in order. The sigma charts provide a unique and quick way of targeting option strike prices based on volatility.

Spotting a Volatility Cone

If a trader spots a volatility cone, then there is an opportunity to detect and conjecture which options are overpriced or undervalued. In the volatility cone chart in Figure 2.34,

TABLE 2.2 Optima Sigma Boundary—Currency Futures

As of Nov-07	Standard Deviations	JYZ07	ECZ07	SFZ07	BPZ07	CDZ07
Today:	+1 Std Dev:	0.0084	0.009	0.0062	0.0136	0.0111
	−1 Std Dev:	0.0083	0.009	0.0062	0.0136	0.0109
	68% H:	0.9226	1.491	0.9119	2.0786	1.0281
	L:	0.9058	1.473	0.8995	2.0514	1.006
	95% H:	0.931	1.5	0.9182	2.0922	1.0391
	L:	0.8975	1.464	0.8932	2.0378	0.9951
	99% H:	0.9394	1.509	0.9245	2.1058	1.0502
	L:	0.8891	1.455	0.887	2.0242	0.9841
20 Days Out:	+1 Std Dev:	N/A	N/A	N/A	N/A	N/A
	−1 Std Dev:	N/A	N/A	N/A	N/A	N/A
To Expiration:	+1 Std Dev:	0.0291	0.031	0.0216	0.047	0.0384
	−1 Std Dev:	0.0282	0.03	0.0211	0.046	0.037
	68% H:	0.9433	1.513	0.9273	2.112	1.0554
	L:	0.8859	1.452	0.8845	2.0188	0.9799
	95% H:	0.9725	1.544	0.9489	2.159	1.0939
	L:	0.8576	1.452	0.8634	1.9728	0.9429
	99% H:	1.0017	1.574	0.9706	2.2062	1.1323
	L:	0.8294	1.392	0.8423	1.9268	0.9058

Note: Shows probability of closing within price range based on implied volatility on subannual basis.
Source: Optima Investment Research, www.oir.com

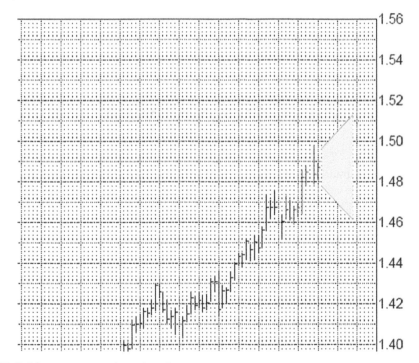

FIGURE 2.33 Sigma Boundary Chart for Euro Forex Dec 2007
Source: Orats.com

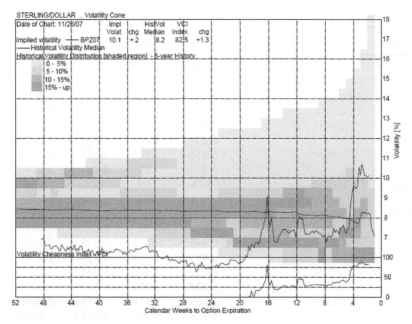

FIGURE 2.34 Volatility Cone for Sterling/Dollar
Source: Orats.com

we can see the historical changes in the volatility by the variation in the shading. We can see that the volatility of the GBPUSD pair has entered into the lowest percentile, signaling a potential buy. The ORATS software provides a quick visualization of volatility cones.

 ASSIGNMENT

Volatility Quotes

Serious forex option traders should look at the CME's volatility quotes on currency pairs. This allows traders to trade volatility directly. While institutions trade volatility directly, retail traders can now do it at the CME: http://www.cme.com/trading/get/files/volquotedimpact.pdf.

SUMMARY

This chapter focused on why volatility is a crucial component of forex option trading and strategies. The concepts of historical and implied volatility were reviewed. Important visualizations of volatility are also available to the trader, and software presenting volatility surfaces and smiles become important elements of trading options on the currencies. To help the trader, many software services are now available that offer sophisticated analytics on volatility.

PART TWO

Forex Market Drivers

S electing a currency pair for option trading is not a result of some canned formula. It is a process resulting from an evaluation of market conditions. The selection process is very much subjective. To be successful, it requires that the trader adopt a preferred direction where he or she has maximum confidence in the result. Gaining confidence about a direction of a forex option trade involves understanding several dimensions, explained in detail in Chapter 3.

Forex Market Drivers

Finding Direction for Your Forex Option Trade

This chapter focuses on how to find direction for a forex option trade and details the importance of several factors, such as interest rate expectations, the role of federal funds futures, and finding the probabilities of Federal Open Market Committee (FOMC) decisions. In addition, you will find an introduction to the binary options on the FOMC decisions as well as instruction on using housing sector data for developing forex option direction decisions.

THE IMPORTANCE OF INTEREST RATE EXPECTATIONS

Of major importance to the forex option trader is anticipating interest rate decisions by central banks. Of all of the factors moving currency prices, this is the most important and will be discussed in greater detail later in this book. The following column appearing in *Bloomberg* is a typical example of commentary throughout the year regarding interest rates and a currency direction.

Jan. 7 (Bloomberg)—Demand for options offering insurance against losses in the U.K. pound has almost quadrupled in the past two months amid speculation the Bank of England will cut interest rates as soon as this week to support its economy.

"The pound probably has further downside to go," said Russell Jones, global head of foreign exchange and fixed-income research at RBC Capital markets in London. "We expect the Bank of England to keep rates unchanged at the meeting, but it would be no big surprise if they did cut. It's an economic story that has started to deteriorate pretty rapidly."

"Sterling will depreciate further versus the dollar and it may weaken substantially as the U.K. economy slows to a greater extent than the U.S.," said Paul Robinson, senior sterling strategist in London at Barclays Capital Inc., in a telephone interview.

To make a decision on anticipated direction, the forex trader can use the interest rate expectation calculator found at www.learn4xi.com/tools.

 ASSIGNMENT

Group These Currencies by Interest Rate Expectations

Check the appropriate box reflecting your expectations.

	(DOWN 0.25)	(NO CHANGE)	(UP 0.25)	(UP 0.50)	(UP 0.75)
USD	☐	☐	☐	☐	☐
EUR	☐	☐	☐	☐	☐
YEN	☐	☐	☐	☐	☐
GBP	☐	☐	☐	☐	☐
CAD	☐	☐	☐	☐	☐
AUD	☐	☐	☐	☐	☐
NZD	☐	☐	☐	☐	☐
CHF	☐	☐	☐	☐	☐
MXN	☐	☐	☐	☐	☐
RENMINBI	☐	☐	☐	☐	☐

HOW TO ANTICIPATE THE DIRECTION OF THE FEDERAL OPEN MARKET COMMITTEE (FOMC)

It's all about the central bank's role to increase or decrease interest rates. Technically, we mean the action the FOMC makes on the federal funds rate at its meetings. These are the interest rates paid on loans made between banks (also known as depository institutions). The Federal Reserve therefore uses the policy tool of increasing or decreasing these loan rates to achieve policy goals.

A currency will strengthen if the market perceives that there is reason for interest rates to increase. The market forms an expectation about the next central bank decision on interest rates. This expectation then governs the sentiment between central bank meetings. So the first thing that a trader needs to do is to group the world of currencies into three groups: currencies with interest rates expected to go up, currencies with interest rates expected to go down, and currencies with interest rates expected to stay the same. The forex trader must consider these correlations between interest rate expectations and direction in shaping the duration of the trade. If the option trade extends beyond a central bank decision window, then the trader needs to anticipate a future meeting decision. There are now very effective ways of anticipating FOMC decisions that we will demonstrate in the next section.

The Role of Federal Funds Futures

What is the probability of a specific interest rate decision by the FOMC? How can the trader answer this question and go beyond just guessing? Answering this question is the focus of a great deal of work throughout the world. For the readers of this book however, there is a very effective way and it is in fact supported by official Federal Reserve Bank analysis. The Federal Reserve Bank of Cleveland stated, "Options on federal funds futures can be analyzed to extract public expectations of future Fed actions."

The Federal Reserve experts have developed a very sophisticated method for calculating the probability of FOMC actions that a reader interested in quantitative methods would consider worthwhile to review.

Calculating the Probability of a 25-Basis-Point FOMC Move

The following simple formula is a useful approximation of what a Chicago Board of Trade (CBOT) 30-day fed fund futures price implies for the probability of an increase in the target fed funds rate:

$$\text{FF futures implied rate} = \text{target} \times d_b/d + [(\text{target} + 0.25) \times p$$
$$+ \text{target} \times (1 - p)] \times d_e/d$$

where

target is the current target fed funds rate.

p is the probability that the FOMC will raise the target rate 25 bps and $(1\text{-}p)$ is the probability that it will leave the target unchanged.

d_b is the number of days in the month for which the current level of the target rate applies, that is, the number of days before and including the FOMC meeting date.

d_e indicates the number of days in the month for which the FOMC's next setting of the target rate will apply, that is, the number of days in the month after the FOMC meeting date.

d is the total number of days in the month. Not that d- $d_b + d_e$

(*Source:* www.wrightson.com)

In any case, by understanding and evaluating options on the federal fund futures contract, the forex trader can shape an expectation about the how the FOMC will be meeting. This important tool should be understood by forex traders.

Exchange (CBT) Chicago Board of Trade		
Name	FED FUND 30 DAY Jan08	
Ticker	FFF8 < CMDTY>	
Price is 100 - Yield		
Contract Size	$ 5,000,000.00	
Value of 1.0 pt	$ 4,167.00	
Tick Size	0.005	
Tick Value	$ 20.84	
Current Price	95.830	100 - yield
Pt. Val x Price	$ 399,323.62	@ 12/28

FIGURE 3.1   Federal Funds Futures Contract Details
Data Source: Bloomberg Finance L.P.

The Federal Funds Futures Contract

Let's first define terms. The fed fund futures contract is cash settled to the simple average overnight fed funds rate (for the delivery month) (see Figure 3.1).

The basis for obtaining a strike price by the subtraction of the targeted rate – 100, allows for the market to bet not only on whether the FOMC will change rates but also on how incremental the change will be.

The options market can be used to estimate the probabilities associated with several possible paths for the target federal funds rate over the next several FOMC meetings. An important study concluded that options on federal funds futures provide a simple but powerful means for extracting market expectations for the possible outcomes of FOMC meetings. In other words, the forex trader who wants to trade the FOMC decision can use the federal funds option information to help identify the probabilities involved in an impending decision. But it's important to keep in mind that it is not a simple prediction of whether the feds will increase, decrease, or stay the same. The trader has to be more quantitative about it. It's not just that rates will go up, down, or stay the same. A better way to express it is that rates can go down or up in increments of 25 basis points (www.clevelandfed.org/Research/workpaper/2005/WP0507.pdf).

The CBOT Binary Options: Using Binary Option Prices to Get Market Expectations of FOMC Decisions

The importance of anticipating currency direction we have said is paramount to the forex option trader. So our focus here is on presenting the best direct tool for enabling the trader to get an informed opinion about what the FOMC will do and also actually trade the FOMC decision directly! The forex option trader is very fortunate because the federal funds contract has a revolutionary option on it—binary options traded on the CBOT. It's important to note that understanding how these options can provide the trader

Exchange (CBT) Chicago Board of Trade		
Name	TARGET FEDFDS SF	Mar08
Ticker	YHH8	<CMDTY>
Price is 100 - Yield		
Contract Size	1,000 metric tons	
Value of 1.0 pt	$ 1,000	
Tick Size	0.005	
Tick Value	$ 5	
Current Price	96.060	100 - yield
Pt. Val x Price	$ 96,060	@ 12/28

FIGURE 3.2 Federal Funds Futures Contract Description
Data Source: Bloomberg Finance L.P.

information is what we are focusing on and not necessarily trading them. A good source for review for those who want to become familiar with binary options on the fed funds is www.clevelandfed.org/research/policy/fedfunds/binary.cfm.

Here is how it works. There are only two payout possibilities. Either the option is right and expires in the money and the trader gets $1000.000 payout or it is wrong and it expires worthless. The option expires on the last day of the FOMC meeting (see Figure 3.2)!

The ticker symbol is BUSC for calls and BUSP for puts. The up-to-date settlement values can be found at: www.cbot.com/cbot/pub/page/0,3181,1525,00.html.

Interpreting the Binary Options

The federal funds rate is targeted by the FOMC. The target is converted into an option strike price. So a target of 4.00 percent gets converted to 100 – 4.00 or 96.00 strike price. In other words, the trade gets strike prices that allow an anticipation of what the FOMC meeting will do.

The binary option is on the underlying federal funds rate directly. This contrasts with options on the average federal fund rate. The contracts also cover the next four meetings, so it provides a longer time frame as well. Also there is no other outcome. The trader either gets 1000 or gets 0. In a regular option purchase, the risk is limited to the premium paid, but the gain can vary. Figure 3.3 compares the payout under the binary option or a call. We can see that the binary option limits the payout. A major advantage is that the binary option also limits the risk on writing the option. A trader can in effect play the house and write an option and have no further risk other than owing the difference between what the trader receives (premium paid by the buyer) and 1000.

The strike prices are then subject to being bought or sold (written). If the trader writes a call at a strike price of 96.00, he is betting that the rates will *not* go down. He

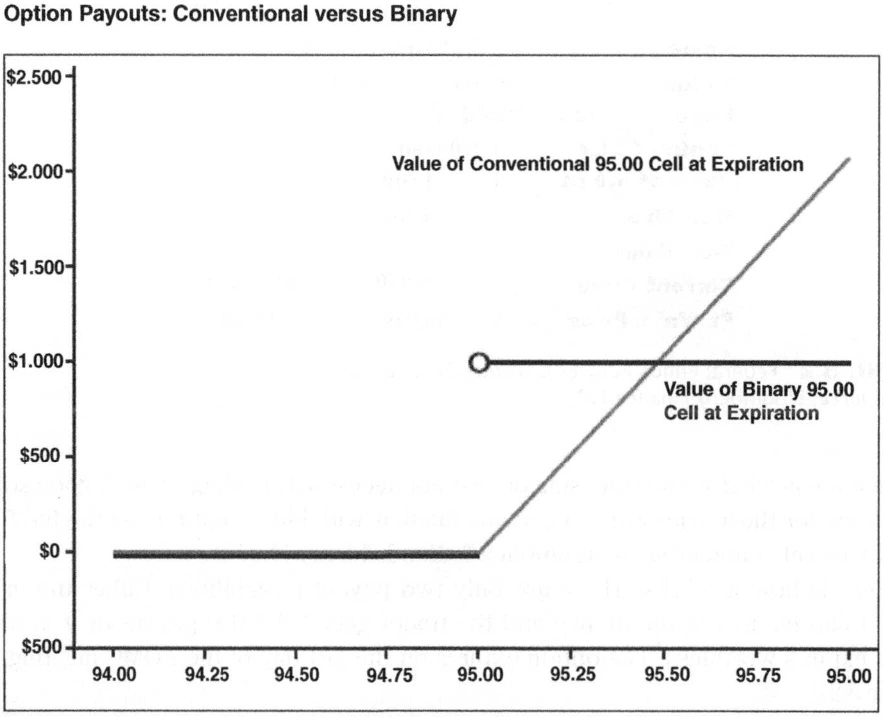

Option Payouts: Conventional versus Binary

FIGURE 3.3 Binary Option Payoffs Compared to Regular Options
Source: Saxo Bank Group at www.saxoeducation.com

receives premium. The buyer of the 96 strike price is paying a premium and betting that the rates will be 100 – 96, or 4 percent. The seller believes it will stay above that. The writer of the contract, unlike a plain vanilla option, will have a risk limited only to the difference between 1000 and the premium price he received.

Figure 3.4 shows how market call option prices on these binary's instantly shows the market opinion of the probability of fed FOMC actions. Here on November 28 was the option price on the December 11 decision. The interpretation of the data below showed that the market is pricing the probability of a cut as 78 percent that the fun rate will be below 4.5 percent and 20 percent that it will move further to a target rate of below 4.30 (see Figure 3.5).

For more important information on binary options, refer to the following sources:

- John B. Carlson, Ben R. Craig, and William R. Melick, "Recovering Market Expectations of FOMC Rate Changes with Options on Federal Funds Futures," *Journal of Futures Markets* 25(12) (December 2005): 1203–42.
- www.cbot.com/cbot/docs/82543.pdf
- www.cbot.com/cbot/docs/75940.pdf

Fed Binary Calls Settlement (BUSC)

as of November 28, 2007 17:01 CST

07Dec settle: 12/12 Click to see Fed Binary Product Calendar Dates

| Quotes | Settlement | Daily Vol | Historical Data | Time & Sales | Spreads |

Electronic

| Calls | Puts |

07Dec

Strike	Opening	High	Low	Closing	Settle	Net Change
94750				99 N	99	Unch
95250				96 N	96	Unch
95500	75	78	75	78	78	+8
95750	20	20	20	20	20	+1

Table generated November 28, 2007 17:01 CST   = Chart   = Option

FIGURE 3.4 Binary Calls Settlement Table
Source: CME Group

What Strategy Would Be Appropriate If the Trader Believes that on the Next FOMC Decision, Nothing Will Happen?

If a trader believes that the FOMC will not do anything, he could write a call and write a put. The trader would receive the premium paid him, which is the most he would gain. The trader would owe the difference between 1000 and the premium received if he were wrong.

The Commitment of Trader Reports and FOMC Decisions

The Commitment of Trader (COT) report is useful in spotting where the "big" money is betting on the FOMC decisions by looking at the latest COT report regarding bonds. Figure 3.6 provided by Lan Turner tracks the COT reports.

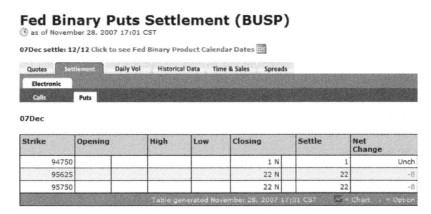

Fed Binary Puts Settlement (BUSP)

as of November 28, 2007 17:01 CST

07Dec settle: 12/12 Click to see Fed Binary Product Calendar Dates

| Quotes | Settlement | Daily Vol | Historical Data | Time & Sales | Spreads |

Electronic

| Calls | Puts |

07Dec

Strike	Opening	High	Low	Closing	Settle	Net Change
94750				1 N	1	Unch
95625				22 N	22	-8
95750				22 N	22	-8

Table generated November 28, 2007 17:01 CST   = Chart   = Option

FIGURE 3.5 Binary Puts Settlement Table
Source: CME Group

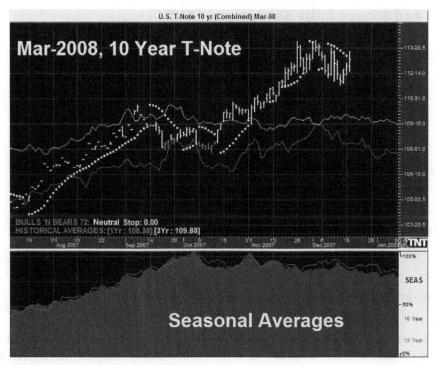

FIGURE 3.6 Tracking the Commitment of Trader Reports
Source: www.trackntrade.com

Taking a look at the COT, we see that the large speculators, banks and hedge fund managers, started loading up on T-bonds around the first of August; and as we can see in Figure 3.6, they continued to hold those positions into year's end 2007. This indicates strong sentiment of a continued decline in interest rates. The COT report is certainly an indicator that forex traders should use to track COT holdings on the 10-year bond.

The power of the binary options is that it allows the trader not only to play a direct decision on the FOMC, but it gives the trader the ability to extract sentiment data and use it in his own trading. This option play allows the trader to trade more than just the next FOMC meeting. He can trade a sequence of events. What if the trade thinks the FOMC will cut or raise rates one more time and then do nothing? A strategy here would be to *buy a put* or sell a call if the trader things rates would go up. Or if the trader thinks rates will go down and the FOMC will lower rates, he would *buy a call* or write a put.

For more information on the CBOT binary options on the federal funds rate, take a look at these web sites:

- www.cbot.com/cbot/pub/cont_detail/0,3206,1415+39173,00.html
- www.cbot.com/cbot/docs/82543.pdf
- www.cbot.com/cbot/pub/cont_detail/0,3206,1415+39173,00.html
- www.cbot.com/cbot/pub/page/0,3181,1563,00.html

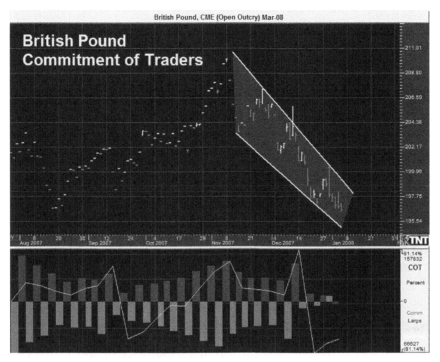

FIGURE 3.7 British Pound Commitment of Traders, January 7, 2008
Source: www.trackntrade.com

Tracking Sentiment on Bank of England's Rate Decisions
COT on the British Pound

The COT can also be used to help predict interest rate decisions on other currencies, particularly as an interest rate decision month is coming up for the market to consider. For example, here is the COT report on the British pound that indicates big money is neutral as to direction. Together with the volatility surface favoring puts, a trader inclined to trade puts on the pound has gained more confirming information.

In the COT graph, as shown in Figure 3.7, you will notice that we have a representation of both the large commercials, in red, and the large speculators, in blue. One of the most powerful capabilities offered to us by the COT is the ability to see a representation of market sentiment by the largest of players. In Figure 3.7, notice that both segments are about to converge at the zero point along our histogram. This is a representation of market equilibrium, using past experience as our gauge; this is generally indicative of two things:

1. Stagnation, as the market tries to determine the next new trend.
2. A breakout will be fueled by both sides trying to jump on the next big move.

(*Source:* Lan Turner)

3 MO EURO EURIBOR Jun 08		95.67			
Ticker	Last	Strikes	Last		Ticker
calls					puts
ERM8 JUN 2008 (Contract Size 1000000)				**ERM8 JUN 2008 (Contract Size 1000000)**	
ERM8C	0.3350	95.3750	0.0450		ERM8P
ERM8C	0.2400	95.5000	0.0750		ERM8P
ERM8C	0.1650	95.6250	0.1250		ERM8P
ERM8C	0.1050	95.7500	0.1900		ERM8P
ERM8C	0.0700	95.8750	0.2800		ERM8P
ERU8 SEP 2008 (Contract Size 1000000)				**ERU8 SEP 2008 (Contract Size 1000000)**	
ERU8C	0.3250	95.6250	0.1250		ERU8P
ERU8C	0.2500	95.7500	0.1750		ERU8P
ERU8C	0.1900	95.8750	0.2400		ERU8P
ERU8C	0.1400	96.0000	0.3150		ERU8P
ERU8C	0.1050	96.1250	0.4050		ERU8P
ERZ8 DEC 2008 (Contract Size 1000000)				**ERZ8 DEC 2008 (Contract Size 1000000)**	
ERZ8C	0.4450	95.6250	0.1350		ERZ8P
ERZ8C	0.3600	95.7500	0.1750		ERZ8P
ERZ8C	0.2900	95.8750	0.2300		ERZ8P
ERZ8C	0.2350	96.0000	0.3000		ERZ8P
ERZ8C	0.1800	96.1250	0.3700		ERZ8P
ERH9 MAR 2009 (Contract Size 1000000)				**ERH9 MAR 2009 (Contract Size 1000000)**	
ERH9C	0.6400	95.5000	0.0950		ERH9P
ERH9C	0.4600	95.7500	0.1650		ERH9P
ERH9C	0.3200	96.0000	0.2750		ERH9P

FIGURE 3.8 3-Month Eurolibor Contract
Data Source: Bloomberg Finance L.P.

Tracking European Central Bank Interest Rate Decisions

When a forex trader is trading the EURUSD, the importance of anticipated European Central Bank (ECB) interest rate decisions is critical to shaping a forex options trade. The trader needs to detect any shift in a consensus of what the ECB under Trichet's leadership will do.

Using futures data, the trader can look at the 3-month Euro Interbank Offered Rate (EURIBOR) interest rate futures contract. It trades on the Liffe Exchange. The contract's movement reflects market sentiment on interest rate changes in the Eurozone. For example, the June 2008 contract price was at 95.665. This translates into (100 – 95.665) or 4.335 percent. This is an implied percentage and if the market was anticipating the EUR rate coming down, this contract would go up in value. But the trader can look at option data to derive some further confirmation regarding a consensus on direction. The option chain table shows calls and puts, and the put/call ratio would be helpful (e.g., see Figure 3.8).

HOW TO USE HOUSING SECTOR DATA FOR DEVELOPING FOREX OPTION TRADE DIRECTION

Housing data is one of the most important components in projecting currency moves and in anticipating a change in interest rate policies. A weak housing market portends a decrease in rates while a strong housing market raises fears of inflation and, therefore, market anticipation of interest rate increases or at least not cutting rates. The trader needs to keep an eye on key sources of housing data and develop a focus on key indicators and data for each currency pair. Luckily, there is a plethora of information available.

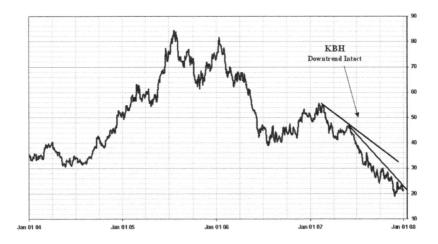

FIGURE 3.9 KB Homes
Data Source: Bloomberg Finance L.P.

KB Homes

For shaping a directional opinion on the U.S. dollar, the trader can track key housing equities to identify whether the prevailing trend is about to change. For example, KB Homes is a leading builder of single-family homes in the United States. Its stock price is a leading indicator of the housing market strengths or weaknesses. We can see in Figure 3.9 that its downtrend was intact by the end of 2007. A forex trader who wants to anticipate whether the FOMC will stop lowering rates or will increase rates will be on high alert if the price breaks its downtrend line. We can see clearly that KB Homes, at the start of 2006, began a downtrend, coinciding with weakness in the overall housing market.

A put on the stock would correspond to a bet that U.S. interest rates would be staying down. A call option just out of the money at $22 would be anticipating an FOMC decision to not lower rates, and therefore, this would be correlated with a recovering in the housing market. A call option playing a $22.50 strike price was priced at a premium of $1.60 compared to an at-the-money put of $2.98. This shows that the sentiment on the housing market recovery was significantly bearish. The forex trader should watch this ratio periodically to see if it changes. If the ratio swings toward the call side, the trader should carefully consider calls on the U.S. dollar because a stronger housing market will reduce any probability of interest rate reductions (see Figure 3.10).

Equity	KBH		
Market Price	21.08		
Date	December 29		
Call Premium	Strike Price	Put Premium	Puts/Calls
1.60	$22.50	2.98	1.8625

Source: Bloomberg

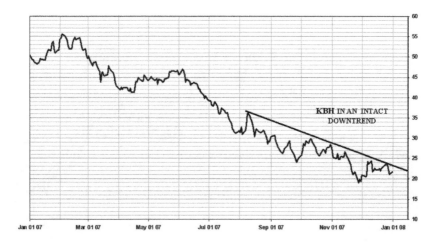

FIGURE 3.10 The Year Downtrend
Data Source: Bloomberg Finance L.P.

In 2007, KB Homes had a 56.89 percent negative return. The forex trader looking for a leading indicator of a housing recovery would want to see the price break the downtrend line. He can also put on an options trade and play a recovery with a purchase of a $25 strike price. The option would need to be longer term to give time for the economy to start recovering. More important is the put/call ratio. It hit a high on December 27 of 31.7, with a moving average of the put/call ratio at 5.7. The average put/call ratio was 3.0. This data showed that the mood of the market was still very bearish (see Figure 3.11).

We can look at one more important piece of information regarding sentiment on this equity. We can compare the premium price of calls and puts. If the trader were to shape an option trade on the recovery of this stock and its breaking of a downtrend, he might consider an April 19 option and determine whether it is indicating the same bear sentiment. We can see that the put/call ratio or premium price is 3.70, which is not a good sign for buying and therefore not a good support for buying U.S. dollars on anticipation that the FOMC would not decrease rates.

Equity	KBH		
Market Price	21.08kb		
Date	April 19		
Call Premium	Strike Price	Put Premium	Puts/Calls
1.50	$25.00	5.60	3.70

Source: Bloomberg

Yet the price pattern and the option data on this equity do point to future conditions that may be leading indicators for a change in U.S. interest rate policy from decreasing rates to that of being neutral. Also, it is beneficial to be looking at the volatility data. The volatility of this option is 65.29 percent. If it starts declining, it could be a sign of a bottoming out. If it coincided with the price probing the trend line and breaking out, the

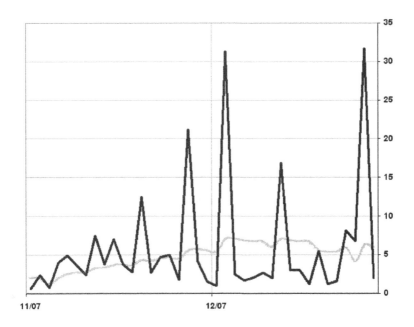

FIGURE 3.11 KB Homes Put/Call Ratio
Data Source: Bloomberg Finance L.P.

market would be telling the trader and the FOMC (who are watching key stocks) that it may be time to no longer cut rates (see Figure 3.12).

Leading U.S. Housing Equities
BHS (BROOKFIELD HOMES CORP)
BZH (BEAZER HOMES USA)
CHB (CHAMPION ENTERPRISES)

KB HOME	21.08 USD	Trade	12/30/07 05:49			Settle	12/30/07
Net Option values							
Price (Total)	169.65377	Currency	USD	Vega	4.37	Time value	169.65
Price (Share)	1.696538	Delta (%)	38.43	Theta	1.28	Gearing	12.43
Price (%)	8.048092	Gamma (%)	4.9858	Rho	1.80	Break-Even (%)	26.64
Single Leg	**Leg 1**						
Style	Vanilla						
Exercise	American						
Call/Put	Call						
Direction	Buy						
Strike	25.00						
Strike % Money	18.60% OTH						
Shares	100.00						
Expiry	04/19/08 16:15						
Time to expiry	111 10:26						
Exercise delay	0						
Model	BS - continuous						
Volatility Market	65.294%						

FIGURE 3.12 KB Homes Call Option
Data Source: Bloomberg Finance L.P.

CTX (CENTEX CORP)
HOV (HOVNANIAN ENTERPRISES)
KBH (KB HOME)
LEN (LENNAR CORP)
MDC (MDC HOLDINGS INC
MTH (MERITAGE HOMES CORP)
PHM (PULTE HOMES INC.)
RYL (RYLAND CORP)
TOL (TOLL BROTHERS INC)

Housing Data outside the United States

Anticipating the direction of interest rates in other countries is a key method for shaping a bullish or bearish sentiment regarding trading currency pairs other than the dollar. The housing sector is a reliable indicator in almost every country that has a floating currency. Let's look at some pairs.

The British Pound   This currency movement went to historic highs against the U.S. dollar and then retraced back. The cause was a fall in housing prices after a decade-long boom (see Figure 3.13).

The direction of the GBPUSD followed a significant slowdown in housing prices and in mortgage approvals in Britain. Seeing this data as a put on the GBPUSD would be following the sentiments of the market. (*Source:* British Bankers' Association, Royal Institution of Chartered Surveyors, Nationwide Building Society.)

FIGURE 3.13   GBPUSD in Downward Channel Break
Data Source: Bloomberg Finance L.P.

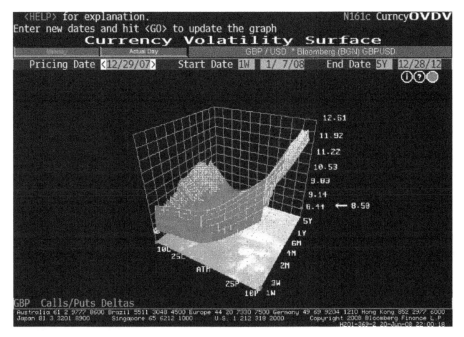

FIGURE 3.14 GBPUSD Volatility Surface
Source: © 2008 Bloomberg L.P. All rights reserved. Used with permission.

Having observed a bearish development in the GBPUSD (Figure 3.13) a further confirmation appears on the GBPUSD's volatility surface. We can see in Figure 3.14 a skew in sentiment toward the put side.

We see a sharp skew in the implied volatility of the puts over the calls. Also, when looking at a the premium prices of options 200 pips away from the spot price, we see a skew of the put premiums nearly twice the calls. Finally, for those who have access to the data, the 25 delta risk reversals show also favoritism for the puts (see Figure 3.15).

	25ΔRR	25ΔFly		5Δ	10Δ	15Δ	20Δ	25Δ	30Δ	ATM	30Δ	25Δ	20Δ
1W	-1.250	0.240	Vol	11.98	11.25	10.86	10.57	10.34	10.10	9.450	9.12	9.09	9.10
			Strike	1.9426	1.9569	1.9655	1.9719	1.9771	1.9817	1.9963	2.0095	2.0132	2.0175
1M	-1.350	0.320	Vol	12.65	11.58	11.02	10.63	10.32	10.04	9.300	8.98	8.97	8.99
			Strike	1.8770	1.9102	1.9296	1.9437	1.9551	1.9650	1.9955	2.0232	2.0313	2.0404
2M	-1.350	0.350	Vol	12.95	11.73	11.11	10.68	10.35	10.05	9.300	9.00	9.00	9.04
			Strike	1.8313	1.8780	1.9048	1.9243	1.9399	1.9534	1.9947	2.0325	2.0438	2.0566
3M	-1.350	0.370	Vol	13.12	11.77	11.10	10.65	10.30	9.99	9.225	8.94	8.94	8.99
			Strike	1.7920	1.8506	1.8839	1.9079	1.9272	1.9437	1.9939	2.0401	2.0541	2.0701

FIGURE 3.15 GBPUSD 25 Delta Risk Reversal
Source: Reprinted with permission of Super Derivatives, Inc.

GBP USD			
Spot	1.9965		
Date	December 29		
Call Strike	2.0265	Premium	1,092 (Pounds)
Put Strike	1.9765	Premium	2.297 (Pounds)

Source: Bloomberg Finance L.P.

Australian Dollar and Housing Data　Another example of how housing data influenced currency price direction and anticipation of interest rate decisions is that of Australia (see Figure 3.16). Here is what *Bloomberg* reported on January 8:

Jan. 8 (Bloomberg)—Australia's dollar rose, reversing a loss, after a government report showed home-building approvals unexpectedly surged in November by the most in nine months.

The currency gained from the weakest in two weeks as traders raised the odds the Reserve Bank of Australia will increase its 6.75 percent key interest rate in

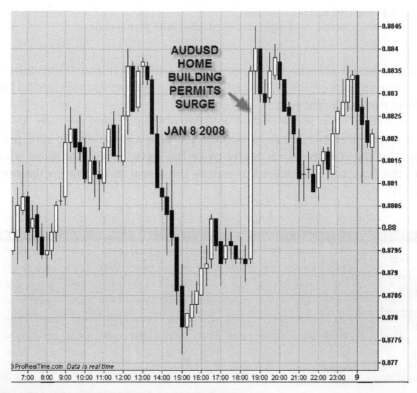

FIGURE 3.16　Aussie Home Building Permits Surge
Source: Reprinted with permission of Super Derivatives, Inc.

the next 12 months. Australia's dollar had declined earlier after a measure of commodity prices fell the most in three weeks yesterday.

"The positive data from Australia is leading to speculation that the RBA will have no choice but to raise rates in February," said Sharada Selvanathan, a currency strategist at BNP Paribas SA in Hong Kong. "That is the main driver for the Aussie," she said, referring to the currency's nickname.

The Australian dollar advanced 0.3 percent to 87.70 U.S. cents at 4:50 P.M. *in Sydney from 87.44 cents late in Asia yesterday. It earlier touched 86.84 cents, the lowest since Dec. 24, and may advance to 90 cents over the next couple of weeks, which would be a good level to sell, Selvanathan said.*

The currency rose to 95.88 yen from 95.74 yen yesterday. Investors expect the central bank will raise its overnight cash-rate target by at least a quarter-percentage point to 7 percent in the next 12 months, according to a Credit Suisse Group index based on trading in interest-rate swaps. The odds of a quarter-point increase within a year were 92 percent yesterday.

Japan Housing Data Traders of the yen will find Japan housing data as an important factor in expectations regarding the Japanese economy. It's important to note that Japan is the second-largest economy in the world. Housing start data provides a potential leading indicator of whether the Japanese economy is declining, stalling, or growing. In 2007 Japan's housing starts reached a 40-year low, adding to a bearish sentiment on the Japanese economy. It is estimated that housing decline had at least a 1 percent reduction in Japanese gross domestic product (GDP). But in January 2008, data showed a bottoming out of residential dwelling started (see Figure 3.17).

Reports in March 2008 indicated that the decline in housing starts in Japan may have reached a bottom. An increase in housing starts is also correlated with related industries such as building materials. Construction orders also rose (see Figure 3.18).

Keeping an eye on Japan housing data makes a lot of sense for formulating longer-term option trades on the yen. A good web site for monitoring Japan economic events is http://japanjapan.blogspot.com/.

New Zealand Housing Data The very strong growth experienced by the New Zealand dollar (NZD) was highly associated with housing prices, which have doubled since 2000. Traders noticing a topping out of housing prices and starts would be justified in selecting a put on the currency pair. Figure 3.19 shows a slowdown in housing prices, and using this data the forex trader could play the slowdown as a leading indictor of the currency's weakening.

Housing statistics data for New Zealand is available from Statistics New Zealand, a government agency. The agency's official web site is www.stats.govt.nz/analytical-reports/housing/Housing+Statistics+Programme.htm.

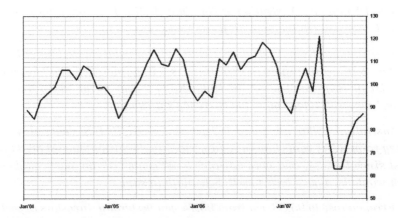

FIGURE 3.17   January 2008 Japan Housing Data
Data Source: Bloomberg Finance L.P.

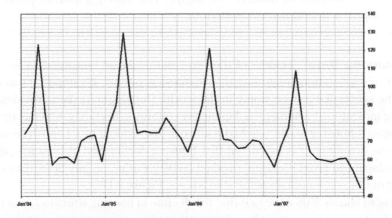

FIGURE 3.18   March 2008 Japan Housing Data
Data Source: Bloomberg Finance L.P.

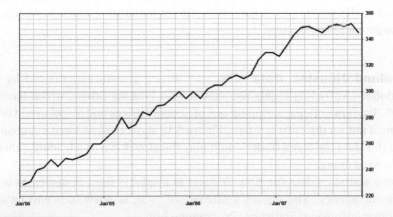

FIGURE 3.19   New Zealand Housing Prices Slow
Data Source: Bloomberg Finance L.P.

Canadian Dollar and Housing Data　Will the Bank of Canada increase its interest rates? That's the question the forex trading Considering the Canadian dollar and its pairs must always ask. Once again, housing data is a key leading indicator about anticipating a central bank decision. The trader needs to look at Canadian housing starts. (*Data source:* Canada Mortgage and Housing Corporation, www.cmhc.ca/en/corp/nero/nere/2008/2008-01-09-0815.cfm.)

> *OTTAWA, January 9, 2008* (*Bloomberg*)—*Housing starts in 2007 are estimated at 229,600, surpassing 2006 starts, and reaching their second highest level in nearly two decades. However, the seasonally adjusted annual rate of housing starts in December decreased to 187,500 units from November's 233,300 units, according to Canada Mortgage and Housing Corporation (CMHC).*

The data showed a slowdown in the housing starts and the currency pair reacted. The trader could use this reaction as a sentiment leading indicator and look to buy calls on the USDCAD pair (see Figure 3.20).

 ASSIGNMENT

Evaluate the price trends of the leading housing equities in Australia, New Zealand, Canada, Germany, and Japan. Are the patterns in a sideways, uptrend, or downtrend market?
　Here is a list of housing country data resources and key equities by country:
Australia
　　Australian Performance of Construction Indicator
　　(Australian Industry Group)
　　Westpac Survey
Canada
　　Housing Mortgage Co Housing Starts
　　Canada Mortgage and Housing Corporation
Germany
　　Federal Statistical Office
　　Axel Weber, head of German Bundesbank and member of the European Central Bank
　　　　Council
Japan
　　Ministry of Land, Infrastructure, and Transport
New Zealand

EVALUATING REAL ESTATE EXCHANGE-TRADED FUNDS (ETFs)

The trader can go further and get a feeling for the market mood and whether it supports a dollar recovery by looking at the Dow Jones U.S. Real Estate Index (DJUSRE).

CANADIAN DOLLAR
FALLS ON WEAK
HOUSING DATA

FIGURE 3.20 Canadian Dollar Falls on Weak Housing Data
Data Source: Bloomberg Finance L.P.

As Figure 3.21 shows, the steep decline indicates that any long-term buy would be difficult to justify, further confirming that the FOMC has a low probability of not increasing rates in this kind of environment.

For those traders who want to confirm a bearish strategy on the U.S. economy and believe that further interest rate cuts are in the cards, there is a contrarian real estate fund. The UltraShort Real Estate (SRS) ETF is a contrarian fund that "seeks daily investment results that correspond to twice (200 percent) the inverse (opposite) of the daily performance of the DJUSRE (www.proshares.com). This fund also has options which makes it more capable of generating useful information to the forex option trader.

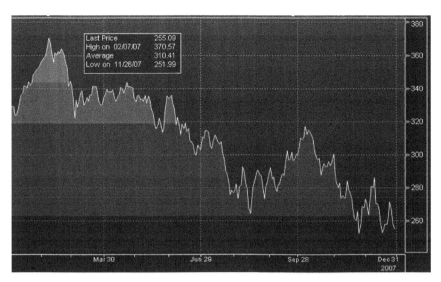

FIGURE 3.21 DJUS Real Estate Index
Data Source: Bloomberg Finance L.P.

This fund makes money as long as the real estate industry is down. Therefore, what would be useful would be evaluating a spread between the DJUSRE and the SRS fund. If the spread is at either end of the bell curve, we can conclude that it's not going to stay there and that the fundamentals that resulted in this wide spread are likely to change (see Figure 3.22).

The results of the spread, seen in Figure 3.23, similar to a bull ETF versus bear ETF, a show very wide spread that is at 97.83 percent in its deviation. This means that it's at a very extreme point that is not likely to last (see Figure 3.24).

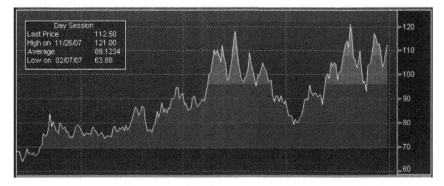

FIGURE 3.22 SRS UltraShort Real Estate Index
Data Source: Bloomberg Finance L.P.

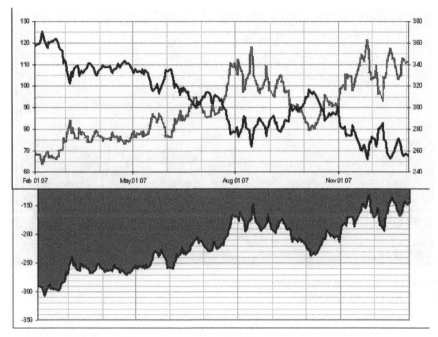

FIGURE 3.23 Spread between the Dow Jones Real Estate Index and the UltraShort Real Estate Index
Data Source: Bloomberg Finance L.P.

Let's go a step further and look at the option sentiment on puts and calls. First locate the at-the-money (ATM) strike price or the one nearest to it. The market price on December 28, 2007, is 112.50. This means that the ATM would be 110.00. Now let's travel at an equal distance from the spot. For example, we can choose a strike price of 115.00 and a strike price of 105.00. Let's choose an April option. The April 115 call is priced at 16.20, while the April 105 put is priced at 13.20. This indicates that the option sentiment is skewing in favor of a bullish recovery by April since the premiums for the calls are higher than the premiums for the puts.

Option sentiment is not a predictor but simply reflects the consensus of opinion. The forex trader needs to be always ready for surprises in the market and use the ETFs on the key housing sector as a strategic alert providing early and leading indication of changes in this important sector (see Figure 3.25).

Strategic Alert: When the Bank Industry ETF Regional Bank HOLDRS (RKH) Breaks

Its own trend line: Buy dollars in the currency markets (see Figure 3.26).

As long as the bank industry ETF stays within its steep downtrend, there is little support to buy dollars.

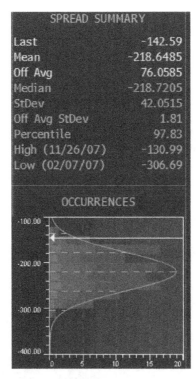

FIGURE 3.24 Standard Deviation of Spread
Data Source: Bloomberg Finance L.P.

SRS US $ C : 112.50 Dec 28 2007					
Ticker	Last	Strikes	Last	Ticker	
calls				puts	
SRS 19 JAN 2008 (Contract Size 100)				**SRS 19 JAN 2008 (Contract Size 100)**	
SRS+AA	7.30	105.00	6.10	SRS+MA	
SRS+AF	7.60	110.00	5.20	SRS+MF	
SRS+AB	6.50	115.00	11.00	SRS+MB	
SRS+AC	3.80	120.00	15.40	SRS+MC	
SRS+AD	2.15	125.00	17.50	SRS+MD	
SRS 16 FEB 2008 (Contract Size 100)				**SRS 16 FEB 2008 (Contract Size 100)**	
SRS+BA	12.00	105.00		SRS+NA	
SRS+BF	10.00	110.00		SRS+NF	
SRS+BB	10.30	115.00		SRS+NB	
SRS+BC		120.00		SRS+NC	
SRS+BD		125.00		SRS+ND	
SRS 19 APR 2008 (Contract Size 100)				**SRS 19 APR 2008 (Contract Size 100)**	
SRS+DA		105.00	13.50	SRS+PA	
SRS+DF	17.70	110.00		SRS+PF	
SRS+DB		115.00		SRS+PB	
SRS+DC	16.50	120.00		SRS+PC	
SRS+DD		125.00	29.00	SRS+PD	
SRS 19 JUL 2008 (Contract Size 100)				**SRS 19 JUL 2008 (Contract Size 100)**	
SRS+GA	25.00	105.00		SRS+SA	
SRS+GF	24.70	110.00	20.80	SRS+SF	
SRS+GB	20.50	115.00		SRS+SB	

FIGURE 3.25 Option Chain on the UltraShort Real ETF
Data Source: Bloomberg Finance L.P.

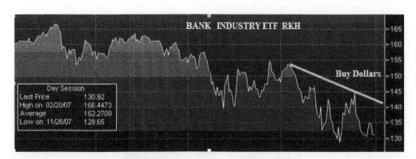

FIGURE 3.26 Bank Industry ETF RKH
Data Source: Bloomberg Finance L.P.

Appendix: Housing Sector ETFs and Charts

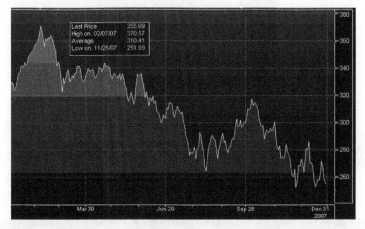

FIGURE 3.27 Dow Jones U.S. Real Estate Index
Data Source: Bloomberg Finance L.P.

FIGURE 3.28 Ultra Real Estate Proshares
Data Source: Bloomberg Finance L.P.

FIGURE 3.29 XHB SPDR S&P Homebuilders ETF
Data Source: Bloomberg Finance L.P.

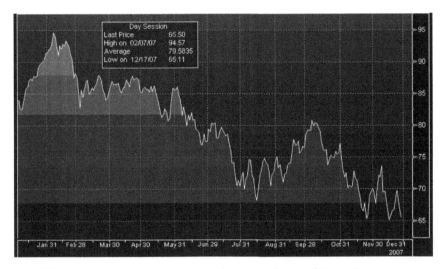

FIGURE 3.30 The Ishares Dow Jones U.S. Real Estate Index Fund (IRY US)
Data Source: Bloomberg Finance L.P.

SUMMARY

This chapter reviewed some key components of formulating option strategies for currency pairs. A major impact on currency direction is the FOMC decisions on interest rates. The chapter reviewed how option strategies can be shaped around the FOMC decisions. Additionally, the chapter focused on how to locate and use housing sector data as a leading indicator for anticipating longer-term currency directions in the currency pairs of the majors.

FIGURE 3.29 Xo8 SPDR S&P Homebuilders ETF
Data Source: Bloomberg Finance L.P.

FIGURE 3.30 The iShares Dow Jones U.S. Real-Estate Index Fund (IYR US)
Data Source: Bloomberg Finance L.P.

SUMMARY

This chapter reviewed some key components of formulating option strategies for currency pairs. A major impact on currency direction is the FOMC decisions on interest rates. The chapter reviewed how option strategies can be shaped around the FOMC decisions. Additionally, the chapter looked at how to locate and use housing sector data as a leading indicator for anticipating future central bank directives to the currency pairs of the majors.

CHAPTER 4

Tracking Fundamental Directions

In this chapter the forex option trader learns to diagnose market conditions in order to develop a currency outlook and directional trading strategy. Two fairly new tools to use are exchange traded funds (ETFs) and exchange-traded notes (ETNs). They provide easy to access information on currencies and key sectors. The role of purchasing power parity (PPP) measurements is reviewed in their ability to help decide an option direction. The trade-weighted index is reviewed as a tool for analysis. The reader will learn more about the currency–commodity connections and how to use commodity and currency intermarket analysis to shape option strategies. Finally, a currency outlook checklist is provided at the end of the chapter.

USING CURRENCY TARGETED EXCHANGE-TRADED FUNDS (ETFs) TO DETERMINE IF THE MARKET IS DOLLAR BEARISH OR BULLISH

We can see that an ETF can be used to derive supportive information about the direction of interest rate policy when the focus is on the housing sector. But ETFs can be used by the forex trader to support a decision on what direction a currency pair should be traded. Many ETFs offer options on the ETFs, and this allows the forex trader to either use the option data for sentiment analysis or even trade the option data.

ETFs on currencies can be grouped as those dealing with the U.S. dollar sentiment; those dealing with a currency pair; and those dealing with a particular sector that has an impact on currency price movements. Let's take a closer look.

Dollar Bull versus Dollar Bear ETFs

UUP PowerShares DB U.S. Dollar Index Bullish Fund is an ETF that employs a bullish dollar strategy. The strategy is to identify opportunities to go long the dollar against several currencies, including the euro, yen, British pound, Canadian dollar, Swedish krona, and Swiss franc. This has not been an easy strategy in recent times. But the point is that this ETF tells a very effective story about the mood of the market. Its price pattern shows a breakdown in any bullish sentiment. In contrast, the UDN US is an ETF with a bearish strategy and we see that the result was very profitable. Using these two ETFs provides support for a trader's being bullish or bearish. They are a good pair to use because they are negatively correlated at −0.96. This means they move in opposite directions and are almost always in negative sync! Comparing these two sides of the coin on U.S. dollar sentiment is an effective way of deriving further insights (see Figures 4.1 and 4.2).

If the forex trader wants insight into whether dollar bearish sentiment is likely to continue or may be nearing a bottom, generating a spread chart would identify if the bulls versus the bears are at their statistical extremes. If the spread is at the widest point, it is likely to narrow. If the spread is narrowing, then it is likely to widen. This likelihood is statistical in nature and based on standard deviation analysis. So what happens when we spread these two different funds? We get an instant picture of the spread being at its widest point. This means that a narrowing of the spread is likely and the strategy

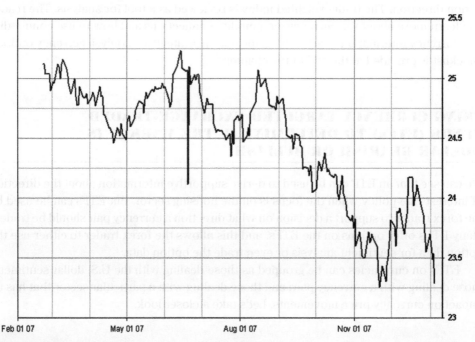

FIGURE 4.1 UDN US PowerShares DB US Dollar—Bearish
Data Source: Bloomberg Finance L.P.

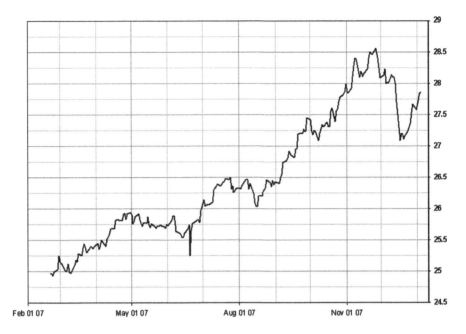

FIGURE 4.2 UUP PowerShares US Dollar Index—Bullish
Data Source: Bloomberg Finance L.P.

that created the wide spread (selling the bull fund) and buying the bear fund will start reverting to the mean.

At the highest the spread was 5.25; at the lowest it was −0.19. Being at 4.12 means that it is in its outer part of the statistical bell curve. Another point to consider is the importance of the spread when it's at the center of its curve at the mean. This would strategically mean that there is a balance between the bulls and bears on the U.S. dollar sentiment, and therefore trading can occur in either direction (see Figures 4.3 and 4.4).

ETFs for Currency Pairs

Traders looking to track and analyze currency pairs via the ETF vehicle can use the following ETFs:

FXF Currency Shares Swiss Franc
FXS Currency Shares Swedish Krona
FXM Currency Shares Mexican Peso
FXY Currency Shares Japanese Yen
FXE Currency Shares Euro Trust
FXB Currency Shares British Pound
FXA Currency Shares Australian Dollar

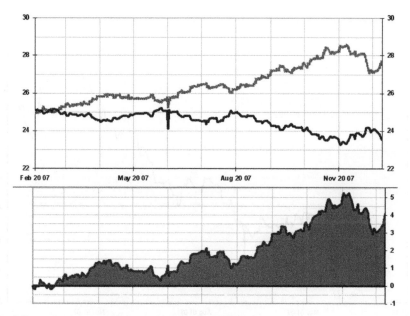

FIGURE 4.3 Spread Range History of UUP versus UDN
Data Source: Bloomberg Finance L.P.

<u>**Spread Summary**</u>

Last	4.12
Mean	1.967
Off Avg	2.153
Median	1.595
St Deviation	1.454
High (11/26/07)	5.25
Low (02/22/07)	-0.19

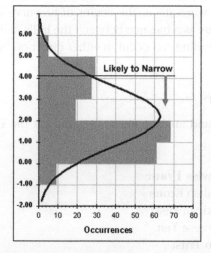

FIGURE 4.4 Standard Deviation for UUP versus UDN
Data Source: Bloomberg Finance L.P.

ETFs and ETNs on Key Sectors

The following ETFs can be used to track sectors relevant to currency trading and analysis. PowerShares is a group of ETFs that track sectors relevant to currency analysis and trading. Some key ones include:

PowerShares DB Agriculture Fund
PowerShares DB Commodity Index Tracking Fund
PowerShares DB US Dollar Index Bullish Fund
PowerShares US Dollar Index Bearish Fund
PowerShares DB Base Metals Fund

ETNs provide a new group of equities that allow for tracking of currency movements and related sectors:

Market Vectors-Renminbi/USD ETN

iPath ETNs provide a large group of securities on commodity sectors as well as currencies (www.ipathetn.com):

iPath EURUSD Exchange Rate ETN
iPath Optimized Currency Carry ETN
iPath JPY/USD Exchange Rate

In addition to ETFs and ETNs, ETCs (Exchange Traded Commodities) are becoming available (on the London Stock Exchange, Deutsche Borse, Euronext Amsterdam, Euronext Paris, Borsa Italiana, Mexican Borsa) significantly increasing the ability of all traders not only to trade intermarket instruments but access valuable price and sentiment information relating to commodities. See www.etfsecurities.com.

DIAGNOSING GLOBAL ECONOMIC CONDITIONS

Generally, the forex trader needs to anticipate the economic growth of the country or region associated with the currency. There are many locations to access up to date data on economic growth. Foremost among them is the central banks themselves. Once again, it is a question of timing. Economies move in cycles and take time to slow down or turn around. This is an area of great ambiguity for the forex trader. The trader has four decision rules:

1. Trade with the current economic cycle.
2. Trade a slowing down of economic growth.

3. Trade a stagnant economy.

4. Trade a growing economy.

If economic growth is projected to be slowing down, then the probability of the central bank's increasing rates must be considered as declining. Central banks do not increase rates when growth is slowing down.

Also, the trader needs to consider the time frame for the option. The longer the time frame, the greater the risk of being wrong. But a longer time frame allows time for fundamentals to work out and express themselves in the price action. The forex option trader chooses a longer time frame to allow for countertrend moves to occur and then resume a fundamental direction. So, whether a forex option trade should be one week or several months is very much a judgment call. However, there are fundamental criteria for choosing a time of duration that should be considered. Depending on the economic conditions, forex option trades can range from very short term to longer term. Basically, a 3-month duration for an option trade will allow a reasonable period of time for fundamental forces to express themselves.

GROUP CURRENCIES BY PURCHASING POWER PARITY (PPP) (BIG MAC INDEX)

Ranking currency pairs for the PPP is a valid use of fundamental data to detect if a currency pair is overvalued. The theory of PPP basically asserts that a good way to detect if a currency is overvalued or undervalued is to compare prices of similar products across countries. A well-known version is the Big Mac index. The idea is that a product like a McDonald's hamburger should have the same cost in different countries. If one compared a global product such as Coca-Cola, the differences in prices in one country compared to another would demonstrate an imbalance in the currency value. To learn more about PPPs, visit the Organisation for Economic Co-operation and Development's web site to read this article: www.oecd.org/dataoecd/61/54/18598754.pdf. (*Source:* Main Economic Indicators, pp. 280–81, March 2008, © OECD 2008.)

Here is how the OEC defines PPP:

PPPs are the rates of currency conversion that equalize the purchasing power of different currencies by eliminating the differences in price levels between countries. In their simplest form, PPPs are simply price relatives which show the ratio of the prices in national currencies of the same good or service in different countries. For example, if the price of a hamburger in France is 2.84 Euros and in the United States it is 2.2 dollars, then the PPP for hamburger between France and the

United States is 2.84 Euros to 2.2 dollars or 1.29 Euros to the dollar. This means that for every dollar spent on hamburger in the United States, 1.29 Euros would have to be spent in France to obtain the same quantity and quality—or, in other words, the same volume—of hamburger.
—www.oecd.org/faq/0,3433,en_2649_34357_1799281_1_1_1_1,00.html#1799063

Economists predict that currency prices will revert to toward the level of purchasing power parity. The task of the forex trader is to access the PPP information in a timely way and use it to determine a potential direction for the trade. Since the process of reverting back to a mean PPP takes time, it is a perfect application of longer-term option trades. Let's look at some recent PPP data that is easily accessible. The most overvalued currency was the Swiss franc, and the most undervalued was the Chinese yuan. The euro appears overvalued by 23 percent and the British pound by 18 percent. Based on the Big Mac theory, one would buy out of the money puts on the EURUSD, GBPUSD, and the USDCHF. In contrast, the Mexican peso, The British pound, the yen, and the yuan were undervalued, suggesting purchasing longer-term calls on these currency pairs. Where the strike prices should be can be suggested by the prediction that these currencies will retrace by at least 50 percent of the amount they are calibrated to be overvalued or undervalued. The duration of the options should be longer term than most, six months to a year! Of course, variations such as put and call spreads can be applied as well as combinations such as shorting the spot underlying and buying protective hedges.

1. *The Big Mac Index,* July 5, 2007, www.oanda.com/products/bigmac/bigmac.shtml (see Table 4.1).

2. *The OECD PPP data.* Detecting very overvalued currencies based on OECD PPP parity measures can lead to longer-term option trades. Figure 4.5 depicts OECD data in a very accessible and understandable format and is available to anyone from the Pacific Forex Service. (*Source* http://fx.sauder.ubc.ca/PPP.html.)
   Figure 4.5 shows which currency pairs are overvalued and undervalued on December 27, 2007, based on OECD data. As a result, the forex trader can play a long-term reversion to the PPP equilibrium by buying puts and put spreads on the overvalued pairs and calls and call spreads on the undervalued pairs. It is worthy to note that the yen and the New Zealand dollar are the closest to their equilibrium point. This suggests trades of a shorter-term nature.

3. *UBS Data on PPPs.* The UBS Bank also provides frequent updates on PPP values. Their data showed that the GBPUSD and AUDUSD were overvalued and that the USDNOK were undervalued (see Figure 4.6). (*Source:* www.ubs.com/1/e/ubs_ch/wealth_mgmt_ch/research/rates.html.)

TABLE 4.1 The Big Mac Index

| | Big Mac Prices | | | Under(−)/Over (+) |
	In Local Currency	In Dollars	Implied PPP	Actual Dollar Exchange Rate July 2	Valuation Against the Dollar (%)
United States	$3.41	3.41			
Australia	A$3.45	2.95	1.01	1.17	−14
Britain	Pound 1.99	4.01	1.71	2.01	−18
Brazil	Real 6/90	3.61	2.02	1.91	+6
Canada	C$3.88	3.68	1.14	1.05	+8
China	Yuan 11.0	1.45	3.23	7.60	−58
Japan	Yen 280	2.29	82.1	122	−33
Mexico	Peso 29.0	2.69	8.50	10.8	−21
New Zealand	NZ$4.60	3.59	1.35	1.28	+5
South Africa	Rand 15.5	2.22	4.55	6.97	−35
Russia	Ruble 52.0	2.03	15.2	25.6	−41
Euro area	3.06	4.17	1.12	1.36	+22
Switzerland	SFr 6.30	5.20	1.85	1.21	+53

Data Source: Bloomberg Finance L.P.

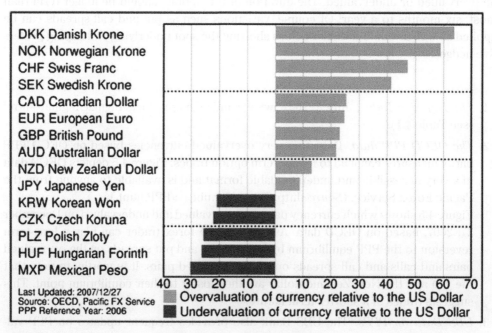

FIGURE 4.5 Over- and Undervalued Currency Pairs by PPP
Source: Purchasing Power Parity chart © 2008 Pacific Exchange Rate Service (fx.sauder.ubc.ca), Prof. Werner Antweiler, University of British Columbia, Sauder School of Business, Vancouver.

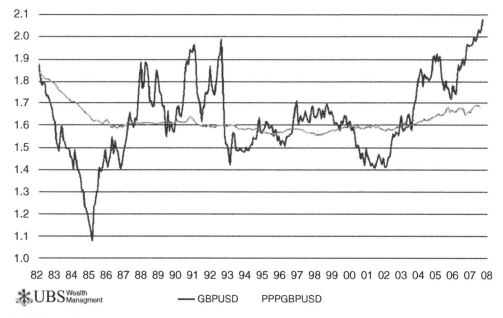

FIGURE 4.6 GBPUSD Overvalued
Source: UBS AG

ASSIGNMENT

Big Mac Theory
Find out the latest cost of a MacDonald's Big Mac in NYC, London, Tokyo, and Beijing. Which are overvalued and undervalued based on the Big Mac theory?

ASSIGNMENT

Scan of the PPPs of Currency Pairs

In this section we see more charts showing PPP on several currency pairs. A useful exercise would be to compare how predictive these charts (Figures 4.7 through 4.15) are compared to what actually happened in the months following the time period captured in the charts.

At the end of 2007, the U.S. dollar bearish sentiment was indeed very bearish and entering an extreme area as measured by the PPP valuations over time. The PPP chart in Figure 4.15 indicates that the U.S. dollar was breaking into extremes of undervaluation. It is based on long-run PPP estimates of the U.S. dollar/euro exchange rate. A forex trader using this chart could put on a long-term call on the dollar for a potential dollar bounce.

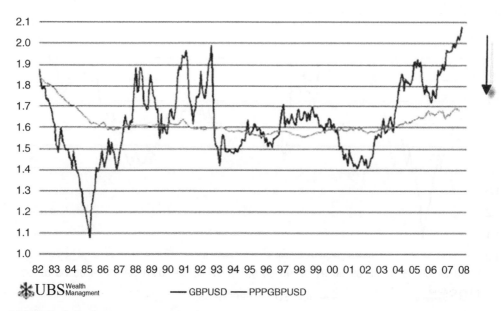

FIGURE 4.7 GBPUSD Is Overvalued
Source: UBS AG

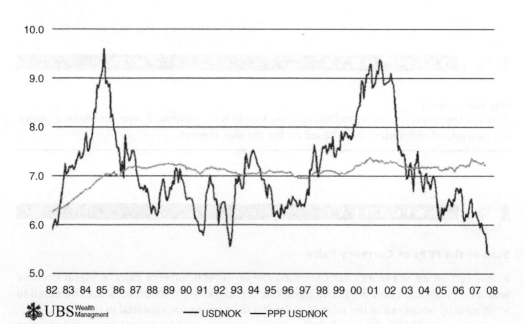

FIGURE 4.8 The Norweigan Krona Is Undervalued
Source: UBS AG

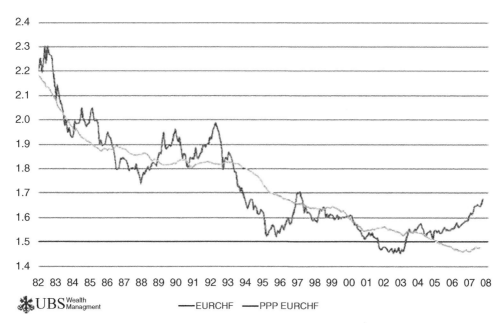

FIGURE 4.9 The EURCHF Cross-Pair Is Overvalued
Source: UBS AG

FIGURE 4.10 The EURGBP Cross-Pair Is Fairly Valued
Source: UBS AG

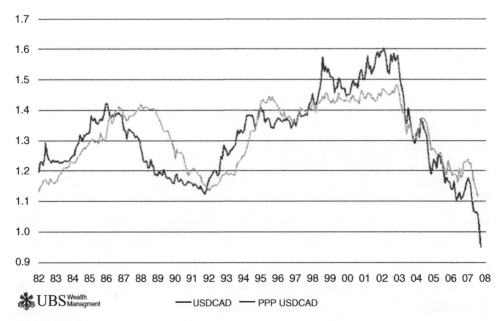

FIGURE 4.11 The USDCAD Is Slightly Undervalued
Source: UBS AG

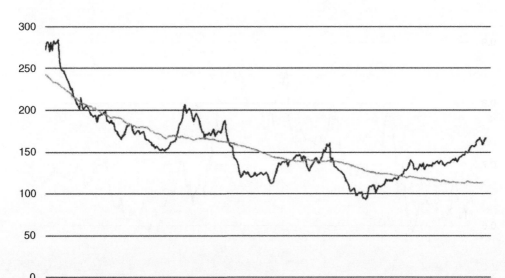

FIGURE 4.12 The EURJPY Is Overvalued
Source: UBS AG

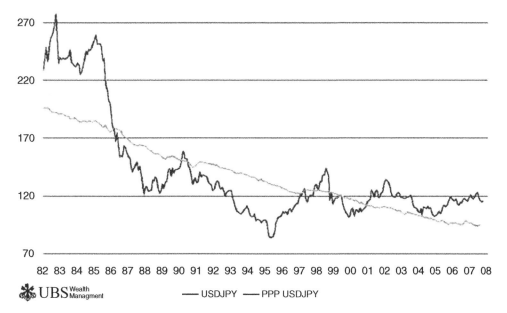

FIGURE 4.13 The USDJPY Is Overvalued
Source: UBS AG

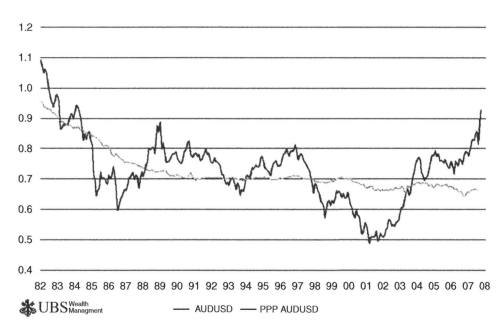

FIGURE 4.14 The AUDUSD Is Overvalued
Source: UBS AG

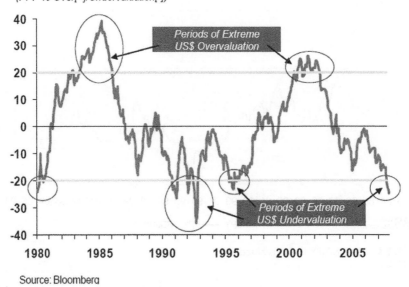

(Based on Long-Run Purchasing Power Parity Estimates of the
U.S. Dollar/Euro Exchange Rate)

Source: Bloomberg

FIGURE 4.15 US$ PPP Over-/Undervaluation
Source: © 2008 Bloomberg Finance L.P. All rights reserved. Used with permission.

Group Currencies by Trade-Weighted Index Patterns

Ultimately, currencies' strength ebbs and flows with global trading patterns. A very useful tool for identifying shifts in the trend of a currency is the currency's trade-weighted index (TWI). These indexes are used by economists and central banks to forecast trend direction and currency strength. In the Forex Trading Course, a detailed exploration of the TWI and how it can be used is presented. However, let's briefly look at how to use them to identify opportunities in forex options. They can be easily accessed at www.iboxx.com. (See Table 4.20.)

The main question facing the forex trader that the TWI can answer is: Is the currency getting stronger or weaker? While traders trade one currency against another, the question of how strong a currency is can be answered in reference to the trade basket of that currency. The trade basket is composed of currencies in a proportion that reflects the country's level of trading with another country. For example, the TWI of Canada shows that the U.S. dollar is its largest component (81.5 percent) because Canada's exports and imports are 81.5 percent with the United States. The TWI baskets generate an index that provides a useful clue as to whether a currency is globally stronger or weaker from its trading point of view.

TABLE 4.2 iBoxx Trade Weights

iBoxxFX TWI	EUR		USD		JPY		GBP		NZD	
Reference Index	EER- 23		Major Currencies Index		BOJ Effective Exchange Rate Index		Sterling ERI		Trade-Weighted Exchange Rate Index	
Baskets and Weights (%)	USD	38.74	EUR	35.52	USD	60.91	EUR	66.59	USD	31.24
	GBP	28.37	CAD	33.39	EUR	25.89	USD	21.47	EUR	26.37
	JPY	16.94	JPY	19.18	GBP	6.33	JPY	5.91	AUD	18.76
	CHF	9.33	GBP	9.12	AUD	3.67	CHF	3.14	JPY	16.67
	SEK	6.62	CHF	2.79	CAD	3.20	SEK	2.89	GBP	6.96
Constant Factor	44.652021		32.917766		12518.63354		43.842134		93.609497	

iBoxxFX TWI	NOK		SEK		CHF		CAD		AUD	
Reference Index	Norges Bank TWI		Swedish TCW Index		Swiss Franc Export-Weighted Exchange Rate Index		CERI		Reserve Bank of Australia TWI	
Baskets and Weights (%)	EUR	47.34	EUR	62.06	EUR	70.43	USD	81.50	JPY	33.36
	SEK	22.49	USD	12.84	USD	15.04	EUR	9.96	EUR	24.92
	GBP	13.67	GBP	12.76	GBP	7.40	JPY	5.64	USD	22.43
	DKK	9.15	DKK	6.18	JPY	5.15	GBP	2.90	NZD	9.80
	USD	7.35	NOK	6.16	AUD	1.98			GBP	9.49
Constant Factor	433.768931		784.550371		120.762281		123.234201		35.358384	

*iBoxxFX TWIs are based on major central banks' basket exchange rates which track the performance of a currency against a defined basket of currencies.
**Each basket is limited to five currencies with the largest weights in the relevant central bank's officially published index.
Source: iBoxx® is a registered trademark of International Index Company Limited.

Let's consider the GBPUSD from a TWI point of view. The TWI chart for 2007 shows a breakdown of a strengthening uptrend in the GBP at the end of July 2007, and thereupon a beginning of a downward channel. This suggested fundamental reason to anticipate a decline of the GBP. The TWI was a leading indicator of this and even though the GBPUSD pair was making historic highs, it sold off and began a significant downtrend by the end of 2007. The forex trader using TWI patterns was able to anticipate a change in direction, if not an immediate one. The TWI patterns can be effectively used to identify

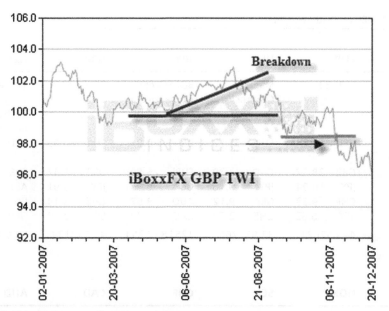

FIGURE 4.16 British Pound's TWI Breakdown
Source: iBoxx® is a registered trademark of International Index Company Limited.

longer-term direction, and then the trade can shape the specific option combination to reflect the diagnosis regarding the currency strength or weakness. The trader should not be surprised that a particular currency pair is moving opposite to the direction suggested by the TWI patterns. Trade patterns take time to impact currency moves. This, however, is a very good sign. The trader can wait for the market to come to him (see Figure 4.16).

ASSIGNMENT

Find the latest TWI charts and formulate a direction for your next option trade.

TRACKING THE CURRENCY–COMMODITY CONNECTION

We know that commodities often are leading indicators regarding currency movements. Among the most important commodity–currency connections are the gold, copper, and oil sectors. Scanning these sector commodity price patterns can give the forex trader early identification of impending changes in the currencies that are closely related to them.

The major commodity–currency connections are important because ultimately they provide very effective data for preparing forex spot and option trading. This makes sense because world trade essentially provides the reason for the currency–commodity connection. A country produces a product and exports it to another country. The producer needs to get paid for the product. This means that the buyers of the product have to take their currency and convert it to the currency of the producer of the product. So when China buys Australian copper, there is money flow converting Chinese renminbi to Australian dollars.

The top commodity–currency connections involve several commodity sectors. These include oil, gold, copper, and agricultural exports such as sugar. It is a rational deduction that the currencies of the countries that produce these commodities will be affected by events that impact those commodities. The correlations between price action in these commodities and currency prices are seen in Figure 4.17.

The close correlation between commodities and currencies can be easily seen in Figures 4.18 and 4.19. We see oil and the Canadian dollar in sync with each other. We can see that the USDX (U.S. dollar index) is inversely related to gold. While oil and gold are the most popular commodities that impact currencies, there are others as well. Chile is the largest producer of copper; however, its currency cannot be traded because it doesn't float. This makes the Australian dollar the currency to watch and trade when it comes

FIGURE 4.17 The Canadian Currency–Crude Oil Connection
Data Source: Bloomberg Finance L.P.

FIGURE 4.18 The U.S. Dollar Index versus Gold
Data Source: Bloomberg Finance L.P.

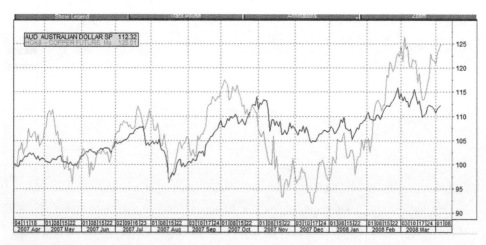

FIGURE 4.19 The AUDUSD and Copper Futures
Data Source: Bloomberg Finance L.P.

to copper since Australia is the second-largest producer of copper and its currency is readily tradable.

Tracking commodity markets is becoming easier for the forex trader. The forex trader doesn't have to access commodity charts but can use the charts and information provided by the ETFs. The ETFs are valuable resources for tracking these commodity patterns. By monitoring ETF price action and option information (when available) the forex trader can obtain an edge in developing an accurate diagnosis of conditions in the commodity markets as they relate to forex price action. There is a growing number of ETFs providing tracking of key commodity sectors. The securities known as iPath DJ, PowerShares, and iShares provide a large percentage of these ETFs. A good idea is to access their web sites for detailed information.

iPath Exchange Traded Notes: www.ipath.com
PowerShares: www.invescopowershares.com
iShares: www.ishares.com

THE CURRENCY OUTLOOK CHECKLIST

This section will present a set of strategies and analytical steps to accomplish this result. There are many dimensions that define the optimal condition for a forex option trade. Certainly, foremost among them is the nature of the price action. But at the start of the process is the overall fundamental environment of the price action. It is essential for the trader to develop a currency outlook for all of the currency pairs. In order to do this, the trader can use the following currency outlook checklist to establish a framework for deciding on the direction of a currency pair. The currency outlook checklist serves to keep the forex trader accountable to assessing fundamental issues. These are too often overlooked. The forex trader will greatly benefit by being able to complete this checklist. Some traders will look to be very detailed, while others will be more cursory in their decision process. Ultimately, anticipating a direction is the key first step in developing a forex option strategy. An Excel spreadsheet input form of the currency outlook checklist is available at www.learn4xi.com/toolschecklist.

Currency Outlook Checklist

1. Expected Economic Growth

   Negative
   Slowing
   Uncertain
   Steady
   Slow growth
   Fast growth
   Decelerating

2. Inflation Latest

   Central bank target
   Actual target

3. Sentiment Indicators

   Consumer sentiment
   Manufacturing sentiment
   Market Sentiment

4. Possible Recession

   Housing starts
   Home price
   Yield curve inversion

5. Central Bank Interest Rate Policies

   Lowering rate mode (.25 basis points, .50 basis points)
   Nothing
   Increase (.25 basis points, .50 basis points)
   Binary option sentiment

6. U.S. Dollar Sentiment

   Central bank currency reserves of dollars
   U.S. dollar index
   Trade-weighted index

7. Commodity Markets

   Gold
   Commodity index
   Oil

8. U.S. Dollar Data

   % Dollar holding of currency reserves of central banks
   Foreign ownership of U.S. Treasuries—declining

SUMMARY

This chapter provided a review of how a forex option trader can build a fundamental knowledge base to help shape a decision on what direction to select for his next option trade. ETFs, ETNs, PPP, and the tradeweighted index are key sources of fundamental data. Important also is analysis of commodity markets. A currency outlook checklist is presented as an aid to analysis.

PART THREE

Timing the Trade with Technical Analysis

O nce a directional decision is made by the forex trade, the critical phase of timing the trade occurs. Chapter 5 reviews important chart patterns that identify conditions for entering a trade and display market sentiment. These patterns include parabolic paths, volatility envelopes, and channel patterns. Trend reversal patterns can be identified using three-line break charts. There are also potential useful applications of Elliott wave theory. Chapter 5 also reviews the role of currency pair correlations in identifying forex option trading opportunities.

Chart Patterns and Trade Entry

Becoming familiar with chart patterns is an essential skill. The most important are parabolic paths, Bollinger bands, channel patterns, and three-line break charts. All provide useful tools in confirming the direction of an option trade and shaping strategies for selecting strike prices and direction.

CHART PATTERNS AND HOW TO USE THEM

The reason for using technical analysis is to effectively describe what the price is doing. While the direction of the option trade can occur based on fundamental analysis, the trader has to compare the conclusion to buy or sell with the reality of the price action. The best way to begin is to detect the presence of patterns in the currency pairs.

Because patterns in forex are not random Brownian motion, they reflect human decisions and crowd behavior and they therefore provide the best clues for diagnosing market sentiment. Since option trades are longer term in nature compared to intraday spot trading, it's a good idea to start by scanning the daily and weekly charts for evidence of direction of the underlying currency pairs. Is the pair in a strong, weak, or stable trend?

Is its price action gaining or losing momentum? Is it exhausting? Is it probing trend lines? Is it confirming reversals? Is there a frequency to the pattern that is repeating an earlier pattern? The answers to the questions provide a virtual map of the price action. Let's review some key patterns the forex option trader needs to know.

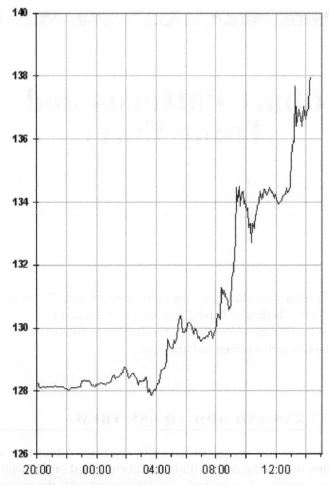

FIGURE 5.1 Typical Parabolic Path
Source: © ProRealTime.com, web-based charting software

Parabolic

This pattern reflects an increasing momentum and is generally an indicator of an unstable event. The parabolic price reaches an apex of nearly 90 degrees and cannot sustain itself. It becomes a prelude to exhaustion and possible reversal (see Figure 5.1).

Extreme Bollinger Bands

A good way to identify exhaustion patterns and the location for whether a strike price is in an area likely to be reached is to use the weekly charts and use extreme Bollinger bands (EBBs). This is a setting of 13 periods and 2.618 standard deviations. It means that the price action is within a 99 percent interval of falling between the bands, compared to

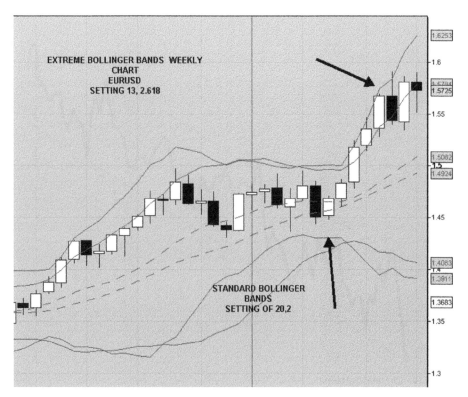

FIGURE 5.2 Extreme Bollinger Bands Weekly Chart
Source: © ProRealTime.com, web-based charting software

a 96 percent interval using regular Bollinger bands. The trader looks for a currency pair to be probing an EBB, and that price area can be used as a strike price that is selected. Let's look at an example in Figure 5.2. We see a EURUSD weekly chart with the standard Bollinger bands and the EBBs. A forex option trader, seeing that the price is hugging the standard band and refusing to bounce off it, would also note that the extreme band has not been touched. This would be a bullish conclusion. The price has room to keep going up. But when the weekly candles started touching the extreme outer Bollinger bands, the trader can start thinking about a retracement possibility or at least the price getting tired. They can use the location of the EBBs as potential areas for selecting an option target. Trades, particularly option strategies anticipating range behavior, can benefit from using the EBBs.

Channel Patterns

Channel patterns can be sideways, uptrending, and downtrending channels (see Figure 5.3). They indicate stability and a persistence of sentiment. Appearing on monthly,

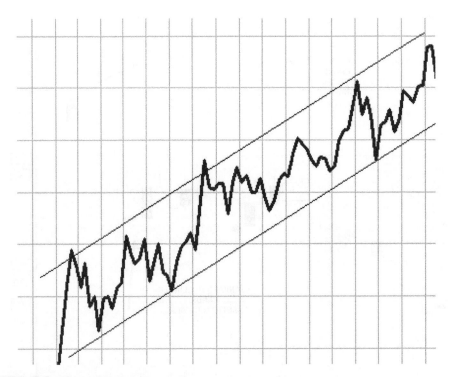

FIGURE 5.3 Channel Pattern
Source: © ProRealTime.com, web-based charting software

weekly, and daily charts, they offer projected levels of resistance and support. The trader can use channel patterns to shape target strike prices for entry and exit.

Three-Line Break

The forex option trader can benefit greatly from the use of three-line break charts. This section will demonstrate the powerful potential of this application.

A three-line break presents consecutive highs and consecutive lows only. The color reverses when a price moves in the opposite direction and takes out the previous highs or lows (see Figure 5.4).

This means that the trader can detect the start of a trend and project the beginning of a new trend (see Figure 5.5).

There are many ways to use a three-line break in helping the forex option trader make some trading strategies and decisions. One of the best ways is to identify where a trend reversal will occur. For example, the EURGBP cross-pair had experienced a significant trend up at the end of 2007. This was fundamentally due to the strengthenin European economy and also the weakening of the British housing market. Figure 5.6

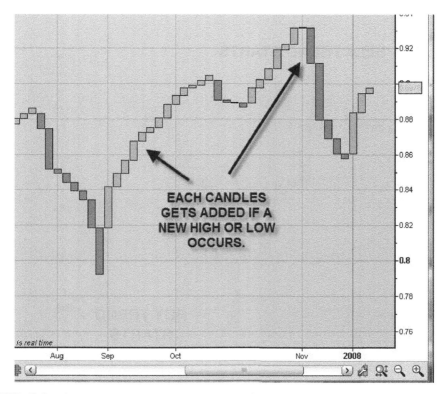

FIGURE 5.4 Three-Line Break Shows Trend Reversals
Source: © ProRealTime.com, web-based charting software

shows that there were, in fact, 16 consecutive weekly highs completed from January 2007 to February 2008. The trader who wants to trade the exhaustion of this trend would be able to use three-line break to identify where it would be over. By definition, the EURGBP trend reversal would be considered to occur if the EURGBP price reversed and passed beyond three previous highs.

This would suggest that the trader put on a 0.73 strike price. A three-month duration would be appropriate to allow time for this kind of event to occur. We can see that three price break projects reversal point locations. However, it does not project when they will occur.

Three-Line Break Trend Continuation Trade   The example of the EURGBP (Figure 5.6) shows that three-line break is also a basis for a trend continuation trade. The forex option trader can employ several strategies. They can go long the EURGBP currency spot and use a 0.73 put strike price to hedge against a trend reversal. This combination of using spot trading with options enables longer-term trading.

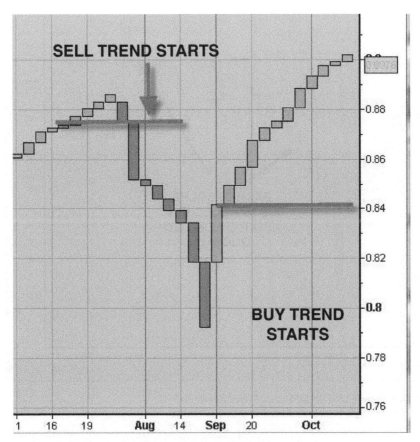

FIGURE 5.5 Three-Line Break Indicating Sell Entry and Buy Enter Locations
Source: © ProRealTime.com, web-based charting software

Fibonacci Patterns

While this book is not a primer on Fibonacci patterns and assumes that the reader is familiar with the "Fibs," there is an effective application of Fib resistance and support lines in shaping an option trade. Here is how to do it:

First, select a day chart in a currency pair. Locate the appropriate origin of a low or a high. If the price is coming from a low, look for the highest high that preceded it. If the price is coming from a low, look for the lowest low that preceded it. Then generate a Fib resistance line. It will project out into time into the future. Look for the 61.8 percent Fib line. The price that is near or crosses that Fib line can be considered as one of the strike prices in an options play on the currency pair. In the example in Figure 5.7, we see a high-to-low wave in the USDCAD day chart. The trader located the 61.8 percent line when the low was created. This projected that at 1.0181 the CAD would

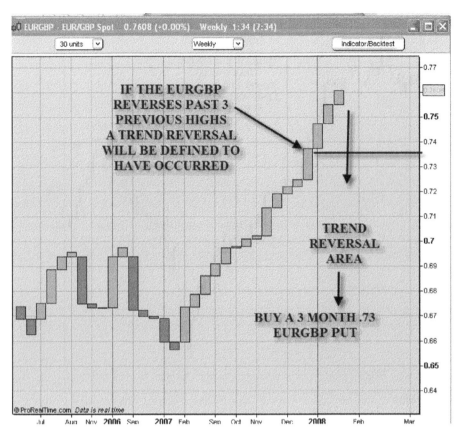

FIGURE 5.6 Confirmation of Trend Continuation with Three-Line Break Charts
Source: © ProRealTime.com, web-based charting software

enter a key area of resistance or support. If the trader had a strategy to buy a retracement or a weakening of the Canadian dollar then a 1.02 would be a key strike price, providing near-term resistance to any move up from the date at which the Fib line was drawn. But the trader can use Fib analysis put on a December or January call option spread by buying a 1.02 and selling a 1.04. The logic of such a move would be that if the price had the energy to go through the 61.8 percent Fib line, then it would follow through and continue, obeying what historical experience shows what happens at this Fib line.

If the trader was anticipating a bounce up, followed by a return down, then 101.80 would become a strike price for a selling a call. If the trader waited until the price actually went to 1.02 and observed a failure of the price to stay above it, then he has a perfect Fib-based bear put strategy and should put on an at-the-money (ATM) put at 1.02! Further, using Fib theory, the trader sees where the 50 percent and the 38.2 percent Fibs are and could use them to select the second leg of a put spread (see Figure 5.7)!

FIGURE 5.7 Using Fibs to Select Strike Prices
Source: © ProRealTime.com, web-based charting software

 ASSIGNMENT

Scan Day Charts and Find Prices Near a 61.8 Percent Fib Line

Elliott Wave Patterns: The Zigzag Pattern

One of the most potentially useful forecasting tools available to the forex trader to help determine a currency pair trade's most probable direction turns out to be based on the application of Elliott wave analysis. Generally speaking, Elliott wave analysis focuses on patterns that recur; these patterns are identified by both their shape and position within a chart and by virtue of specifically defined and consistently reliable rules that govern them. Greg Melick, an expert in Elliott wave, describes the patterns as follows:

There are 11 distinctly different patterns or waves, divided into two major groups: (1) those that move with the trend are known as *impulse* or *motive waves*; (2) those that move against the trend are known as *corrective waves.* There are three motive waves and eight corrective waves. If one believes that this wave pattern is in effect in a currency pair, it becomes a way to project the direction of the currency pair, as well as a future retracement of that pair. The

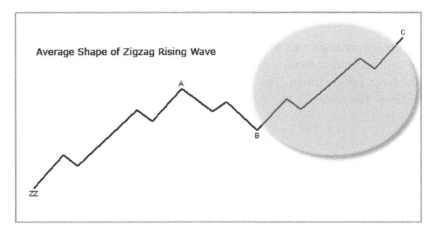

FIGURE 5.8 Elliott Projected C Wave in Rising Forex ZigZag Pattern
Source: C. Gregory Melick

challenge to the forex trader is to be confident in identifying which waves are in place. More importantly, for applications to forex option trading, the best wave to identify would be an incomplete zigzag wave. The incomplete zigzag wave has the highest probability of being fulfilled. In Figure 5.8, we see a downward and an upward zigzag wave projecting a move from point B to point C.

Once the Elliott wave software projects this B-to-C region, the forex option trader can select strike prices within that region and within the projected time frame. (See Figure 5.9.)

The followers of Elliott wave may very well have a tool for forex option trading. A conclusion that Elliott wave patterns work for forex option trading needs further research to be conclusive.

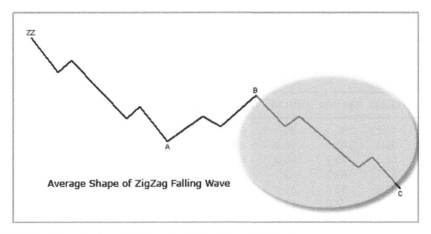

FIGURE 5.9 Elliott Projected C Wave in Falling Forex ZigZag Pattern
Source: C. Gregory Melick

SCANNING FOR VOLATILITY

Since volatility is very important in shaping forex option trading, scanning for volatility conditions and comparing them with technical price patterns is a logical key step to take for the forex option trader. The volatility scan is similar to the price pattern scan in its objectives. The trader is looking for the volatility situations that are probing the extremes.

Find Currencies that Have Drifted from Their Historical Volatilities

The first volatility scan is to find currencies that have drifted from their historical volatilities. Which pairs have their historical volatility greater than the implied volatility? The forex trader is looking for the extremes. There are many ways to find it.

Find Currencies that Have Drifted from Their Historical Correlations

Currency pairs do not move in separate price patterns. Many are correlated to each other. When the trader spots a deviation from the expected correlation, a trade strategy can emerge. While correlations constantly are updated in real time, they historically have shown pairs that are highly correlated (80 percent or more in their movements). This can be a positive correlation where the pairs move together in the same direction, or a negative correlation where they move in opposite directions. We can see in Tables 5.1 and 5.2 that the EURUSD and the USDCHF were detected to be negatively correlated at −0.88 percent hourly (Table 5.1) and 0.963 percent daily (Table 5.2). We can see monthly (Figure 5.10) and three-month correlations (Figure 5.11) for key currency pairs.

TABLE 5.1   Hourly Currency Correlations

	EURUSD	GBPUSD	USDCHF	USDJPY	EURGBP	EURCHF	EURJPY	GBPCHF	GBPJPY
Correlation 1H									
EURUSD	100.1	92.1	−88.0	67.1	−63.6	73.5	94.5	77.5	92.1
GBPUSD	92.1	100.0	−78.9	63.5	−82.8	72.2	87.9	90.0	94.5
USDCHF	−88.0	−78.9	100.0	−62.1	53.9	−32.8	−84.6	−53.0	−81.7
USDJPY	67.1	63.5	−62.1	100.0	−46.0	43.9	87.6	53.5	80.9
EURGBP	−63.6	−82.8	53.9	−46.0	100.0	−51.5	−61.9	−92.5	−82.2
EURCHF	73.5	72.2	−32.8	43.9	−51.5	100.0	66.9	79.9	67.1
EURJPY	94.5	87.9	−84.6	87.6	−61.9	66.9	100.0	74.1	95.6
GBPCHF	77.5	90.0	−53.0	53.5	−92.5	79.9	74.1	100.0	88.0
GBPJPY	92.1	94.5	−81.7	80.9	−82.2	67.1	95.6	88.0	100.0

Data Source: © www.Mataf.net, Forex Trading

TABLE 5.2 Daily Currency Correlations

	Correlation Daily								
	EURUSD	**GBPUSD**	**USDCHF**	**USDJPY**	**EURGBP**	**EURCHF**	**EURJPY**	**GBPCHF**	**GBPJPY**
EURUSD	100.0	53.4	−96.3	−94.5	83.1	−80.0	−61.3	−86.4	−83.1
GBPUSD	53.4	100.0	−46.2	−42.4	7.3	−19.7	1.2	−7.5	−17.9
USDCHF	−96.3	−46.2	100.0	96.8	−87.0	88.1	69.4	89.8	88.9
USDJPY	−94.5	−42.4	96.8	100.0	−87.0	87.4	75.8	89.8	91.0
EURGBP	83.1	7.3	−87.0	−87.0	100.0	−83.5	−73.7	−93.9	−93.9
EURCHF	−80.0	−19.7	88.1	87.4	−83.5	100.0	84.6	92.9	87.6
EURJPY	−61.3	1.2	69.4	75.8	−73.7	84.6	100.0	81.2	77.9
GBPCHF	−86.4	−7.5	89.8	89.8	−93.9	92.9	81.2	100.0	91.3
GBPJPY	−83.1	−17.9	88.9	91.0	−93.9	87.6	77.9	91.3	100.0

Data Source: © www.Mataf.net, Forex Trading

Sites for Correlation Data

http://fxtrade.oanda.com/currencyCorrelations/index.html
www.mataf.net/en/forex/trading/correlation/table/
www.superderivatives.com
www.dukascopy.com (Shakers and Movers)
www.mataf.net/en/forex/trading/correlation/table/

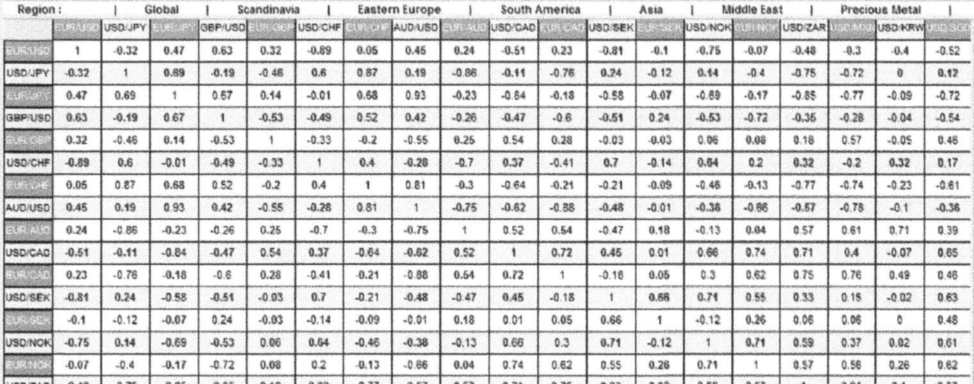
SuperDerivatives

Correlations (implied correlations are highlighted in blue) Close

1 MONTH | 3 MONTH | 6 MONTH | 1 YEAR

Please click on the two currency pairs for a quick reference

Region : | Global | Scandinavia | Eastern Europe | South America | Asia | Middle East | Precious Metal |

	EUR/USD	USD/JPY	EUR/JPY	GBP/USD	EUR/GBP	USD/CHF	EUR/CHF	AUD/USD	EUR/AUD	USD/CAD	EUR/CAD	USD/SEK	EUR/SEK	USD/NOK	EUR/NOK	USD/ZAR	USD/MXN	USD/KRW	USD/SGD
EUR/USD	1	-0.32	0.47	0.63	0.32	-0.89	0.05	0.45	0.24	-0.51	0.23	-0.81	-0.1	-0.75	-0.07	-0.48	-0.3	-0.4	-0.52
USD/JPY	-0.32	1	0.69	-0.19	-0.46	0.6	0.87	0.19	-0.86	-0.11	-0.76	0.24	-0.12	0.14	-0.4	-0.75	-0.72	0	0.12
EUR/JPY	0.47	0.69	1	0.67	0.14	-0.01	0.68	0.93	-0.23	-0.84	-0.18	-0.58	-0.07	-0.69	-0.17	-0.85	-0.77	-0.09	-0.72
GBP/USD	0.63	-0.19	0.67	1	-0.53	-0.49	0.52	0.42	-0.26	-0.47	-0.6	-0.51	0.24	-0.53	-0.72	-0.35	-0.28	-0.04	-0.54
EUR/GBP	0.32	-0.46	0.14	-0.53	1	-0.33	-0.2	-0.55	0.25	0.54	0.28	-0.03	-0.03	0.06	0.08	0.18	0.57	-0.05	0.46
USD/CHF	-0.89	0.6	-0.01	-0.49	-0.33	1	0.4	-0.28	-0.7	0.37	-0.41	0.7	-0.14	0.64	0.2	0.32	-0.2	0.32	0.17
EUR/CHF	0.05	0.87	0.68	0.52	-0.2	0.4	1	0.81	-0.3	-0.64	-0.21	-0.21	-0.09	-0.46	-0.13	-0.77	-0.74	-0.23	-0.61
AUD/USD	0.45	0.19	0.93	0.42	-0.55	-0.28	0.81	1	-0.75	-0.62	-0.88	-0.48	-0.01	-0.36	-0.66	-0.57	-0.78	-0.1	-0.36
EUR/AUD	0.24	-0.86	-0.23	-0.26	0.25	-0.7	-0.3	-0.75	1	0.52	0.54	-0.47	0.18	-0.13	0.04	0.57	0.61	0.71	0.39
USD/CAD	-0.51	-0.11	-0.84	-0.47	0.54	0.37	-0.64	-0.62	0.52	1	0.72	0.45	0.01	0.66	0.74	0.71	0.4	-0.07	0.65
EUR/CAD	0.23	-0.76	-0.18	-0.6	0.28	-0.41	-0.21	-0.88	0.54	0.72	1	-0.18	0.05	0.3	0.62	0.75	0.76	0.49	0.46
USD/SEK	-0.81	0.24	-0.58	-0.51	-0.03	0.7	-0.21	-0.48	-0.47	0.45	-0.18	1	0.66	0.71	0.55	0.33	0.15	-0.02	0.63
EUR/SEK	-0.1	-0.12	-0.07	0.24	-0.03	-0.14	-0.09	-0.01	0.18	0.01	0.05	0.66	1	-0.12	0.26	0.06	0.06	0	0.48
USD/NOK	-0.75	0.14	-0.69	-0.53	0.06	0.64	-0.46	-0.38	-0.13	0.66	0.3	0.71	-0.12	1	0.71	0.59	0.37	0.02	0.61
EUR/NOK	-0.07	-0.4	-0.17	-0.72	0.08	0.2	-0.13	-0.66	0.04	0.74	0.62	0.55	0.26	0.71	1	0.57	0.56	0.26	0.62
USD/ZAR	-0.48	-0.75	-0.85	-0.35	0.18	0.32	-0.77	-0.57	0.57	0.71	0.75	0.33	0.06	0.59	0.57	1	0.94	0.1	0.57
USD/MXN	-0.3	-0.72	-0.77	-0.28	0.57	-0.2	-0.74	-0.78	0.61	0.4	0.76	0.15	0.06	0.37	0.56	0.94	1	-0.21	0.55
USD/KRW	-0.4	0	-0.09	-0.04	-0.06	0.32	-0.23	-0.1	0.71	-0.07	0.49	-0.02	0	0.02	0.26	0.1	-0.21	1	0.15
USD/SGD	-0.52	0.12	-0.72	-0.54	0.46	0.17	-0.61	-0.36	0.39	0.65	0.46	0.63	0.48	0.61	0.62	0.57	0.55	0.15	1

FIGURE 5.10 1-Month Currency Correlations
Source: Reprinted with permission of Super Derivatives, Inc.

SD-FX Correlations - Windows Internet Explorer

http://www.superderivatives.com/Content800/Correlation/Correlation.asp?Sess=86665219

SuperDerivatives

Correlations (Implied correlations are highlighted in blue)

1 MONTH | 3 MONTH | 6 MONTH | 1 YEAR   Please click on the two currency pairs for a quick reference

Region:	EUR/USD	USD/JPY	EUR/JPY	GBP/USD	EUR/GBP	USD/CHF	EUR/CHF	AUD/USD	EUR/AUD	USD/CAD	EUR/CAD	USD/SEK	EUR/SEK	USD/NOK	EUR/NOK	USD/ZAR	USD/MXN	USD/KRW	USD/SGD
EUR/USD	1	-0.3	0.5	0.64	0.31	-0.89	0.1	0.5	0.2	-0.51	0.26	-0.81	-0.09	-0.74	-0.02	-0.48	-0.28	-0.52	-0.51
USD/JPY	-0.3	1	0.88	-0.18	-0.35	0.57	0.74	0.17	-0.69	-0.07	-0.54	0.25	-0.13	0.18	0.03	-0.54	-0.62	-0.01	0.18
EUR/JPY	0.5	0.88	1	0.54	0.14	0.01	0.66	0.84	-0.23	-0.73	-0.1	-0.55	-0.03	-0.56	-0.07	-0.75	-0.73	-0.09	-0.59
GBP/USD	0.64	-0.18	0.54	1	-0.54	-0.5	0.31	0.44	-0.3	-0.45	-0.47	-0.53	-0.15	-0.55	-0.46	-0.32	-0.35	-0.17	-0.55
EUR/GBP	0.31	-0.35	0.14	-0.54	1	-0.27	-0.16	-0.24	0.24	0.24	0.33	-0.13	0.01	-0.06	0.15	0.07	0.25	-0.09	0.24
USD/CHF	-0.89	0.57	0.01	-0.5	-0.27	1	0.37	-0.3	-0.45	0.38	-0.27	0.72	0.11	0.61	0.35	0.29	-0.12	0.34	0.21
EUR/CHF	0.1	0.74	0.66	0.31	-0.16	0.37	1	0.68	-0.32	-0.5	-0.15	-0.26	-0.03	-0.28	-0.16	-0.61	-0.65	-0.22	-0.46
AUD/USD	0.5	0.17	0.84	0.44	-0.24	-0.3	0.68	1	-0.75	-0.61	-0.69	-0.5	-0.4	-0.35	-0.47	-0.55	-0.6	-0.18	-0.36
EUR/AUD	0.2	-0.69	-0.23	-0.3	0.24	-0.45	-0.32	-0.75	1	0.58	0.5	0.13	0.16	0.1	-0.04	0.65	0.71	0.5	0.48
USD/CAD	-0.51	-0.07	-0.73	-0.45	0.24	0.38	-0.5	-0.61	0.58	1	0.71	0.45	0.36	0.64	0.58	0.67	0.42	0.06	0.54
EUR/CAD	0.26	-0.54	-0.1	-0.47	0.33	-0.27	-0.15	-0.69	0.5	0.71	1	0.19	0.04	0.33	0.5	0.59	0.51	0.4	0.48
USD/SEK	-0.81	0.25	-0.55	-0.53	-0.13	0.72	-0.26	-0.5	0.13	0.45	0.19	1	0.65	0.72	0.58	0.51	0.29	0.16	0.61
EUR/SEK	-0.09	-0.13	-0.03	-0.15	0.01	0.11	-0.03	-0.4	0.16	0.36	0.04	0.65	1	0.34	0.3	0.42	0.14	0.25	0.59
USD/NOK	-0.74	0.18	-0.56	-0.55	-0.06	0.61	-0.28	-0.35	0.1	0.64	0.33	0.72	0.34	1	0.69	0.61	0.27	0.07	0.61
EUR/NOK	-0.02	0.03	-0.07	-0.46	0.15	0.35	-0.16	-0.47	-0.04	0.58	0.5	0.58	0.3	0.69	1	0.48	0.01	0.2	0.62
USD/ZAR	-0.48	-0.54	-0.75	-0.32	0.07	0.29	-0.61	-0.55	0.65	0.67	0.59	0.51	0.42	0.61	0.48	1	0.89	0.09	0.59
USD/MXN	-0.28	-0.62	-0.73	-0.35	0.25	-0.12	-0.65	-0.6	0.71	0.42	0.51	0.29	0.14	0.27	0.01	0.89	1	0.01	0.4
USD/KRW	-0.52	-0.01	-0.09	-0.17	-0.09	0.34	-0.22	-0.18	0.5	0.06	0.4	0.16	0.25	0.07	0.2	0.09	0.01	1	0.18
USD/SGD	-0.51	0.18	-0.59	-0.55	0.24	0.21	-0.46	-0.36	0.48	0.54	0.48	0.61	0.59	0.61	0.62	0.59	0.4	0.18	1

FIGURE 5.11 3-Month Currency Correlations
Source: Reprinted with permission of Super Derivatives, Inc.

SD-FX Correlations - Windows Internet Explorer

http://www.superderivatives.com/Content800/Correlation/Correlation.asp?Sess=86665219

SuperDerivatives

Correlations (Implied correlations are highlighted in blue)

1 MONTH | 3 MONTH | 6 MONTH | 1 YEAR   Please click on the two currency pairs for a quick reference

Region:	EUR/USD	USD/JPY	EUR/JPY	GBP/USD	EUR/GBP	USD/CHF	EUR/CHF	AUD/USD	EUR/AUD	USD/CAD	EUR/CAD	USD/SEK	EUR/SEK	USD/NOK	EUR/NOK	USD/ZAR	USD/MXN	USD/KRW	USD/SGD
EUR/USD	1	-0.29	0.52	0.64	0.3	-0.89	0.17	0.53	0.16	-0.48	0.3	-0.81	-0.08	-0.77	-0.06	-0.5	-0.24	-0.52	-0.51
USD/JPY	-0.29	1	0.66	-0.17	-0.3	0.54	0.72	0.11	-0.59	-0.03	-0.39	0.25	-0.19	0.18	-0.17	-0.5	-0.49	0.07	0.12
EUR/JPY	0.52	0.66	1	0.51	0.13	-0.01	0.63	0.72	-0.19	-0.53	-0.01	-0.53	-0.02	-0.53	-0.09	-0.59	-0.59	-0.14	-0.47
GBP/USD	0.64	-0.17	0.51	1	-0.54	-0.5	0.23	0.48	-0.3	-0.47	-0.13	-0.54	-0.15	-0.57	-0.26	-0.35	-0.17	-0.2	-0.46
EUR/GBP	0.3	-0.3	0.13	-0.54	1	-0.34	-0.15	-0.16	0.25	0.13	0.31	-0.2	0.02	-0.12	0.13	0.08	0.05	0.07	0.03
USD/CHF	-0.89	0.54	-0.01	-0.5	-0.34	1	0.3	-0.33	-0.35	0.33	-0.39	0.72	0.09	0.64	0.08	0.32	-0.1	0.32	0.27
EUR/CHF	0.17	0.72	0.63	0.23	-0.15	0.3	1	0.5	-0.34	-0.35	-0.18	-0.17	-0.01	-0.22	-0.14	-0.55	-0.55	-0.1	-0.28
AUD/USD	0.53	0.11	0.72	0.48	-0.16	-0.33	0.5	1	-0.75	-0.56	-0.33	-0.48	-0.2	-0.39	-0.32	-0.4	-0.4	-0.27	-0.38
EUR/AUD	0.16	-0.59	-0.19	-0.3	0.25	-0.35	-0.34	-0.75	1	0.46	0.44	0.05	0.1	0.12	-0.04	0.46	0.45	0.37	0.32
USD/CAD	-0.48	-0.03	-0.53	-0.47	0.13	0.33	-0.35	-0.56	0.46	1	0.69	0.44	0.19	0.5	0.4	0.56	0.4	0.05	0.45
EUR/CAD	0.3	-0.39	-0.01	-0.13	0.31	-0.39	-0.18	-0.33	0.44	0.69	1	-0.12	0.07	0.07	0.33	0.29	0.32	0.1	0.16
USD/SEK	-0.81	0.25	-0.53	-0.54	-0.2	0.72	-0.17	-0.48	0.05	0.44	-0.12	1	0.64	0.73	0.34	0.44	0.27	0.12	0.53
EUR/SEK	-0.08	-0.19	-0.02	-0.15	0.02	0.09	-0.01	-0.2	0.1	0.19	0.07	0.64	1	0.31	0.28	0.25	0.13	0.04	0.32
USD/NOK	-0.77	0.18	-0.53	-0.67	-0.12	0.64	-0.22	-0.39	0.12	0.5	0.07	0.73	0.31	1	0.69	0.49	0.28	0.18	0.51
EUR/NOK	-0.06	-0.17	-0.09	-0.28	0.13	0.08	-0.14	-0.32	-0.04	0.4	0.33	0.34	0.28	0.69	1	0.31	0.16	0.22	0.31
USD/ZAR	-0.5	-0.5	-0.68	-0.35	0.08	0.32	-0.55	-0.56	0.46	0.56	0.29	0.44	0.25	0.49	0.31	1	0.84	0.12	0.54
USD/MXN	-0.24	-0.49	-0.59	-0.17	0.05	-0.1	-0.55	-0.4	0.45	0.4	0.32	0.27	0.13	0.28	0.16	0.84	1	0.03	0.38
USD/KRW	-0.52	0.07	-0.14	-0.2	0.07	0.32	-0.1	-0.27	0.37	0.05	0.1	0.12	0.04	0.18	0.22	0.12	0.03	1	0.21
USD/SGD	-0.51	0.12	-0.47	-0.46	0.03	0.27	-0.28	-0.38	0.32	0.45	0.16	0.53	0.32	0.51	0.31	0.54	0.38	0.21	1

FIGURE 5.12 1-Year Currency Correlations
Source: Reprinted with permission of Super Derivatives, Inc.

TABLE 5.3 Expensive and Cheap—Based on Implied Volatility Percentile

Expensive (Based on Implied Vol. Percentile)			Cheap (Based on Implied Vol. Percentile)		
Symbol	Last Price	Current Impl. Vol.	Percentile	Symbol	Last Price	Current Impl. Vol.	Percentile
GC8Q	860.9	22.84	100	CT8H	67.89	16.27	0.5
GC8M	855.3	22.95	100	CC9H	2090	21.47	0.7
W9N	743	32.04	100	CC9K	2096	21.41	0.72
GC9M	886	21.62	100	CC8Z	2075	21.79	1
GC8J	849.3	24.09	100	CC8N	2064	22.65	1.5

Source: eztrade.com

Track Volatility Option Extremes in Currency Option Futures

The futures markets offer options on currency futures and therefore provide the ability to identify options that may be attractive because they are either overvalued or undervalued.

A quick way of accessing this information is by locating a free list offered by www.eztrade.com. This firm scans all options and produces a table. The trader can use this table every day to find currency options that may appear on their list. Its also very useful in finding options on related commodities such as bonds, gold, and the U.S. dollar index, which give the forex option trader directional insight. Let's look at what one day's report indicated.

In Table 5.3, we see expensive versus cheap options. The criterion used is the implied volatility and whether it the implied volatility was in its highest percentile. We see that gold options appear at the top. The forex option trader would see this as a confirming indicator of being dollar bullish. The gold option is too expensive, and therefore is a leading indicator for being bullish on the dollar. If gold declines, the dollar goes up. Table 5.4 tracks overvalued and undervalued options relative to their 20 day historical volatility.

TABLE 5.4 Overvalued and Undervalued Options—20 Days' Historical Volatility

Overvalued (Based on 20 Days' Hist. Vol.)				Undervalued (Based on 20 Days' Hist. Vol.)			
Symbol	Last Price	Current Impl. Vol.	20 Days Hist. Vol.	Ratio (in %)	Symbol	Last Price	Current Impl. Vol.	20 Days Hist. Vol.	Ratio (in %)
US8M	115.0625	79.3	17.13	462	ED9M	96.435	1.14	2.39	47
C9H	478	25	10.98	227	ED9U	96.27	1.14	2.41	47
C8U	472.25	31.06	13.7	226	YU8M	9950	12.45	25.79	48
OJ8H	144.35	56.89	25.49	223	YU8H	9860	12.75	26.03	48
KC8H	133.1	30.96	14.63	211	ED9H	96.555	1.13	2.24	50

Source: eztrade.com

TABLE 5.5 Overvalued and Undervalued Options—100 Days Historical Volatility

	Overvalued (based on 100 Days' Hist. Vol.)				Undervalued (based on 100 Days' Hist. Vol.)			
Symbol	Last Price	Current Impl. Vol.	100 Days Hist. Vol.	Ratio (in %)	Symbol	Last Price	Current Impl. Vol.	100 Days Hist. Vol.	Ratio (in %)
DA8V	16.45	20.43	7.89	258	SM8Z	292.5	25.57	882.19	2
DA8Z	16.2	20.05	7.9	253	SION	1621.2	28.18	879.49	3
DA8X	16.26	20.29	8.37	242	SIOZ	1642.5	27.82	879.48	3
DA8N	16.6	21.09	9.58	220	SI9Z	1590.5	28.43	879.49	3
DA8U	16.89	20.57	9.57	214	SI9N	1569.2	28.93	879.48	3

Source: eztrade.com

Table 5.5 tracks overvalued and undervalued options relative to their 100 day historical volatility.

SUMMARY

You have now been introduced to the important role that chart patterns can play in identify conditions for shaping a forex option strategy. You have also been introduced to Elliott wave theory and patterns, including the zigzag pattern, which promises to be the most important pattern for forex option traders. Finally the importance of detecting volatility conditions and correlations between currency pairs and which pairs are out of their statistically correlations has been discussed. Chapter 6 will show you how to go one step further by using expert sources to shape your trading decisions.

Using Experts to Shape Trading Decisions

A very useful way for the forex trader to make a directional decision on a forex option trade is to tap into the opinions of the "gurus." Survey opinion is an established method for forecasting economic direction. It is used by governments all over the world and authoritative economic institutions. One example is the Reuters Tankan Poll, which is a monthly survey of leading Japanese companies.

The Internet is full of accessible information. For example, on the last day of 2007, the following forecast was on the Net:

> *Robert Shiller, Professor of Economics at Yale University, predicted that there was a very real possibility that the US would be Splunged into a Japan-style slump, with house prices declining for years. Professor Shiller, co-founder of the respected S&P Case/Shiller house-price index, said: "American real estate values have already lost around $1 trillion [£503 billion]. That could easily increase threefold over the next few years. This is a much bigger issue than sub-prime. We are talking trillions of dollars' worth of losses."*
>
> —Suzy Jagger, "Top Economist Says America Could Plunge into Recession,"
> December 31, 2007,
> http://business.timesonline.co.uk/tol/business/economics/article3111659.ece

Among the top sources of publicly free accessible polling of experts are Reuters and Bloomberg. They provide frequent polling of economists and experts about potential currency price movements. For example, to retrieve information on guru forecasts, the trader should try to enter in a search engine, such as Google News, a term like "Bloomberg Survey." One gets back a list of the most recent surveys of expert opinion. They are very useful in shaping a directional opinion.

FORECASTING ACCURACY?

The forex option trader needs to keep in mind that forecasting accuracy on forex price movements is really about accuracy in a given period of time. One can be very accurate predicting a key decision of the central banks for the next day, but as the forecasting period extends into the future, uncertainty becomes a factor and forecast accuracy is very uncertain. One can see this factor in a survey by Bloomberg regarding economists' predictions on whether the Bank of England (BOE) would leave rates the same. The forecast came out the same day and predicted no change in the rates. It was correct.

> *Jan. 10 (Bloomberg)—The Bank of England will probably resist calls for another interest-rate cut today as policy makers gauge the effects of last month's reduction on the economy, a survey of economists shows. The nine-member Monetary Policy Committee, led by Governor Mervyn King, will keep the bank rate at 5.5 percent, according to 40 of 50 economists in a Bloomberg News survey. The rest forecast a quarter-point cut. The bank will announce the decision at noon in London.*

But what happens if the forecast is for several months out? The consensus among experts will reflect less agreement. For example, Figures 6.1 and 6.2 show that the

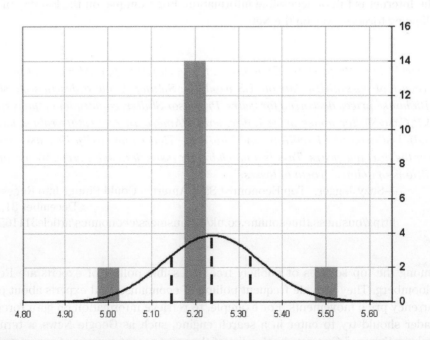

FIGURE 6.1 Central Tendency of Forecasts for First Quarter 2008
Data Source: Bloomberg Finance L.P.

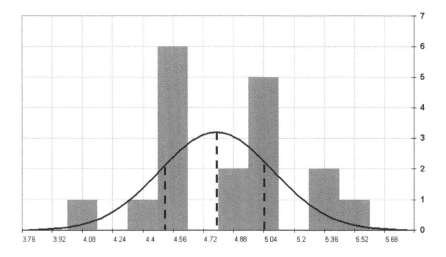

FIGURE 6.2 Central Tendency for Forecasts for Fourth Quarter 2008
Data Source: Bloomberg Finance L.P.

central tendency of forecasts for the first quarter 2008 on BOE rates was clearly in the center between 5.17 and 5.27 percent.

But when the forecast horizon is extended to the fourth quarter of 2008, the agreement among economists gets dispersed.

PROFESSIONAL SOURCES OF EXPERT FOREX OPINION

Of course, the trader can choose to follow the path of professional organizations that provide expertise by subscription. These services are mainly used by institutions but have migrated to the public as well. Some of the leading services are described in this section.

ActionEconomics.com

This site provides daily updates and analytical reports. The key test is whether the forecasts translate it into actionable knowledge. For example, a recent forecast of this site projected an increase in housing starts in February 2008, shown in Table 6.1. This suggests a potential dollar strengthening into the spring if the trader used this projection to shape an option trade. In using these projections as an aid to shaping strategy, a good idea is to give the trade a longer period of time for the projected fundamentals to take hold.

TABLE 6.1 Using Housing Forecasts to Shape Option Trades

Housing Indicators	Jul-07	Aug-07	Sep-07	Oct-07	Nov-07	Dec-07	Jan-08	Feb-08	Mar-08	Apr-08
Housing starts (min)	1.371	1.327	1.182	1.232	1.187	1.170	1.180	1.190	1.200	1.210
Housing permits (min)	1.389	1.322	1.261	1.170	1.152	1.179	1.180	1.190	1.200	1.210
Housing completions (min)	1.520	1.501	1.386	1.402	1.344	1.330	1.320	1.320	1.320	1.320
New home sales (min)	0.796	0.701	0.699	0.711	0.647	0.650	0.665	0.670	0.675	0.685
Median sales price (y/y %ch)	3.4%	-3.0%	4.9%	-8.3%	-0.4%	-6.8%	-10.0%	-10.3%	-10.1%	-6.0%
Existing home sales (min)	5.750	5.40	5.030	4.980	5.00	5.030	5.050	5.080	5.110	5.140
Median sales price (y/y %ch)	-0.7%	0.2%	-4.8%	-5.5%	-3.30%	-3.9%	-4.2%	-5.0%	-4.8%	-6.7%
S&P Case-Shiller Comp—20 m/m	-0.4%	0.7%	-0.8%	-1.4%	-1.0%	-1.0%	-0.8%	-0.8%	-0.8%	-0.5%
S&P Case-Shiller Comp—20 y/y	-3.8%	-4.3%	-4.9%	-6.1%	-6.7%	-7.1%	-7.4%	-7.7%	-8.2%	-8.5%
Pending home sales index	91.4	85.5	86.7	89.9	87.6	87.8	88.2	88.7	89.5	90.4
MBA Purch. Mort. Index	434.6	439.9	432.6	419.5	440.8	412.4	421.0	423.5	423	421.5
NAHB Composite Index	24	22	20	19	19	19	20	20	21	22

Source: actioneconomics.com

2 ■ BLUE CHIP ECONOMIC INDICATORS ■ JANUARY 10, 2008

2008 Real GDP Consensus Forecast Stays At 2.2%

JANUARY 2008 Forecast For 2008 SOURCE:	Real GDP (Chained) (2000 $)	GDP Price Index	Nominal GDP (Cur $)	Consumer Price Index	Indust. Prod (Total)	Dis Pers. Income (2000 $)	Personal Cons Exp (2000 $)	Non-Res Fix Inv (2000 $)	Corp Profits (Cur $)	Treas Bills 3-mo.	Treas Notes 10-Year	Unempl. Rate (Cur)	Housing Starts (Mil.)	Auto & Light Truck Sales (Mil.)	Net Exports (2000 $)
RBS Greenwich Capital	2.8 H	2.3	5.1	3.3	2.2	2.2	2.4	6.2	3.8	3.9	4.3	4.8	1.22	16.0	-523.0
ClearView Economics*	2.8 H	2.2	5.0	3.2	2.2	2.6	2.5	6.2	1.3	2.8	4.0	4.7	1.09	16.2	-528.0
Argus Research Corp.	2.7	3.2 H	6.0 H	3.1	2.6	3.0	2.4	6.1	5.5	3.0	4.2	4.8	1.15	16.3	-540.3
Wells Capital Management	2.6	2.4	5.1	2.6	2.8	2.8	2.4	5.0	5.6	3.1	4.1	4.9	1.31	16.1	-544.0 L
FedEx Corporation	2.6	2.3	4.9	3.1	2.1	2.6	2.5	5.8	5.6	3.6	4.4	5.1	1.49 H	16.4	-532.5
Eaton Corporation	2.6	2.0	4.7	3.0	2.4	2.4	2.0	5.0	-0.7	3.4	4.4	5.4	1.00	15.9	-463.5
Conference Board*	2.6	1.8	4.5	3.3	5.3 H	3.7 H	2.5	5.1	0.1	4.1	4.2	4.6 L	1.18	16.0	-503.6
National City Corporation	2.6	1.8	4.5	2.3	2.3	3.1	2.3	4.0	-0.1	3.5	4.3	4.8	1.22	15.9	-486.9
Bear, Stearns & Co., Inc.	2.5	2.6	5.2	3.2	1.9	2.3	2.1	5.3	3.6	3.8	4.8 H	4.7	1.20	16.5 H	-498.1
Macroeconomic Advisers, LLC**	2.5	2.3	4.9	3.1	2.2	2.2	2.1	5.5	3.9	3.7	4.5	4.9	1.13	15.9	-512.9
Mesirow Financial	2.5	2.3	4.8	3.1	2.2	2.1	2.1	5.8	3.7	3.7	4.5	4.9	1.11	16.2	-511.9
Wayne Hummer Investments LLC*	2.5	2.2	4.8	2.8	2.6	2.8	2.3	4.2	4.5	3.3	4.3	5.0	1.14	15.8	-474.0
J P MorganChase	2.5	2.2	4.7	2.8	2.0	2.6	2.3	4.5	0.7	3.6	4.3	4.8	1.13	16.0	-518.7
Chrysler	2.5	1.7	4.2	2.8	3.1	2.9	2.2	4.4	6.5	3.7	4.5	4.9	1.22	na	-497.0
J.W. Coons Advisors	2.4	2.5	5.0	3.2	0.6	2.1	2.5	2.4	-1.7	3.1	4.3	5.0	1.10	15.9	-510.0
Stanford Washington Research Group*	2.4	2.3	4.8	3.1	2.2	2.0	2.1	5.7	6.8	3.6	4.1	4.9	1.06	15.9	-508.0
Fannie Mae	2.4	2.3	4.7	3.1	1.8	2.0	2.0	5.0	7.0 H	3.3	4.2	5.0	1.13	na	-510.0
Nomura Securities	2.4	2.2	4.7	3.4	2.2	2.0	2.3	6.0	3.8	3.4	4.4	4.9	1.08	16.2	-494.5
National Assn. of Realtors	2.4	2.1	4.5	2.7	2.0	2.2	1.9	5.1	1.5	3.6	4.3	5.0	1.15	16.2	-509.0
Barclays Capital	2.3	2.4	4.8	3.2	2.3	1.9	2.5	4.0	-2.8	3.6	4.7	4.8	1.09	15.9	-500.0
Wachovia	2.3	2.4	4.7	3.6 H	1.6	2.6	2.2	4.6	5.2	3.6	4.2	5.1	1.07	16.0	-490.3
General Motors Corporation	2.3	2.3	4.7	3.2	1.9	2.0	1.9	5.1	3.4	3.6	4.5	5.0	1.09	na	-505.4
Moody's Investors Service	2.3	2.1	4.5	2.8	2.2	2.0	2.0	3.0	4.2	3.4	4.1	4.9	1.12	16.0	-485.8
U.S. Chamber of Commerce	2.3	2.1	4.4	3.1	2.0	2.8	1.9	6.1	5.0	3.7	4.4	4.9	1.10	na	-540.9
Turning Points (Micrometrics)	2.3	1.8	4.1	3.3	2.9	2.7	2.3	4.2	-1.3	3.4	4.5	4.8	1.16	16.3	-525.0
Georgia State University*	2.3	1.8	4.1	2.4	2.2	3.5	2.1	4.5	-2.0	3.3	4.1	5.1	1.18	15.3	-500.8
Inforum - Univ. of Maryland	2.2	2.7	4.9	3.3	1.4	2.4	2.1	3.8	-1.3	3.7	4.6	5.0	1.16	15.9	-499.0
Action Economics	2.2	2.5	5.0	2.8	1.9	3.1	2.9	4.3	3.7	4.4 H	4.6	4.6 L	1.35	16.1	-555.0
Bank of America*	2.2	2.3	4.5	3.3	1.0	1.7	2.3	2.3	2.0	3.2	4.4	5.1	1.15	16.2	-485.0
National Assn. of Home Builders	2.2	2.1	4.4	2.7	2.2	2.6	2.0	4.5	2.5	3.4	4.3	4.9	1.08	15.9	-520.0
Moody's Economy.com	2.2	1.8	4.1	2.5	1.5	2.8	1.5	7.1 H	1.1	4.0	4.8 H	5.1	0.99	15.9	-504.7
Naroff Economic Advisors	2.1	2.5	4.6	2.4	2.9	2.5	2.7 H	2.5	3.3	3.0	4.6	5.0	1.30	16.3	-495.0
DuPont***	2.1	1.9	4.0	2.5	1.0	2.2	2.1	3.9	3.5	3.6	4.4	5.0	1.10	16.1	-532.0
Comerica Bank*	2.1	1.8	4.0	2.5	1.7	1.9	2.4	3.5	3.0	3.6	4.4	5.1	1.07	15.9	-505.0
UBS Warburg	2.1	1.8	3.9	2.6	0.8	2.0	1.8	4.1	na	3.3	4.2	5.1	1.03	na	-495.0
UCLA Business Forecasting Proj.*	2.0	1.6 H	3.7	2.0 L	1.4	2.9	1.8	3.2	-0.9	3.1	4.2	5.0	0.97	15.8	-467.6
SOM Economics, Inc.	1.9	2.7	4.6	2.9	1.1	2.6	2.1	1.1	-3.0	3.0	4.0	5.0	1.17	15.8	-496.0
Credit Suisse	1.9	2.4	4.3	3.2	0.9	na	1.8	4.3	3.7	na	4.0	5.1	na	na	-455.0
Lehman Brothers	1.9	2.0	3.9	2.6	1.1	1.8	1.6	3.9	2.2	3.2	4.3	5.1	1.05	15.8	-508.1
BMO Capital Markets	1.9	1.9	3.9	3.2	2.4	2.2	1.9	3.1	1.6	2.9	4.0	5.1	0.97	15.5	-497.0
Standard & Poors Corp.*	1.9	1.8	3.7	2.2	1.6	2.7	2.0	2.8	-4.9	2.9	4.2	5.1	1.02	15.5	-464.5

FIGURE 6.3   Real GDP Consensus Forecasts of Blue Chip
Source: Blue Chip Consensus

Professional Projections: Using Blue Chip Economic Indicators

Blue Chip Economic Indicators polls America's top business economists, collecting their forecasts of U.S. economic growth, inflation, and interest rates. It produces a monthly consensus report on gross domestic product (GDP) and reports expert opinion on key economic variables and their projected values into the coming year. The following forecast was issued on Blue Chip in its January 10, 2008, survey of opinion (see Figure 6.3).

In the report, Blue Chip reported a consensus on housing:

> *Prospects for the housing sector remain grim. The consensus now expects total housing starts in 2008 to only 1.11 million units, down about 17% from last year's total and almost 50% less than the totals put in place in 2004 and 2005. Combined inventories of new and existing unsold homes remain near a record high, lending standards have tightened considerably foreclosures will likely accelerate this year as adjustable rate mortgages resets surge and the unemployment rate increases. Real residential investment may continue to subtract more than a full percentage point form the rate of real GDP growth during the first half of 2008. The drag from residential investment should ease, perhaps considerably, in the second half*

of 2008. Nonetheless, residential investment will continue to subtract from GDP growth until at least the Q4 of this year according to about 75% of our panelists and a third say it will not happen until later.

Based on this consensus of opinion, further decreases in U.S. interest rates would be projected by the trader. The trader should be careful about concluding that this news justifies dollar selling. Remember, currency pairs are trades of one currency versus another. In the same report, Blue Chip reported on forecasts of a slowing of other economies:

International Commentary. Consensus forecasts of inflation-adjusted economic growth abroad also have fallen over recent months The consensus now predicts real GDP in the Eurozone will grow only 1.9% this year versus October's projected growth rate of 2.2%. Japan's economy is forecast to grow just 1.5% in 2008, 0.6 of a point less than estimated in October. Forecasts of GDP growth in Canada and Mexico also have dropped, most likely in response to the downgrading of U.S. growth prospects. In contrast, consensus forecasts of global inflation this year have increased; reflecting sharp increases in energy and food costs.

—www.aspenpublishers.com/PDF/SS01934600.pdf

Following this kind of analysis, the trader could strategize that in 2008 the USDCAD and USDMXN will be finding more ranging like price patterns because each economy was slowing down.

The trader using this kind of guru survey can develop well-informed views on whether a particular currency pair can be strengthening, weakening, or will be range-bound.

What is most impressive and useful is the ability to find the highest and lowest forecasts, and a trader can align himself with one of them as well. The list also tracks the accuracy of the forecasters, enabling a trader to put more emphasis on some sources. For example, DuPont and Macroeconomic Advisors LLC were the most accurate of projector.

Of exceptional utility are Blue Chip Consensus's forecasts of exchange rates. They provide two-year projections of rates. See Table 6.2 for an example of the USDJPY in 2008.

TABLE 6.2 Blue Chip Dollar/Yen Exchange Rate Forecasts

Japan	2008	2009
January consensus	109.5	106.9
Top 3 avg.	114.4	114.7
Bottom 3 avg.	103.5	98.7
Last month avg.	109.3	n/a
	Latest	**Year Ago**
Actual	112.9	110.4

Source: Blue Chip Consensus

Using these forecasts, a trader would find a sentiment low of 103.5 and a high of 114.5. One strategy would be to be contrarian and reject the highs and lows, and therefore one strategy would be to a sell strangle where one can sell 114 calls and also sell 103 puts praying that the gurus are wrong!

Consensus Economics

Consensus Economics is a company that polls over 240 economists to obtain their forecast (www.consensuseconomics.com). The Consensus Survey of June 9 shows that the likelihood of a Federal Reserve interest rate change (from a 2 percent rate) on the June 25 FOMC meeting was projected as follows:

Economists Predicting an Increase: 5.1%
Economists Predicting No Change: 86.1%
Economists Predicting an Increase: 8.7%

Those predicting no change were correct. (*Source*: Consensus Forecasts.)

The trader needs to assess how accurate the analysts have proven to be before they blindly follow their recommendations. For example, Bloomberg often surveys analysis and also tracks their performance. As 2007 ended, Bloomberg surveyed 27 traders on projections of gold prices. The survey reported that 14 of 27 analysts recommended buying gold. The survey accuracy was 117 out of 190 weeks on the direction. That is 62 percent. This is an example of an effective use of following the gurus.

Let's look at a powerful example of accessing guru opinion in shaping a trade regarding the British pound. A scan of the Internet using Google search/news showed several headlines and then detailed items regarding forecasts on the pound. Let's compare what a trader read in the articles to what actually happened. On November 29, the headline and article read:

Projections on British Pound: World Economy Heading for "Perfect Storm"
(Alex Brummer, Daily Mail 29 November 2007, 8:16 A.M.)

One of the world's leading financial experts warned yesterday that a "perfect storm" could be about to hit Western economies. Economic adviser David Kern warns the risks have increased and the correct policy response to avoid a nasty downturn is to cut interest rates soon, even if some of the cuts will have to be reversed at a later date.

Kern believes rates will be shaved to at least 5.25% before the middle of next year but a reduction to 5% is a realistic prospect, particularly if the credit crisis worsens.

FIGURE 6.4 GBP USD Day Chart
Source: © ProRealTime.com, web-based charting software

He forecasts a sharp slowdown in UK average GDP growth, from 3.1% in 2007 to 1.9% in 2008 and believes the slowdown could be even sharper if the Bank of England decided not to cut interest rates in the next few months.

Reading this, the forex trader could on November 29 formulate a directional view of the GBP. Following the forecast meant that selling the GBP would be the strategy. Since the forecast isn't specific as to how far the GBP would weaken, there would be many ways to implement this view in an option strategy. These will be discussed in a later chapter but, clearly, closely tracking the forecast (see Figure 6.4) is compelling as to which way to trade.

FOLLOW THE HOUSING PRICES

Housing price data is among the most important sources for forming a directional view on a currency pair. This is because when housing prices are increasing, the probabilities of decreasing interest rates are very low. Central banks fear inflationary pressures would be strengthened with any decrease in rates. The rate of change in housing prices is one

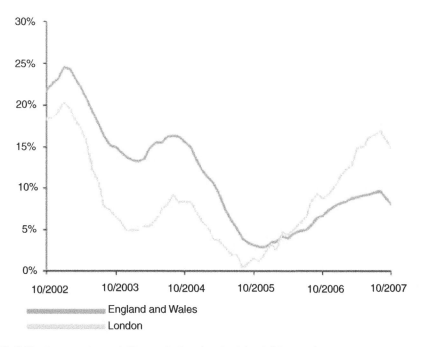

FIGURE 6.5 Average Annual Change in London Residential Properties
Source: landregistry.gov.uk

of the leading indicators watched by central banks to shift their policy. The forex trader should look very closely to track housing data.

For example, the headline "London House Prices Fall as Slowdown Hits" occurred on November 28. Figure 6.5 shows the average prices of residential properties falling.

Several weeks later, on December 6, the BOE decided to cut rates. It is worthwhile reading its statement:

News Release: Bank of England Reduces Bank Rate by 0.25 Percentage Points to 5.5%

Although output in the United Kingdom has expanded at a brisk pace for the past two years, there are now signs that growth has begun to slow. Forward-looking surveys of households and businesses suggest spending is moderating, broadly in line with the projections contained in the November Inflation Report. But conditions in financial markets have deteriorated and a tightening in the supply of credit to households and businesses is in train, posing downside risks to the outlook for both output and inflation further ahead.

CPI inflation was 2.1% in October. Higher energy and food prices are expected to keep inflation above the target in the short term. Although upside risks to inflation remain, which the Committee will continue to monitor carefully, slowing demand growth should ease the pressures on supply capacity, bringing inflation back to target in the medium term.

The trader following housing data in Australia saw a sharp contrast to conditions in the United States and Britain's strong housing market. Westpac senior economist Andrew Hanlan referred to the Aussie situation as: "Dwelling approvals are up 10 per cent in the last 10 months. At least for now the immediate outlook is for housing construction to actually be stronger than it has been." (*Source:* "Demand for Housing 'Yet to Be Dampened,'" December 10, 2007, http://news.theage.com.au/demand-for-housing-yet-to-be-dampened/20071210-1g3a.html.)

This kind of data leads to expectation of strength in the Australian dollar and a directional strategy of going long that currency. Housing data such as lending for construction of new homes issued by the Australian Bureau of Statistics should be followed for traders following the aussie.

FOLLOW THE THINK TANKS

For traders who want a think tank or guru opinion, Westpac is a major bank that provides ongoing economic data.

There are many think tanks that scan the world economy. Among them are the International Monetary Fund (IMF), the Organisation for Economic Co-operation and Development (OECD), and the World Bank. They come out with key reports about the economies of different countries. In October 2007 the IMF's World Economic Outlook report forecasted lower U.S. economic growth in 2007. This suggestion would spark interest in puts on the U.S. dollar.

Some of the best think tank sources are also major banks. These banks issue forecasts of their economies. The trader should scan and read bank reports. (*Source of DBS group research:* www.dbs.com.) Here is a list of important banks and think tanks for forecasting economic direction:

Bank/Institution	Country
HSBC	Britain
British Chamber of Commerce	Britain
Scotia	Canada
Ubs.com	Switzerland
Bank of New York	United States
Westpac	Australia

TABLE 6.3 Global Foreign Exchange Outlook

December 5, 2007		Actual	Q1a 07	Q2a 07	Q3a 07	Q4 07	Q1 08	Q2 08	Q3 08	Q4 08
Euro	EUR/USD	1.48	1.34	1.35	1.43	1.49	1.54	1.52	1.50	1.48
	Consensus		1.33	1.35	1.42	1.42	1.41	1.40	1.38	1.37
Yen	USD/JPY	109.8	118	123	115	108	106	104	103	103
	Consensus		118	124	115	114	113	113	112	112
Sterling	GBP/USD	2.06	1.97	2.01	2.05	2.07	2.10	2.08	2.07	2.04
	Consensus		1.96	2.01	2.04	2.02	2.00	1.97	1.95	1.93
Canadian	USD/CAD	1.00	1.15	1.07	0.99	0.98	0.94	0.96	0.98	0.95
dollar	Consensus		1.15	1.06	0.99	1.02	1.03	1.04	1.06	1.06
Australian	AUD/USD	0.88	0.81	0.85	0.89	0.91	0.97	0.97	0.93	0.89
dollar	Consensus		0.81	0.85	0.89	0.86	0.85	0.84	0.84	0.83
Mexican	USD/MXN	10.92	11.04	10.81	10.94	11.00	11.07	11.15	11.22	11.30
peso	Consensus		11.01	10.79	10.93	11.00	11.07	11.14	11.21	11.27

Source: Foreign Exchange Outlook (August 2008), Scotiabank

FOLLOW THE BANK FORECASTS

Forecasts and projections on the direction of the currencies for longer-term option plays can be derived by scanning bank forecasts. For example, in the Global Currency Forecast issued by Scotia Capital, a trader can convert the forecast into a strategy of being bullish or bearish a currency pair. Table 6.3 shows that Scotia Capital sees on December 5, 2007, an end-of-year price of 108 for the USDJPY pair and a second quarter strengthening to 104. Following this projection, one can generate a put spread where a trader would buy a 108 strike price and then sell a 104 strike price. For the EUR, using the Scotia Capital forecast, the bank forecast an end-of-2007 price at 1.49 and then a strengthening to 1.54 by the end of the first quarter. But the forex trader could also choose to be a contrarian. Bank global forecasts may also be wrong. Following a particular bank forecasts record of accuracy would be advisable before leaping into shaping a trading action based on one report. But as 2007 ended, compare the forecast prices against the actual prices.

For those traders wanting a longer-term view, Scotiabank offered a 3-month, 6-month, and 1-year outlook. This generates many potential trades. For the EURUSD, if

TABLE 6.4 Currency Trends Forecast by Scotiabank at End of 2007

	Going Back			Spot	Outlook			
Forex rate	12 m	6 m	3 m	5-Dec	3 m	6 m	12 m	FX Rate
EUR/USD	1.32	1.354	1.427	1.476	1.54	1.52	1.48	EUR/USD
USD/JPY	119.1	123.2	114.8	109.8	106	104	103	USD/JPY
GBP/USD	1.959	2.009	2.047	2.062	2.1	2.08	2.04	GBP/USD

Source: Foreign Exchange Outlook (August 2008), Scotiabank

TABLE 6.5 Mellon Bank Forecasts of Exchange Rates in November 2007

Currency	11/5/2007	Q4 07	Q1 08	Q2 08	Q3 08	Q4 08
AUD/USD	0.9205	0.9400	0.9600	0.9700	0.9500	0.9300
GBP/USD	2.0801	2.1000	2.1300	2.1500	2.0800	2.0200
USD/CAD	0.9337	0.9200	0.8800	0.8700	0.9000	0.9300
USD/DKK	5.1528	5.0533	4.8876	4.8400	4.9691	5.1404
EUR/USD	1.4468	1.4750	1.5250	1.5400	1.5000	1.4500
USD/JPY	114.26	114.00	112.00	108.00	106.00	105.00
NZD/USD	0.7685	0.7850	0.8000	0.8050	0.7900	0.7700
USD/NOK	5.3942	5.2881	5.0820	5.0000	5.1000	5.2414
USD/SEK	6.4131	6.3051	6.0852	6.0130	6.1600	6.3586
USD/CHF	1.1529	1.1400	1.1100	1.1000	1.1200	1.1400

Source: The Bank of New York Mellon

TABLE 6.6 Crosses and Exchange Rate Projections for November 2007

Currency	11/5/2007	Q4 07	Q1 08	Q2 08	Q3 08	Q4 08
EUR/GBP	0.6956	0.7024	0.7160	0.7163	0.7212	0.7178
EUR/JPY	165.30	168.15	170.80	166.32	159.00	152.25
EUR/CHF	1.6679	1.6815	1.6928	1.6940	1.6800	1.6530
EUR/DKK	7.4536	7.4536	7.4536	7.4536	7.4536	7.4536
EUR/SEK	9.2732	9.3000	9.2800	9.2600	9.2400	9.2200
EUR/NOK	7.8027	7.8000	7.7500	7.7000	7.6500	7.6000
EUR/CAD	1.3512	1.3570	1.3420	1.3398	1.3500	1.3485
EUR/AUD	1.5720	1.5691	1.5885	1.5876	1.5789	1.5591
EUR/NZD	1.8828	1.8790	1.9063	1.9130	1.8987	1.8831
GBP/JPY	237.66	239.40	238.56	232.20	220.48	212.10
GBP/CAD	1.9421	1.9320	1.8744	1.8705	1.8720	1.8786
GBP/CHF	2.3979	2.3940	2.3643	2.3650	2.3296	2.3028
GBP/DKK	10.718	10.612	10.411	10.406	10.336	10.384
GBP/SEK	13.340	13.241	12.962	12.928	12.813	12.844
GBP/NOK	11.220	11.105	10.825	10.750	10.608	10.588
CHF/JPY	99.100	100.000	100.901	98.182	94.643	92.105
AUD/NZD	1.1979	1.1975	1.2000	1.2050	1.2025	1.2078
AUD/JPY	104.790	107.160	107.520	104.760	100.700	97.650
NOK/SEK	1.1889	1.1923	1.1974	1.2026	1.2078	1.2132
CAD/JPY	122.40	123.91	127.27	124.14	117.78	112.90
NZD/JPY	87.835	89.490	89.600	86.940	83.740	80.850

Source: The Bank of New York Mellon

TABLE 6.7 Mellon Bank Projections of Exchange Rates in December 2007

Currency	12/17/2007	Q4 07	Q1 08	Q2 08	Q3 08	Q4 08
AUD/USD	0.8576	0.9400	0.9600	0.9700	0.9500	0.9300
GBP/USD	2.0222	2.0600	2.1000	2.1300	2.0800	2.0200
USD/CAD	1.0044	1.0000	0.9700	0.9600	0.9500	0.9400
USD/DKK	5.1762	5.0592	4.8933	4.8456	4.9749	5.1464
EUR/USD	1.4416	1.4750	1.5250	1.5400	1.5000	1.4500
USD/JPY	112.86	114.00	112.00	108.00	106.00	105.00
NZD/USD	0.7549	0.7850	0.8000	0.8050	0.7900	0.7700
USD/NOK	5.5445	5.2881	5.0820	5.0000	5.1000	5.2414
USD/SEK	6.5615	6.3051	6.0852	6.0130	6.1600	6.3586
USD/CHF	1.1487	1.1400	1.1100	1.1000	1.1200	1.1400

Source: The Bank of New York Mellon

TABLE 6.8 Mellon Bank Cross-Rate Projections of Exchange Rates in December 2007

Currency	12/17/2007	Q4 07	Q1 08	Q2 08	Q3 08	Q4 08
EUR/GBP	0.7129	0.7160	0.7262	0.7230	0.7212	0.7178
EUR/JPY	162.66	168.15	170.80	166.32	159.00	152.25
EUR/CHF	1.6560	1.6815	1.6928	1.6940	1.6800	1.6530
EUR/DKK	7.4623	7.4623	7.4623	7.4623	7.4623	7.4623
EUR/SEK	9.4540	9.3000	9.2800	9.2600	9.2400	9.2200
EUR/NOK	7.9885	7.8000	7.7500	7.7000	7.6500	7.6000
EUR/CAD	1.4481	1.4750	1.4793	1.4784	1.4250	1.3630
EUR/AUD	1.6803	1.5691	1.5885	1.5876	1.5789	1.5591
EUR/NZD	1.9088	1.8790	1.9063	1.9130	1.8987	1.8831
GBP/JPY	228.20	234.84	235.20	230.04	220.48	212.10
GBP/CAD	2.0309	2.0600	2.0370	2.0448	1.9760	1.8988
GBP/CHF	2.3230	2.3484	2.3310	2.3430	2.3296	2.3028
GBP/DKK	10.467	10.422	10.276	10.321	10.348	10.396
GBP/SEK	13.269	12.988	12.779	12.808	12.813	12.844
GBP/NOK	11.212	10.894	10.672	10.650	10.608	10.588
CHF/JPY	98.005	100.000	100.901	98.182	94.643	92.105
AUD/NZD	1.1346	1.1975	1.2000	1.2050	1.2025	1.2078
AUD/JPY	97.085	107.160	107.520	104.760	100.700	97.650
NOK/SEK	1.1835	1.1923	1.1974	1.2026	1.2078	1.2132
CAD/JPY	112.37	114.00	115.46	112.50	111.58	111.70
NZD/JPY	85.230	89.490	89.600	86.940	83.740	80.850

Source: The Bank of New York Mellon

you choose to follow the outlook, the EUR is forecast to rise to a high of 1.54 in the first three months, and then fall within a year to 1.48. The yen was forecast to strengthen.

Mellon Bank Is a Source for Forecasts

The Mellon Bank provides monthly forecasts and analysis. When using this kind of data, it is important to track each month's forecast and then identify where changes have occurred. This can lead to trading ideas. Tables 6.5 through 6.8 show what they projected on November 5 and December 17.

It's a good idea to maintain a habit of accessing bank forecasts. They provide good confirming information about the fundamental forces that will affect forex prices. As a result, they will enable the forex option trader to generate many new trading ideas.

SUMMARY

The ability to access expert research and opinion by the average trader is easier now than ever before. Finding expert forecasts and using them to shape forex trades and option strategies is a more effective methodology than just relying on one's own judgment. The trader should use expert opinion to develop alternative scenarios. This chapter reviewed some of the sources of "guru" opinion.

Forex Options Strategies

N ow that we have provided a comprehensive review of key elements in deciding the direction of forex option trades, the objective of Part Four is to guide the reader through different forex option strategies and tactics. The key is to match the strategy and tactic with the underlying price patterns and fundamental conditions. Option spreads reviewed here involve calendar spreads and vertical spreads. Part Four also covers commodity currency correlations that provide sources for spread strategies. Option strategies for carry traders are presented to stimulate thinking. Finally, this section details the importance of "the Greeks" and how they are used for forex option trades.

CHAPTER 7

Vanilla, Spreads, and Volatility Strategies

This chapter provides a review of the basic option strategies used in forex trading. This includes what are called plain vanilla calls and puts. Trading option spreads forms a step into more sophisticated trading.

PLAIN VANILLA STRATEGIES

Buying calls and puts becomes the first base for trading forex options. As indicated earlier, a call or a put allows a leveraged position where the trader tries a directional play with limited risk to the premium paid. The major advantage is to avoid being stopped out of a position and having time for the position to work out. Time also is the enemy of the option trader who buys a position. Each trader in considering a call or put needs to have high confidence that the directional move of the underlying currency will be powerful enough to take the underlying into the money at the time of expiration.

Trading Forex Option Spreads

Trading forex option spreads is a directional play that limits both the gains and the cost of participating. The most a trader can make is the difference between the strike prices. Spread trades offer the advantage of conserving trading capital. Their disadvantage is that in the case the underlying currency went beyond the strike prices, the trader could not participate in the move.

Hugh, a forex option trader just starting out, put on the spreads on the Canadian dollar currency pair and the Australian dollar seen in Table 7.1. He did this in his equity account using an option trade through the Philadelphia Stock Exchange (PHLX).

TABLE 7.1 USDCAD Put Option Trade

Description	Price	Cost		Date
CDD DEC 100 Put	0.30	270.00		7/26/07
CDD DEC 105 Put	1.85	(1880.00)		7/26/07
		(1610.00)	Cost	
CDD DEC 100 Put	0.85	(880.00)		9/12/07
CDD DEC 105 Put	2.75	2720.00		9/12/07
		1840.00	Reward	
		230.00	Net	
CDD NOV 104 Put	1.18	221.06		8/30/07
CDD NOV 105 Put	1.73	(360.96)		8/30/07
		(139.90)	Cost	
CDD NOV 104 Put	4.30	(874.96)		9/20/07
CDD NOV 105 Put	5.00	985.06		9/20/07
		110.10	Reward	
		(29.80)	Net	
XDA MAR 2008 86 Call	1.90	(979.90)		9/13/07
		(979.90)	Cost	
XDA MAR 2008 86 Call	2.20	1070.10		9/19/07
		1070.10	Reward	
		90.20	Net	

Data Source: Bloomberg Finance L.P.

Calendar Spreads

This option trade allows the trader to put on a call or put spread with both legs at the same or different strike prices but at different months. In a call calendar spread, the trader anticipates that the currency pair will increase in value during this period of time. In a put spread, the idea is that the currency pair will decrease in value over the period of time. The advantage of the calendar spread over a regular spread is that in currency pairs, it allows a play on fundamental events that may take a bit longer.

Calendar spreads can be used to play a country going through a shift in its economic cycle or sector or a seasonal effect that can occur in a currency. For example, there is a year-end tendency of the yen to rise because exporters would be paying up year-end bills. "The yen rose against 15 of the world's 16 most active currencies on speculation. Japan's exporters purchased it to pay bills due at the end of the year" (Bloomberg, December 25, 2007).

Example: Buy Yuan June, Sell September   Calendar spreads can also be used as a way to trade a contraction of volatility. When the trader spots a condition where short-term volatility is unusually higher than long-term volatility, he has detected a volatility smile. If he expects a contraction in this volatility, then a calendar spread would be an appropriate play on this.

Straddles

This option trade is defined as buying a put and buying a call. The trader anticipates a very big move and would make money if the move occurs beyond the cost of the premium. The advantage of this strategy is that it doesn't require the trader to predict which way the market will go. But if the move is not big enough, there is the strong risk of not being profitable.

CURRENCY PAIR SPREADS: PLAYING THE CORRELATIONS AND DIVERGENCIES

A very effective source of trades for forex option traders are cross pairs. These are currency pairs that do not have the dollar in them. One of the best strategies for cross pairs involves playing a reversion to the mean. This is a high-probability play when the spread between the currency movements is at an "outlier" and is in the tails of the bell curve.

The way to start putting on this kind of currency pair spread is to first observe the charts. An overlay chart where the first pair is compared to the second will provide a quick visualization to the trade. In Figure 7.1, we see that the aussie and the NZD track each other closely. Most of the time, the spread is within a narrow range. But there are

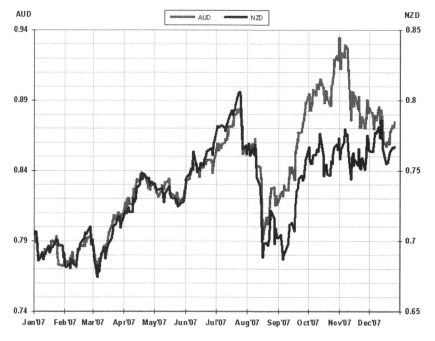

FIGURE 7.1 AUDUSD versus NZDUSD
Data Source: Bloomberg Finance L.P.

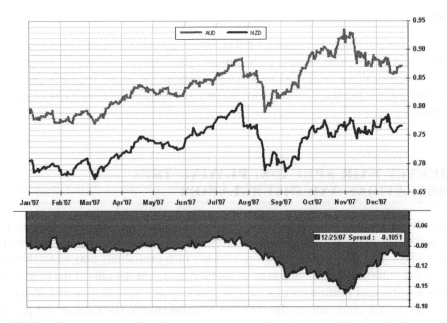

FIGURE 7.2 AUDUSD versus NZDUSD
Data Source: Bloomberg Finance L.P.

times that the spread has widened beyond the norm. That is when an option trade playing a narrowing of the spread can be put on. The trader needs to scan the price charts to observe pairs that usually are in close correlation are going outside their historical correlations (see Figures 7.1 through 7.3).

Australian Dollar versus Euro/Yen

A very closely correlated currency combination is the Australian Dollar (AUDUSD) versus the euro/yen (EURJPY). Three-month correlation data shows these are 85 percent positively correlated (superderivatives.com). The chart showing a 3-year overlay between them tracks this close correlation for everyone to see. It also shows that the strategy of waiting for these pairs to widen and then playing a narrowing of the spread works very well if given enough time. A 3-month and 6-month option play would be appropriate.

We can surmise that there is more room for the spread to narrow. In fact, the deviation data shows that the spread is at 52 percentile (see Figures 7.4 and 7.5). The trader would not take a spread trade in these conditions but wait for more extreme widening.

Euro versus Swiss Franc

A more frequently traded opportunity occurs between the euro (EUR) and the Swiss franc (CHF). These pairs are nearly 90 percent correlated. This means that when the

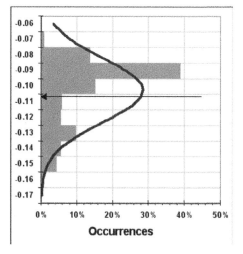

Spread Summary

Last	-0.1051
Mean	-0.1022
Off Avg	-0.0029
Median	-0.0939
St Deviation	0.0206
High (07/03/07)	-0.0736
Low (10/21/07)	-0.1607

FIGURE 7.3 AUDUSD versus NZDUSD
Data Source: Bloomberg Finance L.P.

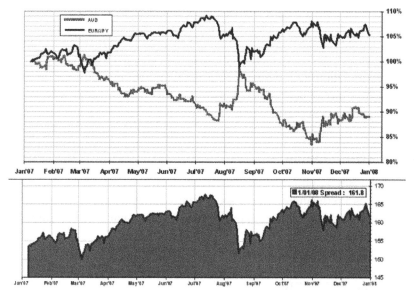

FIGURE 7.4 AUDUSD versus EURJPY
Data Source: Bloomberg Finance L.P.

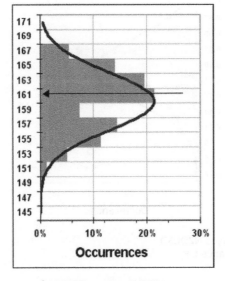

Spread Summary

Last	161.8
Mean	160.22
Off Avg	1.54
Median	161.13
St Deviation	3.94
High (07/12/07)	167.6
Low (03/05/07)	149.9

FIGURE 7.5 Spread Summary of AUDUSD versus EURJPY
Data Source: Bloomberg Finance L.P.

spread is at its widest, the trader has a built-in option play. By looking at Figures 7.6 and 7.7, we see the wide "mouth." It statistically is too wide. The spread graph actually shows (see the arrow) the spread is at a 15.17 percent. In this case the option trade would be a play on narrowing of the spread.

Euro versus British Pound

The euro and the British pound (GBP) often are in sync and then move away from this pattern. In Figures 7.8 through 7.10 we see an extreme widening of the spread between them. The spread is actually in the 8th percentile. Playing a narrowing would be an effective option play.

Tactically, there are several choices:

- Put on puts on the EURGBP.
- Put on a put spread on the EURGBP.
- Buy a put on the EURUSD and buy a call on the GBPUSD.

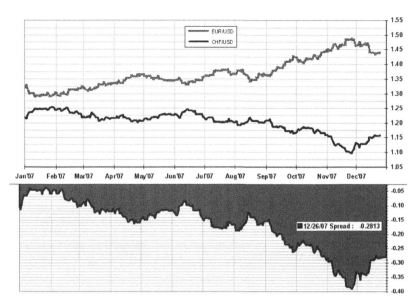

FIGURE 7.6 EURUSD and USDCHF Spread Pattern
Data Source: Bloomberg Finance L.P.

Spread Summary

Last	-0.2813
Mean	-0.1678
Off Avg	-0.1135
Median	-0.1459
St Deviation	0.0888
High (01/26/07)	-0.0379
Low (11/26/07)	-0.3904

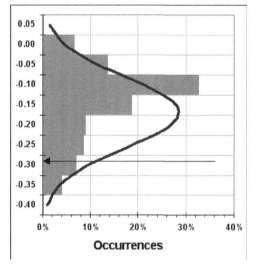

FIGURE 7.7 EUR and CHF Spread at Extremes
Data Source: Bloomberg Finance L.P.

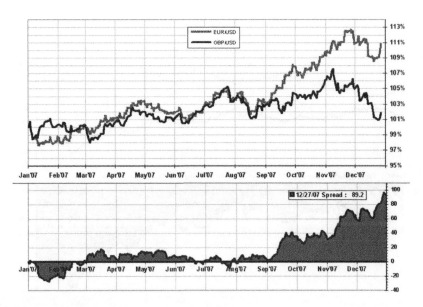

FIGURE 7.8 EUR and GBP Spread Widens Greatly
Data Source: Bloomberg Finance L.P.

Spread Summary

Last	89.2
Mean	16.1453
Off Avg	73.0547
Median	8.0963
St Deviation	25.3251
High (12/27/07)	81.228
Low (01/22/07)	-27.6392

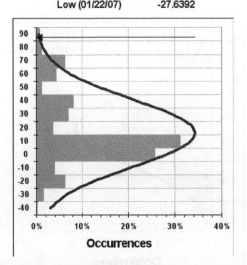

FIGURE 7.9 EUR USD versus GBPUSD Spread at an Extreme Tail
Data Source: Bloomberg Finance L.P.

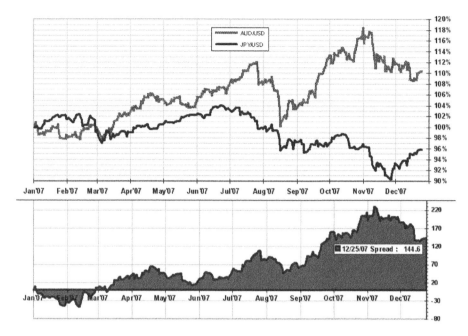

FIGURE 7.10 AUDUSD and USDJPY Spread
Data Source: Bloomberg Finance L.P.

Australian Dollar versus Japanese Yen

These two pairs are nicely correlated and therefore deviate from their correlation. In Figure 7.10 we see a narrowing of the spread as an option trade, and in Figure 7.11 the bell curve shows that the spread value is moving back from the outside tail. The trader should notice that the narrowest point was 6 months before in August. This means time is necessary for the spread to narrow back. It would therefore be appropriate to use a 3-month duration. The trade would be to buy the USDJPY at the money (ATM) and sell the AUDUSD ATM. A variation would be to do an out-of-the-money trade.

COMMODITY–CURRENCY SPREAD STRATEGIES

Several currencies are intimately related to commodities such as gold and copper. By carefully observing when correlations between them are out of sync, trades can emerge. Let's take the example of the South African rand and gold. In Figures 7.12 and 7.13, the trader can see that the spread between gold and the rand is very wide and out of the norm. The strategy would be to trade a narrowing of the spread. Since the puts are being favored on the volatility surface, the trader would go with a buying of gold and a selling of the rand, choosing a gold call and a rand put.

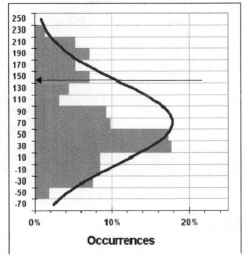

Spread Summary

Last	144.6
Mean	72.0417
Off Avg	72.5711
Median	52.9094
St Deviation	71.3045
High (11/07/07)	229.63
Low (02/12/07)	-46.8243

FIGURE 7.11 AUDUSD and USDJPY Spread Near Extreme
Data Source: Bloomberg Finance L.P.

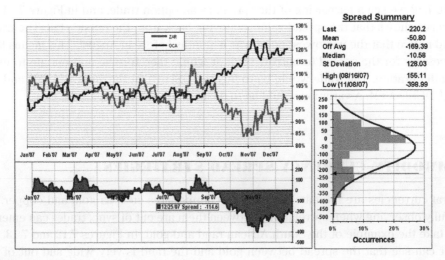

Spread Summary

Last	-220.2
Mean	-50.80
Off Avg	-169.39
Median	-10.58
St Deviation	128.03
High (08/16/07)	155.11
Low (11/08/07)	-398.99

FIGURE 7.12 South African Rand versus Gold
Data Source: Bloomberg Finance L.P.

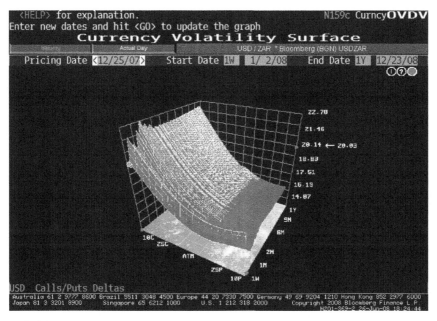

FIGURE 7.13 South African Rand Volatility Surface
Source: ©2008 Bloomberg L.P. All rights reserved. Used with permission.

Australian Dollar and Gold

The spread between the Australian dollar and gold is also very wide in Figures 7.14 suggesting a temporary situation. Using a fundamental understanding that the aussie is expected to strengthen its interest rates, one would look to buy a call on the aussie USD pair but would have to be careful because the volatility surface showed an extreme skew to the put side in Figure 7.15.

Australian Dollar and Commodity Index

In Figure 7.16 we see the Australian dollar against the Reuters Commodity Index. This is a useful index showing general commodity prices. Here, we see a very wide period in this spread. However, on the date of this chart creation (January 7, 2008), there was surprise news that the aussie home building was very strong, leading to a bullish sentiment on the aussie. This spread is fundamentally, then, not likely to last and also technically extreme. Betting on a narrowing is a logical trade. The trade can be expressed as buying a call on the AUDUSD.

Technically, while a trader can visually see that spread is wide, it turned out that it was quite wide, in fact at 98.09 percentile! The bet that it would narrow is a logical option strategy (see Figure 7.17).

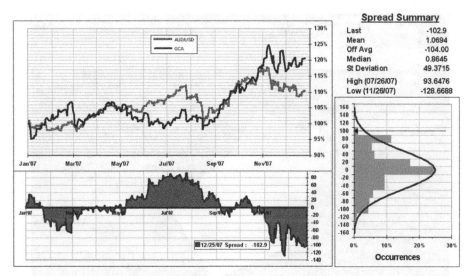

FIGURE 7.14 Australian Dollar versus Gold
Data Source: Bloomberg Finance L.P.

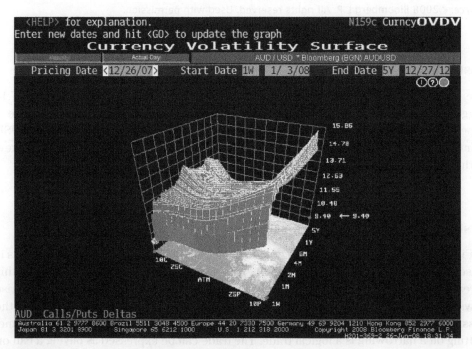

FIGURE 7.15 Australian Dollar Volatility Surface
Source:

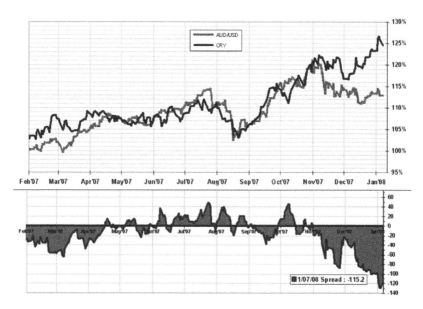

FIGURE 7.16 Australian Dollar versus Reuters/Jefferies Commodity Index
Data Source: Bloomberg Finance L.P.

Spread Summary

Last	-115.2
Mean	-16.074
Off Avg	-99.09
Median	-10.13
St Deviation	35.098
High (07/24/07)	49.34
Low (01/04/08)	-129.5

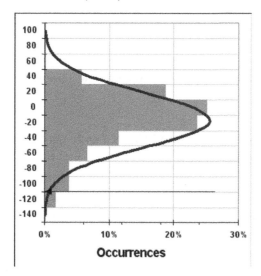

FIGURE 7.17 Australian Dollar and Reuters Jefferies Commodity Index Spread Percentile
Data Source: Bloomberg Finance L.P.

CARRY TRADE OPTION STRATEGIES

Forex traders know that a major trading strategy used by large funds is the carry trade. This strategy involves buying a currency that possesses a high interest rate and selling a currency that has a lower interest rate. The selling of the lower rate currency is often leveraged. Since the yen has the lowest interest rate of 0.50 percent, it has been the source of nearly 1 trillion of carry trade volume.

Popular carry trade pairs are the GBPJPY and NZDJPY. Another carry trade that is common is in Europe where the Swiss franc (CHF) is borrowed (sold) and a currency with a higher rate is purchased. The attraction of the carry trade is the large return on the interest rate difference. The risk of the carry trade is the potential for very large drawdowns. In 2007, there were many drawdown events, and if the forex trader wants to participate in a carry trade, forex options can help.

First, to avoid such drawdowns, the forex trader can use spread analysis. Let's look at an example of the CHF versus the Hungarian forint (HUF) carry trade.

Swiss Franc versus Hungarian Forint

The HUF is allowed to float plus or minus 15 percent against a middle rate fixed at 282.36. This pair can be traded on the Chicago Mercantile Exchange (CME). The spread analysis shows that the pair is about right in its relationship to each other (see Figure 7.18). This indicates a stability of the underlying spots.

If the carry trade was put on, the spread analysis shows that there is a likelihood of an increase in the spread because it is at an extreme in its percentile score (see Figure 7.19). To protect against losses, the trader would look to buy a call option on the CHFHUF. This requires trading on the CME.

Swiss Franc versus Iceland Krona

In this carry trade example of the CHF versus the Iceland krona (ISK), we can see that the spread is exactly at the median and requires no option action (see Figures 7.20 and 7.21).

Japanese Yen versus British Pound Carry Trade and Option Protection Using Spread Analysis

The popular Japanese yen (JPY) versus the British pound (GBP) carry trade has been tempting many traders. But selling the JPY and buying the GBP has encountered many drawdowns. We can see this in the chart below. The spread trader would want the GBPJPY to remain in a sideways channel or to go up. But if the trader were to put on the carry trade by selling the JPY and buying the GBP on January 8, an option trade to improve the situation would be suggested by the spread results. The spread is too high and is likely to narrow, just based on statistical history. But if the forex trader would add some fundamental knowledge regarding weakness in the GBP (due to a decline in

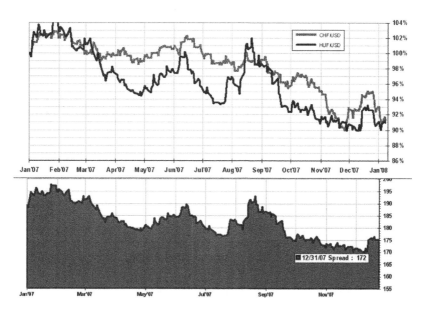

FIGURE 7.18 CHF versus HUF Carry Trade Example
Data Source: Bloomberg Finance L.P.

Spread Summary

Last	172
Mean	182
Off Avg	-10
Median	182
St Deviation	7.2
High (01/25/07)	197.8
Low (11/28/07)	170.1

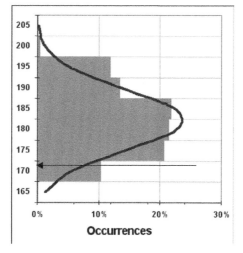

FIGURE 7.19 CHF versus HUF Spread Percentile Analysis
Data Source: Bloomberg Finance L.P.

FIGURE 7.20 Iceland Krona versus Swiss Franc
Data Source: Bloomberg Finance L.P.

Spread Summary

Last	62.27
Mean	62.9
Off Avg	-0.6
Median	62
St Deviation	3.1
High (01/10/07)	71.8
Low (11/06/07)	57.5

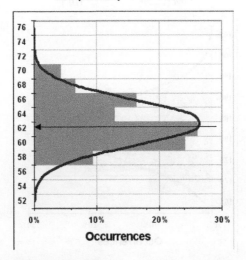

FIGURE 7.21 CHF and ISK Spread Analysis
Data Source: Bloomberg Finance L.P.

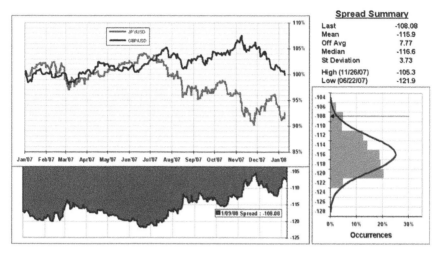

FIGURE 7.22 USDJPY and GBPUSD
Data Source: Bloomberg Finance L.P.

interest rates), a suggested option trade would be to put on a near term (1- to 3-month) option combination of buying a put on the GBP and buying a call on the JPY (see Figure 7.22).

TRADING DELTA CALL/PUT RATIOS

Traders often compare delta call options with delta put options. When the premiums of call and put options for the same expiry date and then same notional amount with the same delta are not equal, and form a ratio favoring one or the other, the forex trader needs to be alerted to a skewing of the market sentiment. The emergence of a skew in the call/put ratio is an opportunity for shaping a trading strategy.

In Figure 7.23, for the USDJPY we see a comparison of the deltas along different strike prices and the volatility. We can detect a skew toward puts. Just compare the implied volatility of similar delta puts versus calls. For example, the 3-month term has a 25 delta 11.11 percent implied volatility for the put, and an 8.46 percent implied volatility for the call, clearly favoring a strengthening of the yen. A trader seeing this could decide to go with the flow and buy USDJPY puts. A trader seeing this would also consider a risk reversal trade.

Using Put/Call Ratios

It is a popular belief supported by scholarly research that the put-to-call volume ratio (PCR) can be an indicator for market sentiment. The trader using this information should

Ⓖ SuperDerivatives

! Negative 25ΔRR means favor USD put   🔁 Refresh   📋 Calculate F2   📊 Chart   ⊗ Close   ❓

Click on the strike to open the pricing page   NY 10:00am

📋 Term Structure   Trade date ▼ Wed. 26 Dec 2007 ▲   Currency pair ❓ USD ↻ JPY ❓   Spot ▼ 114.17 ▲

25ΔRR	25ΔFly		5Δ	10Δ	15Δ	20Δ	25Δ	30Δ	ATM	30Δ	25Δ	20Δ	15Δ	10Δ	5Δ
1W -1.100	0.200	Vol	11.33	10.72	10.39	10.15	9.95	9.74	9.175	8.88	8.85	8.85	8.87	8.93	9.08
		Strike	111.17	111.92	112.38	112.73	113.01	113.26	114.06	114.80	115.01	115.25	115.53	115.89	116.45
1M -2.000	0.230	Vol	13.26	12.24	11.63	11.19	10.83	10.49	9.525	8.93	8.83	8.76	8.71	8.68	8.73
		Strike	106.99	108.84	109.95	110.76	111.42	111.98	113.68	115.22	115.64	116.10	116.65	117.35	118.43
2M -2.350	0.250	Vol	14.02	12.77	12.01	11.47	11.03	10.62	9.500	8.80	8.68	8.59	8.52	8.49	8.57
		Strike	103.22	106.07	107.77	109.01	109.99	110.82	113.28	115.51	116.12	116.79	117.58	118.59	120.19
3M -2.650	0.250	Vol	14.50	13.11	12.24	11.61	11.11	10.66	9.400	8.60	8.46	8.35	8.27	8.24	8.34
		Strike	100.52	104.06	106.19	107.71	108.92	109.94	112.88	115.51	116.23	117.02	117.94	119.13	121.05
6M -3.150	0.260	Vol	15.24	13.58	12.48	11.70	11.08	10.53	9.050	8.11	7.93	7.81	7.73	7.73	7.98
		Strike	94.26	99.39	102.50	104.72	106.44	107.88	111.81	115.30	116.25	117.30	118.54	120.18	122.98
9M -3.400	0.265	Vol	15.65	13.83	12.64	11.77	11.09	10.48	8.900	7.89	7.69	7.57	7.52	7.58	7.94
		Strike	89.59	95.84	99.64	102.35	104.45	106.20	110.80	114.93	116.05	117.31	118.81	120.86	124.48
1Y -3.500	0.270	Vol	15.82	13.89	12.66	11.77	11.06	10.42	8.800	7.77	7.56	7.46	7.43	7.55	8.02
		Strike	86.03	93.11	97.41	100.47	102.86	104.85	109.93	114.55	115.83	117.28	119.04	121.49	125.92
2Y -3.900	0.280	Vol	15.84	13.96	12.89	11.74	10.99	10.31	8.450	7.29	7.09	6.98	6.96	7.09	7.58
		Strike	75.46	84.20	89.72	93.73	96.86	99.48	106.68	113.35	114.99	116.87	119.18	122.47	128.61
			5Δ	10Δ	15Δ	20Δ	25Δ	30Δ	ATM	30Δ	25Δ	20Δ	15Δ	10Δ	5Δ

FIGURE 7.23 USDJPY Delta and Maturities from 1 Week To 2 Years
Source: Reprinted with permission of Super Derivatives, Inc.

track the PCR over time to detect if the ratios are not only unusually high, but statistically outside their means.

Developing a Risk Reversal Trade

A common practice is to compare an out-of-the money (OTM) call with a delta of 25 and an OTM put with a delta of 25. There are equal amounts on both and they have the same expiration date. If implied volatility were the same, the market sentiment would be considered neutral. Traders will come across quotes on risk reversals that can be informative. A 25 delta risk reversal of +2 percent indicates that the market provides a higher probability to a rise in the underlying spot rate. It is called *risk reversal* because the market is willing to pay more to protect against a fast rise in the currency. Many professional forex option traders develop risk reversal strategies because they interpret the presence of a risk reversal skew as predictive of direction. The *Financial Times* of London called it "the Market's best guess of market direction." How does a risk reversal strategy work?

A risk reversal trade is the:

- Simultaneous sell of a put and purchase of a call (on the same underlying asset with the same expiry date and notional amounts) or
- Simultaneous purchase of a put and sell of a call

This kind of a trade insulates the position from the effects of volatility and time.

The trader can take a 1-month option and find the strike prices that are OTM and have each 25 percent delta. The cost of buying the put is offset by the premium received from selling the call. The strategy makes money if the direction is correct. The strategy involves risk if the market is going the other way because selling a call exposes the risk to the trader. There are ways to limit this risk, however, which we will discuss shortly.

A contrarian approach to risk reversal trades is also worth exploring. The skewing of a market revealed by the risk reversal may be interpreted as being not technically extreme but reflecting a fundamental reason for it. In other words, a contrarian risk reversal trade would be to trade in the direction of the skew!

There is no definitive agreement among experts regarding which way is better!

Risk Reversal Trade Example   In Figure 7.24 for the AUDJPY currency pair, we see that the premium for puts is greater than the premiums for calls given equal distances from the ATM spot. This provides an opportunity for a volatility skew trading strategy.

A reasonable interpretation is that the market is therefore skewed to the put side. So if the trader believes that this is temporary, he would put on the following trade. Go out 3 months and sell a 25 delta put (strike 93.4) and buy a 25 delta call (103.5) (see Figure 7.25).

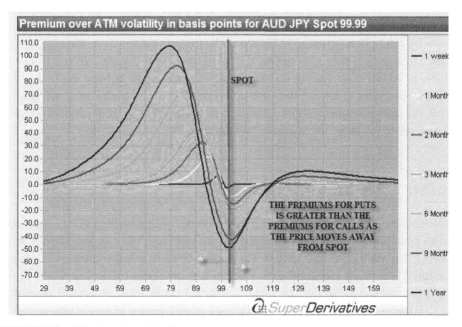

FIGURE 7.24   Delta Premium Graph
Source: Reprinted with permission of Super Derivatives, Inc.

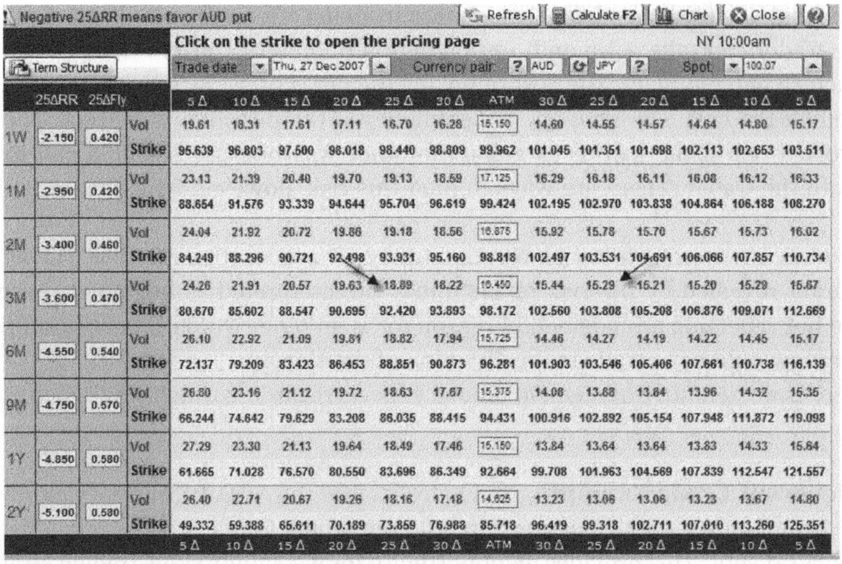

	25ΔRR	25ΔFly		5 Δ	10 Δ	15 Δ	20 Δ	25 Δ	30 Δ	ATM	30 Δ	25 Δ	20 Δ	15 Δ	10 Δ	5 Δ
1W	-2.150	0.420	Vol	19.61	18.31	17.61	17.11	16.70	16.28	15.150	14.60	14.55	14.57	14.64	14.80	15.17
			Strike	95.639	96.803	97.500	98.018	98.440	98.809	99.962	101.045	101.351	101.698	102.113	102.653	103.511
1M	-2.950	0.420	Vol	23.13	21.39	20.40	19.70	19.13	18.59	17.125	16.29	16.18	16.11	16.08	16.12	16.33
			Strike	88.654	91.576	93.339	94.644	95.704	96.619	99.424	102.195	102.970	103.838	104.864	106.188	108.270
2M	-3.400	0.460	Vol	24.04	21.92	20.72	19.86	19.18	18.56	16.875	15.92	15.78	15.70	15.67	15.73	16.02
			Strike	84.249	88.296	90.721	92.498	93.931	95.160	98.818	102.497	103.531	104.691	106.066	107.857	110.734
3M	-3.600	0.470	Vol	24.26	21.91	20.57	19.63	18.89	18.22	16.450	15.44	15.29	15.21	15.20	15.29	15.67
			Strike	80.670	85.602	88.547	90.695	92.420	93.893	98.172	102.560	103.808	105.208	106.876	109.071	112.669
6M	-4.550	0.540	Vol	26.10	22.92	21.09	19.81	18.82	17.94	15.725	14.46	14.27	14.19	14.22	14.45	15.17
			Strike	72.137	79.209	83.423	86.453	88.851	90.873	96.281	101.903	103.546	105.406	107.661	110.738	116.139
9M	-4.750	0.570	Vol	26.80	23.16	21.12	19.72	18.63	17.67	15.375	14.08	13.88	13.84	13.96	14.32	15.35
			Strike	66.244	74.642	79.629	83.208	86.035	88.415	94.431	100.916	102.892	105.154	107.948	111.872	119.098
1Y	-4.850	0.580	Vol	27.29	23.30	21.13	19.64	18.49	17.46	15.150	13.84	13.64	13.64	13.83	14.33	15.84
			Strike	61.665	71.028	76.570	80.550	83.696	86.349	92.664	99.708	101.963	104.569	107.839	112.547	121.557
2Y	-5.100	0.580	Vol	26.40	22.71	20.67	19.26	18.16	17.18	14.625	13.23	13.06	13.06	13.23	13.67	14.80
			Strike	49.332	59.388	65.611	70.189	73.859	76.988	85.718	96.419	99.318	102.711	107.010	113.260	125.351
				5 Δ	10 Δ	15 Δ	20 Δ	25 Δ	30 Δ	ATM	30 Δ	25 Δ	20 Δ	15 Δ	10 Δ	5 Δ

FIGURE 7.25 AUDJPY Deltas and Maturities from 1 Week To 2 Years
Source: Reprinted with permission of Super Derivatives, Inc.

Delta Neutral Trading Example

An advanced strategy for forex option traders is delta neutral trading. This involves buying an ATM straddle, which essentially results in a delta combination of zero. In a delta neutral strategy, we would buy the straddle (and have a positive gamma) if we believed the spot rate would fluctuate much. We would be making money from these moves (selling if spot rate goes higher and buying if it goes lower). In Figure 7.26 the trader buys 10 million EURUSD calls and 10 million EURUSD puts. Here is how the hedge would work. If the spot went to 1.4950, then the trader would be long 3 million. If the spot went to 1.4550, the trader would be short 4.5 million and would buy it. If the spot "visited" first 1.4950, the buyer would be short 7.5 million euros.

TRADING VEGA OR VOLATILITY

We have discussed how important volatility is in forex option trading. As a result, option traders in general have looked at volatility as tradable itself. It can and should, in fact, be treated as an asset class and traded. The trader needs to ask the question: Is volatility high or low? Is it at an extreme? Is it expected to increase or decrease? Once these questions are answered, the trader can choose to benefit from increased volatility by buying straddles or strangles or selling straddles or strangles when volatility is expected to come down.

Trade date:	Fri, 11 Jan 2008	▲	Spot date:	
Currency pair:	? EUR ↻ USD ?		Spot Mid ↻ :	

	Option 1 Data		Option 2 Data	
Option Class:	vanilla	▼	vanilla ▼	
Call / Put:	EUR Call ↻		EUR Put ↻	
Strike:	1.4781		1.4781	
Trigger 1:				
Trigger 2:				
Expiry:	Wed, 13 Feb 2008 🗓		Wed, 13 Feb 2008 🗓	
Delivery:	Fri, 15 Feb 2008		Fri, 15 Feb 2008	
Volatility: ATM ↻	9		9	
Forward Points:	-0.00005		-0.00005	
25Δ RR (%):	0.3 EUR Put ↻		0.3 EUR Put ↻	
25Δ Bfly (%):	0.25		0.25	
Notional in: EUR ↻	Buy 10,000,000		Buy 10,000,000	

FIGURE 7.26 Delta Neutral Option Table
Source: Reprinted with permission of Super Derivatives, Inc.

Volatility plays can coincide with fundamental events. For example, an upcoming election in a country will be accompanied by increased uncertainty and therefore increased volatility. A world crisis leading to an expectation of war will increase volatility.

There are many option volatility strategies. Generally, if vega is net positive in a spread combination, the trader wants volatility to rise. If the net vega is negative, you want to see volatility fall.

A favorite strategy for trading volatility involves spreads. Calendar spreads, call ratios, and put backspreads are used. Call ratios are used to sell volatility (negative vega). Put backspreads are a strategy used to buy volatility (positive vega). Calendar spreads are a very effective way to trade volatility. Let's look at a volatility calendar spread.

Volatility Calendar Spread on the USDJPY

Volatility calendar spreads are forex option trades that can occur frequently. Figure 7.27 shows the volatilities for the USDJPY.

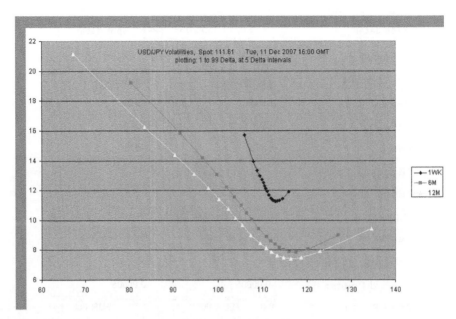

FIGURE 7.27 USDJPY Volatility for 1 Week, 6 Months, and 12 Months
Source: Reprinted with permission of Super Derivatives, Inc.

The following plot shows the volatility for the and 1 year periods for the USDJPY. If the trader thinks that the volatilities will converge, a calendar spread could be put on. In the example below the calendar spread is:

- Buy USDJPY Strike Price 100 June 12 08
- Sell USDJPY Strike Price 100 Dec 11 08

—Source: Trader Udi Sela at superderivatives.com

The trading idea is that the between these months the trade's objective is to capture the volatility difference since the strikes are equal (see Figure 7.28).

Volatility Smile Trading

If a volatility smile is detected, the trader can use the smile to follow it or construct a contrarian trade anticipating that the smile is unusual and temporary. One has to be careful about that in forex. Smiles in forex occur because they reflect not only sentiment in the market but conditions that are fundamental in nature. The skew may be long term and not be reverting quickly. So in contrarian trading a volatility smile, it's a good idea to have longer-duration trades to give the trader time to be right!

Consider Figure 7.29. We see a volatility smile favoring the calls. This suggests a trade of selling the EUR and buying the GBP.

In Figure 7.30 we see an extreme skew favoring the puts on the USDJPY.

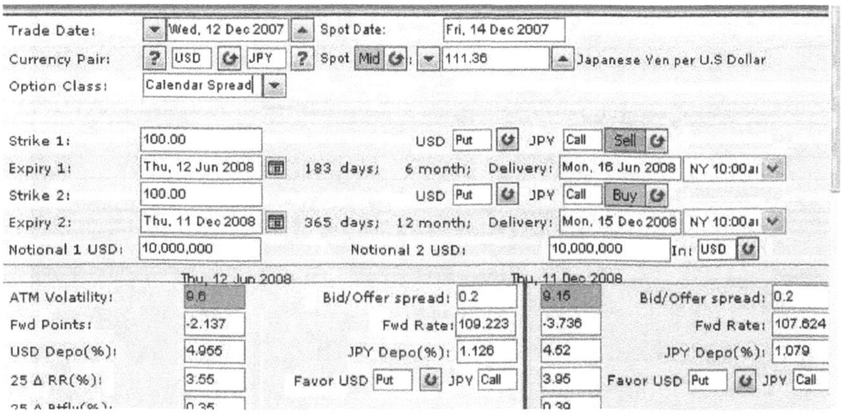

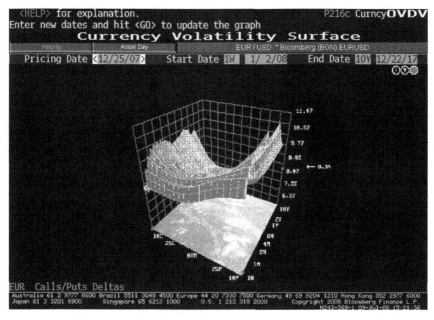

FIGURE 7.28 Calendar Spread Table for USDJPY
Source: Reprinted with permission of Super Derivatives, Inc.

There are three basic ways of trading a volatility skew:

1. Trade a continuation of the skew with puts on the USDJPY.
2. Trade a reversal of the skew with calls on the USD JPY.
3. Trade first a continuation of the skew and then a reversal of the skew with a put spread initially and then a call spread when the put spread is completed.

FIGURE 7.29 Volatility Surface of EURGBP Tilted to Calls
Source: © 2008 Bloomberg L.P. All rights reserved. Used with permission.

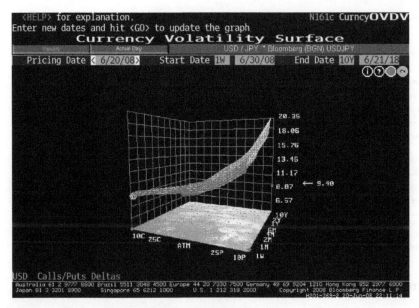

FIGURE 7.30 Volatility Surface of USDJPY Tilted to Puts
Source: ©2008 Bloomberg L.P. All rights reserved. Used with permission.

Implied Volatility and Spreads

The forex option trader should try to match the implied volatility conditions to an option strategy. Straddles and strangles are popular strategies for anticipated low-volatility conditions. Selling straddles and strangles is popular for high-volatility conditions. In Table 7.2 we see the option strategies matched to the volatility conditions.

GAMMA SPREAD TRADING

In gamma trading the ideal scenario is when the markets are very nervous. A high gamma means that there will be a high delta and therefore frequent moves. This is not uncommon

TABLE 7.2 Volatility Conditions and Associated Option Strategies

Volatility Conditions	Option Strategy
Low implied volatility	1. Long straddles and strangles
	2. Long calendar and diagonal spreads
	3. Short butterfly spreads
	4. Ratio backspreads
High implied volatility	1. Short straddles and strangles
	2. Long butterfly spreads
	3. Short calendar and diagonal spreads

in forex. In constructing spreads, a combination resulting in a positive gamma benefits the trader if the underlying moves very quickly up or down. When a spread combination is negative gamma, the trader wants the underlying to move slowly up or down. The trader should also look for implied volatility conditions. If implied volatility is *below* historical, there is a chance that the market is about to move violently, and therefore the trader would look to go long gamma. In a declining gamma situation, where there is expected declining volatility, a calendar spread where one buys an ATM call and sells a same strike further out would be a potential play.

A Gamma Trade Example by a Professional Forex Option Trader

Generally, gamma trading is a very professional type of trade done by hedge funds and sophisticated investors, because it requires very precise measurements that are not offered by retail forex firms.

Figure 7.31 shows an example offered by Udi Sela, a professional forex option trader at Superderviatives.com. The scenario involves putting on a USDJPY call with a 2-day expiration. The idea of the trade is to trade the gamma. The amount traded here is $500 million, not unusual in forex hedge funds. The gamma value in dollars is $192,413. Udi indicates that the strategy of the trade would be as follows:

If the USDJPY spot rate goes higher by 1 percent, you sell almost US$200 million. If the spot afterwards weakens by 1 percent, you buy them back. Each round would be worth US$2 million. If this happens more than once, you recover the initial premium

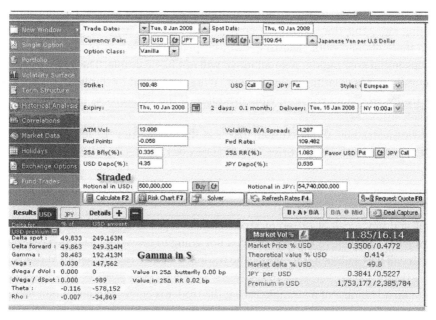

FIGURE 7.31 USDJPY Gamma Trade Table of Values
Source: Reprinted with permission of Super Derivatives, Inc.

paid. Each additional "round" is pure benefit. As a buyer, your maximum loss would be a premium. Who would sell this option?

- A trader already long gamma.
- A trader who estimates that the volatility is too high and expects the underlying spot won't fluctuate as much as the market predicts.

KEY FOREX OPTION COMBINATIONS AND COMPONENTS

There are many combinations of option strategies that can be used. This chapter reviews straddles, strangles, and more exotic strategies such as the seagull, the condor, and the butterfly. It also presents some examples of professional option trades using these strategies.

Straddles

One of the most used strategies in forex options trading is the straddle. Straddles are responses to volatility conditions. If the trader anticipates a big move but doesn't know which way, a straddle strategy can be placed. It involves buying a call and buying a put with the same strike price. One can vary the strategy by placing the call and put ATM or OTM.

The main advantage of the straddle is that it guarantees that the trader will be on the winning side. But this guarantee comes with a cost. The cost is the premiums to purchase the calls and puts. The trade will be profitable only if the underlying moves beyond this initial cost region. A small move will not be desirable. The straddle therefore best occurs in a low-volatility environment. When historical or implied volatility is at a low, the trader would consider buying straddles. If the volatility is high, the trader can think to sell straddles.

In buying a straddle, the maximum loss is at the strike price. In selling a straddle, the maximum profit is at the strike price (see Figure 7.32).

Strangles

Buy a put and buy a call at different strikes or *sell* a put and sell a call with a different strike prices. If you believe that the price is not going to move big. This is a combination of selling a call and selling a put. Again, the trader can place the trades ATM or OTM (see Figure 7.33).

The main advantage of a strangle is that the trader receives income when the market is range bound or very narrow. The risk is that the currency pair will move beyond the strike prices and begin to expose the trader to losses.

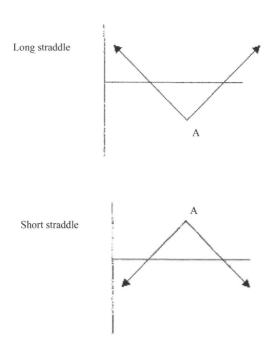

FIGURE 7.32 Straddle Example

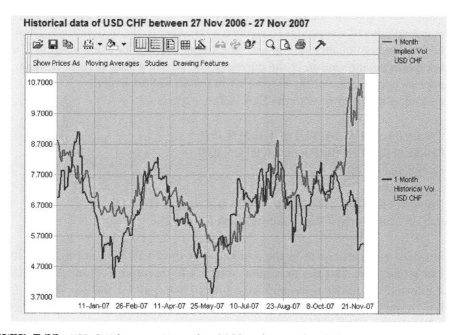

FIGURE 7.33 USD CHF between November 2006 and November 2007
Source: Reprinted with permission of Super Derivatives, Inc.

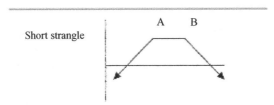

FIGURE 7.34 Strangle Example
Source: Reprinted with permission of Super Derivatives, Inc.

The buyer of the strange faces the maximum loss if the price stays between the strike prices. The seller of the strangle gets a maximum profit if the price stays between the strikes (see Figure 7.34).

Reduced and Zero Cost Strategies for Forex Option Trades: The Seagull

A great advantage of option instruments is that they can be suited to the risk appetite of the trader. The trader that wants to reduce the costs of an option (and thereby reduce the profit potential) can put on combinations of puts and calls that result in a minimal or zero cost for the trade. Among the most famous of these is called the seagull.

The general idea of a seagull is to achieve a zero cost to the option trade. The trader sells calls and puts to finance the option. The trader can buy or sell a seagull. A trader who anticipates a depreciation of the currency will put on a long seagull. A trader who anticipates an appreciation of the currency will put on a short seagull.

Let's look at an example with the EURUSD:

Leg 1: Trader buys EURUSD PUT at 1.4220 @ 1215
Leg 2: Trader sells EURUSD Put at 1.4000 @539.00
Net cost of spread = $676
Creates a put spread
Leg 3: TradersSells EURUSD CALL at 1.5275 and receives $695.00
Total cost of Trade is +$19 Essentially a Break even trade.

The trader will participate in the weakness of the EURUSD until it hits 1.40, the lower put strike price. But the maximum return will therefore be 1.40. The selling of the call allowed the trader to receive premium to help pay for the put spread. In the preceding example, it paid for the whole amount and left some money over. The risk is that the EURUSD could go above the 1.5275 strike price and therefore expose the trader to having the trade lose money.

The trader could also make this an ATM seagull and would therefore immediately participate in the direction of the currency pair. An instructive description of the use of seagulls can be seen in the following examples of its application to a Brazilian currency and how it has been applied to the Yen.

Example of Professional's Application of Seagull to Brazilian Currency

A seagull option may be the best route for a Brazilian subsidiary needing to hedge its exposure as fears over Iraq and Venezuela bite, says Douglas Bongartz-Renaud, global head of forex options at ABN Amro in Amsterdam:

> *PROBLEM: The Brazilian subsidiary of a US multinational has US dollar–denominated debt. At the beginning of each year, it typically rolls its hedges over using forwards. However, this year the subsidiary would like to explore other hedging alternatives involving options. The treasurer believes that spot will weaken significantly in the short term, with volatility changing negligibly. Spot is relatively high, in the 3.50–3.54 per dollar range, and volatility is around 26%. The main worries over the near term are that the possible war with Iraq and the ongoing Venezuelan crisis will put even more pressure on the Brazilian real, while worst-case scenarios in the medium term of spot reaching well over 4.00 per dollar are deemed unlikely at the moment. What would be a suitable structure to hedge this exposure while taking advantage of the currency view and introducing the potential to benefit from favourable movements in the currency?*

> *SOLUTION: Given the currency view that the real would weaken significantly in the short term and that medium-term protection against strong devaluation is currently not necessary, the subsidiary could use a seagull option strategy to hedge their dollar payables. With the seagull strategy, the subsidiary could fully fund the cost of purchasing a six-month 3.75/4.00 dollar call/real put spread by selling a six-month 3.39 dollar put/real call for net zero upfront premium. With this strategy, the subsidiary is protected from a weakening in the real up to 4.00, while it leaves open room for the real to strengthen toward 3.39. However, the subsidiary only participates in any strengthening of the real between 3.70 and 3.40.*

Example of Seagull Trade Recommendation on Yen On

> ***MAY 7 2001***—*The JPY has strengthened recently on foreign buying of Japanese equities and optimism regarding Koizumi's reforms. . . . Indeed, the price action appears to be on the verge of creating strong USD/JPY bearish technical signals. . . . However, we continue to believe that portfolio outflows by Japanese investors after Golden Week, combined with the end of the market's "honeymoon" with Koizumi, will cause USD/JPY to strengthen significantly. Below are alternatives using options that take advantage of the view that USD/JPY will*

appreciate sharply in the next month. Tenor: one-month Spot reference: 121.39 One-month Forward: 120.95 for reference, a one-month, 121.00 USD call/JPY put can be purchased for 1.31% USD notional and has a breakeven level of 122.59. This relatively expensive choice pays for complete protection from any decline in USD/JPY below 121. Further, it pays for unlimited appreciation, despite our view that spot will move to 125 in one month. Below is a more precisely tailored structure:

Position 1: *USD/JPY Bullish Seagull*
Buy: 121 USD call/JPY put
Sell: 125 USD call/JPY put
Sell: 118 USD put/JPY call
Premium: 0.56% USD
Breakeven: 121.68

This structure allows the investor to participate in USD appreciation up to 125, our one-month forecast. The premium is reduced by selling away participation above 125 and also by incurring downside risk in the event that spot falls below 118. Note that this "tailored" structure costs less than 1/2 of the plain vanilla call.

—www.forexhsi.com/forexnews/news0501/news_132384.phpg)

Zero Cost Cylinder

This type of option involves buying a call and selling a put, or selling a call and buying a put at the same strike price. This involves a zero cost result. They both have the same maturity and notional amounts. Buying the call will generate participation in the strengthening of the currency. Selling the put obligates the trader to buy the currency at a pre-determined rate if it gets there. This is used if you anticipated a limited decline or a limited rise.

The Butterfly Spread

Reuters Financial Glossary provides this definition of a *butterfly spread:*

This is a famous combination of options. It involves the sale/buy of an At The Money Straddle and the purchase/sell of an Out Of The Money Strangle. The trader will get the greatest gain if the underlying instrument remains stable. It also limits the risk if there is a big move. Selling a butterfly spread can be used when the currency pairs are in sideways ranges and they are most likely applied to cross pairs because they tend to be more stable. This is a low volatility or low Vega trading condition. They trader should actually try to adjust the spread to a 0 Vega position.

Maximum profit conditions are achieved if the spot pair on expiration stays at the strike prices of the ATM straddle, which was sold. The trader's maximum profit is equal to the net premium received, minus, of course, any commission fees. Maximum loss is limited to at or below the lower strike of the put purchased or rise above or equal to the higher strike of the call purchased. In either situation, maximum loss is equal to the difference in strike between the calls (or puts) minus the net credit received when entering the trade.

Break-Even Points   Assuming no delta hedge has been done, there are two break-even points for the iron butterfly. The break-even points can be calculated using the following formulae.

- Upper break-even point = Strike price of short call + Net premium received
- Lower break-even point = Strike price of short put − Net premium received

Figures 7.35 and 7.36 are examples from our trader Udi at Superderivatives, who was asked to think about an example advanced Butterfly trade. Udi states: "I chose USD/CNY with low volatility and where historical volatility is below implied volatility."

I priced the butterfly in Figure 7.36 (the ATM strike is 6.9500).

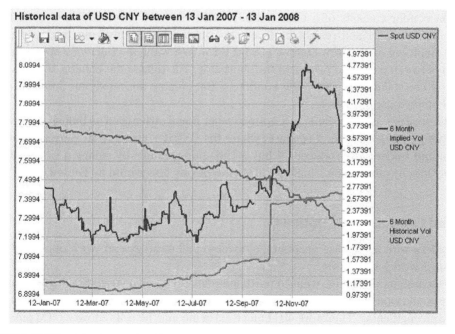

FIGURE 7.35   Volatility on the Chinese Yuan
Source: Reprinted with permission of Super Derivatives, Inc.

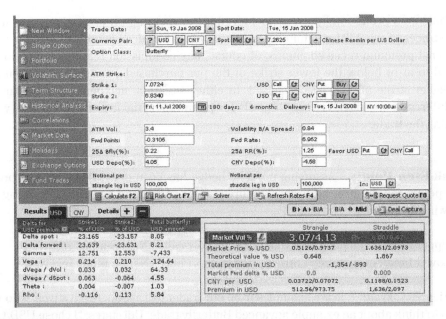

FIGURE 7.36 Butterfly on the Chinese Yuan
Source: Reprinted with permission of Super Derivatives, Inc.

The Condor

An iron condor consists of a bear call and bull put credit spreads. It is important to understand support and resistance levels as you will be placing your trades at these levels. Each leg of the iron condor is sold OTM. We want the currency spot price to stay in between the strike prices on the short side. The tighter the condor, the less max loss you can incur. The wider the condor is, the greater the maximum loss. (*Source:* www.hotstockmarket.com.)

The strategy used by the Forex option trader could structured as bullish or bearish. For example, let's consider a scenario where the USDJPY goes lower. Here is what pro analyst and trader Udi produced: "I buy a USD put—finance by selling a USD call and lock my loss by purchasing a higher USD/CALL (so my loss would be limited).

Writing Covered Forex Options

For traders with larger size accounts, a covered call strategy can work out to achieve income. It works as follows:

Let's assume the trader want to participate in a long-term strengthening of the yen. Therefore, he would sell in the spot market the USDJPY. He expects a rather stable trend toward strengthening. Therefore, to achieve extra income, he sells a lower OTM put. This means that the trader is receiving a premium for selling the put. The trader, however, is really obligating himself if the underlying pair goes to the put price to purchase the underlying. In other words, he would be out of the position. The trader is not worried about that event since it would be profitable. However, the trader wants to actually never go to that strike price and in that case he would keep the premium.

SUMMARY

The option strategies in this section covered the major tools for the forex trader. The level of sophistication is up to the trader. The beginning forex option trader can progress from first putting on plain vanilla strategies, to spreads. The more sophisticated strategies using multiple legs could be tried after one becomes proficient.

CHAPTER 8

Binary Option Strategies

Exotic options are a major tool for professional institutions in forex trading. They are known as exotics because they are in contrast to the plain vanilla calls and puts. There are many kinds of exotics and they have been developed to provide tools for shaping trades under all kinds of conditions. Most of the exotic options are used by hedge funds and institution to customize their option trades in relationship to their specific risks. However, the first-generation options, called binary options, are the focus of this book. They are becoming available to the retail forex trader and offer powerful new trading opportunities. This book focuses on binary options and how to use them to enhance forex trading and forex options trading.

Types of Exotic Options
Barrier
Binary
European digital
Partial/Window barrier
Average options
Structured products
Accrual/Floaters
Fader
Accumulator
Basket
Compound
Quanto
Cross-asset barrier
Forward start

Variance swap
Chooser
Loan related
Multiperiod barriers

Binary Option Types
One touch
No touch
Double one touch
Double no touch
One touch with knock-out
No touch with knock-in
Barrier option types
Knock-out
Knock–in
Ladders
Reverse knock-out
Reverse knock-in
Double knock-out
Double knock-in
Knock-in and knock-out

WHAT IS A BINARY OPTION?

A binary option is an option where a trader specifies an amount of payout that he will receive if he is correct about the targeted price action. This target is known as a barrier. If the trader is wrong, he receives nothing at all. So it's an all-or-nothing situation. In contrast, then, to a plain vanilla call or put, it doesn't matter how far the price is in the money, the trader receives only the amount specified. The trader also sets the time to expiration. Another key difference is that in the binary option, the underlying contract is not the spot currency, but rather is the event itself.

One of the major questions facing the firm and the trader of barrier options is whether there has been a "touch" event. To avoid controversy about whether a barrier has been reached, there is an authoritative foreign exchange committee that has set forth specific conditions that define the "touch" event. For example:

> *Transactions must occur between 5:00* A.M. *Sydney time on Monday and 5:00* P.M. *New York time on Friday. The opening time in Sydney has been advanced by one hour from the Barrier Options Subcommittee's previous recommendation (of 6:00* A.M. *Sydney time) because it is now recognized in the global financial markets that the Sydney spot market opens at 5:00* A.M. *Sydney time.*

The barrier options determination agent may use cross-currency rates to determine whether a barrier has been breached in respect of a currency pair that is not commonly quoted. The barrier options determination agent should use two or more substantially contemporaneous transactions in the most liquid applicable currency pairs to calculate the cross rate. In those cases where more than three currencies are to be used to determine the cross rate, the Committee recommends that the parties agree in advance which currency pairs will be used to calculate such a rate.

—www.mathfinance.de/wystup/papers/OT_derivativesweek.pdf;
www.ny.frb.org/fxc/fxann000217.html

Let's define the types of binary options:

One touch (lock-in). If at any time the price hits the one-touch target, the buyer of the option gets the payout. The payout is paid in the base currency. In Figure 8.1 we can see that the binary payout is different than a payout in a call option because the binary payout will not vary once the trader's anticipated price move occurs. In Figure 8.2, the payoff to the trader shows it is a triggered event and not linear. When compared to a standard call or put option, we can see in Figure 8.1 through Figure 8.3 that the binary trader puts a ceiling on the potential profits.

No touch (lock-out). If at any time the price doesn't hit the target, the buyer of the option gets paid.

Double one touch. This option requires the target to hit either of two price points (a targeted resistance and a targeted support). In other words, the double one touch pays the buyer if the price breaks out of a predetermined range.

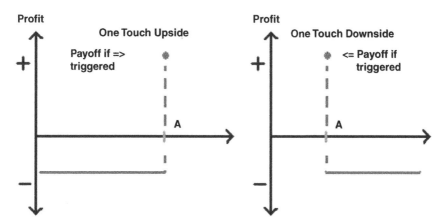

FIGURE 8.1 Binary Option Payoff Diagram
Source: Saxo Bank Group at www.saxoeducation.com

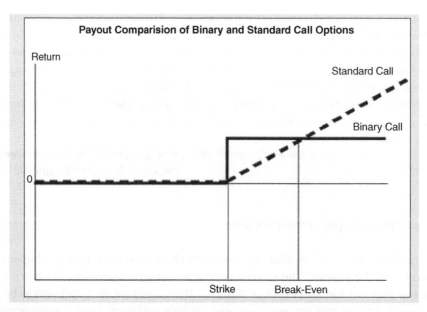

FIGURE 8.2 Payout Comparison of Binary and Standard Call Options
Source: From *The Dictionary of Financial Risk Management* by Gary L. Gastineau and Mark P. Kritzman © 1992, 1996, and 1999. Reprinted with permission of John Wiley and Sons, Inc.

Double no touch. This is the opposite of double one touch. The trader specifies a resistance and support level and an amount to be received. If the price doesn't hit either barrier, the trader gets paid.
Expiration of exotics. Each firm will provide the terms of expiration. The trader has to confirm what exact time will be used.

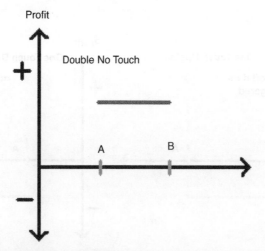

FIGURE 8.3 Double No Touch Payoff Diagram
Source: Saxo Bank Group at www.saxoeducation.com

Premiums of Exotic Options and Risk/Reward

Exotic option premiums are priced as percentage of the amount requested to be received. The trader needs to realize that the premium prices of binary options are not based solely on the standard Black-Scholes model. The Black-Sholes model assumes constant volatility and interest rates, and this is not a real-world condition for options in currencies. Therefore, coming up with premium prices for binary options is computationally challenging, and there is no single accepted set of equations that generate binary option valuations. In fact, there is a market for competing sources of effective pricing engines. Superderivatives.com is a leading world provider of exotic option pricing and supplies many of the exchanges and firms. But their equations are not standardized. A firm can, in fact, develop its own pricing engine. This means that the premiums can vary significantly from firm to firm and the trader can't easily determine whether the premium for a binary option is fair.

This leads to an easy risk-reward calculation. In Figure 8.4 we see a one-touch trade where the payout is 1000 to the trader if the price touches the target of 116.07 on a USDJPY trade. The premium paid is 493.00. The reward to risk ratio is therefore 1000/493.00 or 1:2.

Examples of Binary Option Uses and Price Patterns

Range behavior—double no touch. If a currency pair is anticipated to be in a range, the double-no-touch option provides the ability to benefit from this situation. Unlike a strangle, which would involve the risk of the price action going in the money against the trader on one side, a double no touch involves only a predetermined known risk.

Breakouts—double one touch. If a currency pair is anticipated to break out, but the trader doesn't want to predict which way, a double one touch would provide a payout if the currency pair broke out of either one of the sides. Playing economic data releases is an appropriate implementation of the double one touch.

Trend continuation—one touch. When a currency pair has a strong trend pattern, a one-touch option provides the ability to play a continuation of the pair. The premium will, as in regular options, increase in price as time to expiration increases, as you'll see in Figure 8.6.

Consolidation—no touch. This is appropriate when the pattern is falling into a Fibonacci retracement pattern.

Fed funds interest rate decision. Unique application of binary options.

Ladders—This is a variation of a binary where the firm offers a range of levels that the trader bets the price will be above or below. IGmarket.com offers this form of option.

Comparative Advantages of Exotics versus Plain Vanilla

Using exotics provides the opportunity to contain risk. In each case, the risk is totally limited to the amount paid. This is particularly valuable to the trader who would be

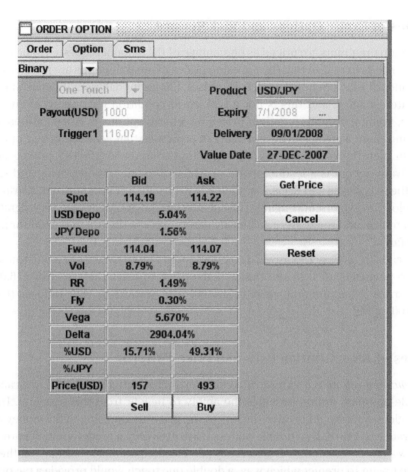

FIGURE 8.4 Binary Option One-Touch Price at 116.07 Quote on USDJPY
Source: Priced by Finotec and reprinted with permission from www.finotec.com.

writing calls or puts, but wants to avoid the huge and unlimited risks associated with being wrong.

USING EXOTICS TO DERIVE MARKET SENTIMENT

One of the most useful applications of exotics is to use them to confirm market senti-ment. If a trader forms a belief about a direction of a currency pair, that belief can be further supported by evaluating exotics. The trader does not have to trade an exotic to use it as a source of market sentiment. We saw that in the binary options on the federal funds rate, the premium prices represent the probability the market is giving the price action meeting the strike price. This means that the trader can observe what the market believes is the probability associated with different kinds of price action.

TABLE 8.1 One-Touch Option Trade—Currency Pair USDJPY

	Market Price: 114.07	
	116.07 Resistance	**112.07 Support**
15 Days	41.25%	49.3
30 Days	55.35%	55.6%
92 Days	73.09%	67.04%

Source: Copyright BeTonMarkets

Let's look at an example where a trader wants to determine market sentiment regarding the yen. On December 22 the USDJPY was at 114.07. To test market sentiment the trader enters a tentative order for two one-touch trades. First, he enters an order for a one-touch option with a strike price of 116.07 and then a one-touch option with a strike price at 112.07. The trader can specify any time duration. Let's assume a 15-day time duration. It's important to remember that the goal here is not to put on the trade, but to see what, if any, differences there are in the price of the binary option. If the market sentiment was neutral, the cost of the premium of a one-touch option in either direction with the same duration and same strike price would be equal. We see in Table 8.1 that the market sentiment favored a strengthening of the yen for the targeted 15 days because the price (which is also the percentage probability) of the binary was 49.3 percent if it touched 112.07, versus a price of 41.25 percent if it touched 116.97. In Table 8.2, we see a market sentiment bias for a weakening pound for 15 days, and then—while still a bias for a weaker pound—this bias declines from 1.11 percent to 1.04 percent. The binary option ratios for the EURUSD in Table 8.3 showed a very strong 30 percent imbalance favoring a weakening of the EUR. It's important to note that these binary premiums are not predictions, but they reflect what the firms offering these options require as payment for the ability of a person to receive payment if they were right.

Another key aspect of using binary options to detect market sentiment is to see the variation in prices over different duration targets. Figure 8.5 shows that a one-touch binary price for a 116.07 target for the USDJPY (spot was 114.19) for a September 1, 2008, expiration is priced at $493. When the date extends another three months to December 24, Figure 8.6 shows that the price increases to $556, indicating that market sentiment was favoring a weakening of the yen.

TABLE 8.2 One-Touch Option Trade—Currency Pair GBPUSD

	Market Price: 1.9836		
	2.0036 Resistance	**1.9636 Support**	**Ratio**
15 Days	62.51	69.54	1.11%
30 Days	75.29	82.07	1.09%
92 Days	87.82	91.84	1.04%

TABLE 8.3   One-Touch Option Trade—Currency Pair EURUSD

	Market Price: 1.4380		
	1.4580 Resistance	1.4180 Support	Ratio
15 Days	44.15	57.25	1.29%
30 Days	60.71	70.03	1.15%
92 Days	78.84	84.85	1.07%

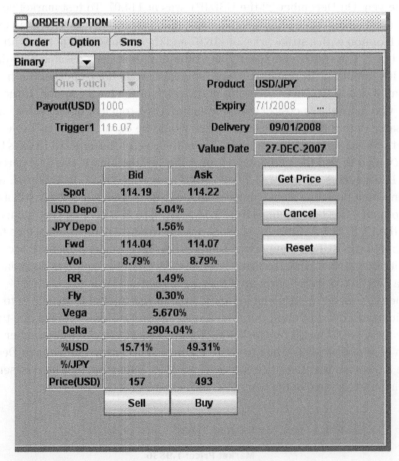

FIGURE 8.5   One-Touch Binary at 116.07 Prices for USDJPY
Source: Priced by Finotec and reprinted with permission from www.finotec.com.

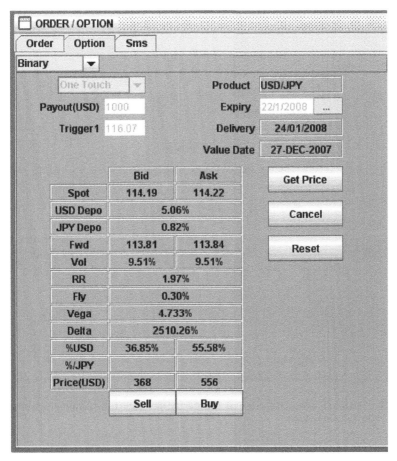

FIGURE 8.6 One-Touch Binary at 116.07 USDJPY Price Increases with a Three-Month Increase in Expiration
Source: Priced by Finotec and reprinted with permission from www.finotec.com.

Using the service of BetonMarkets.com, we can derive market sentiment for a short-duration play of 15 days. In Figure 8.7, we have the spot at 114.07, the price of a one touch at 116.07 was $41.25, while as seen in Figure 8.8, the price of a one touch at 112.07 for the same duration of 15 days was $50.61. The price difference means that the market sentiment favored a strengthening of the yen.

COMBINING BINARY OPTIONS WITH PLAIN VANILLA AND SPOT TRADING

The forex trader should always be looking to reduce the risk of the trade. An effective use of binary options is in a combination with a plain vanilla option trade. A one-touch

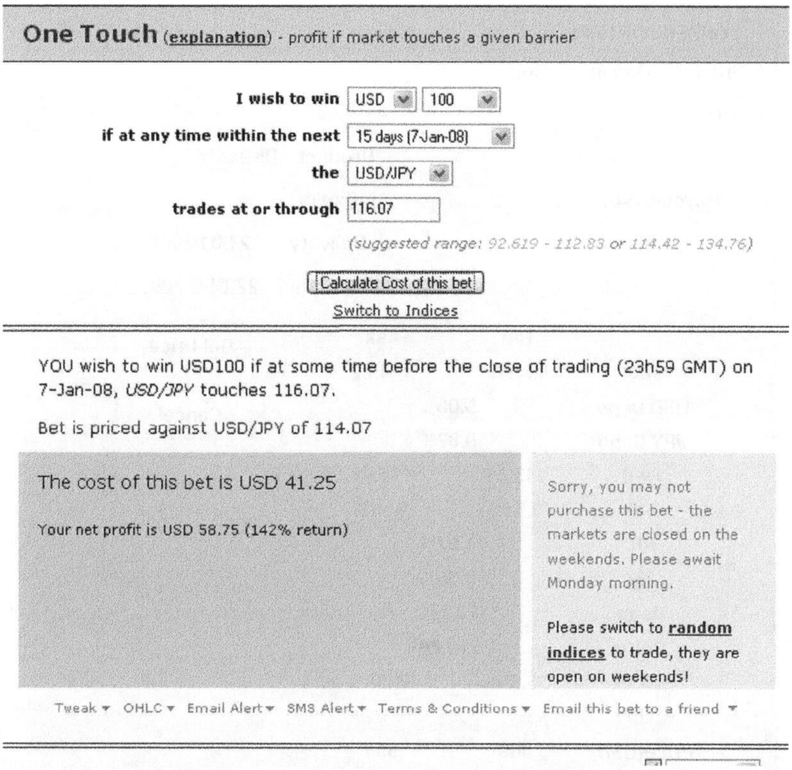

One Touch (explanation) - profit if market touches a given barrier

I wish to win USD ⌄ 100 ⌄

if at any time within the next 15 days (7-Jan-08) ⌄

the USD/JPY ⌄

trades at or through 116.07

(suggested range: 92.619 - 112.83 or 114.42 - 134.76)

[Calculate Cost of this bet]

Switch to Indices

YOU wish to win USD100 if at some time before the close of trading (23h59 GMT) on 7-Jan-08, USD/JPY touches 116.07.

Bet is priced against USD/JPY of 114.07

The cost of this bet is USD 41.25

Your net profit is USD 58.75 (142% return)

Sorry, you may not purchase this bet - the markets are closed on the weekends. Please await Monday morning.

Please switch to **random indices** to trade, they are open on weekends!

Tweak ▾   OHLC ▾   Email Alert ▾   SMS Alert ▾   Terms & Conditions ▾   Email this bet to a friend ▾

FIGURE 8.7   15-Day One-Touch Option of 116.07 USDJPY Bullish Direction Probabilities
Source: Copyright BeTonMarkets

One Touch (explanation) - profit if market touches a given barrier

I wish to win USD ⌄ 100 ⌄

if at any time within the next 15 days (7-Jan-08) ⌄

the USD/JPY ⌄

trades at or through 112.07

(suggested range: 92.619 - 112.83 or 114.42 - 134.76)

[Calculate Cost of this bet]

Switch to Indices

YOU wish to win USD100 if at some time before the close of trading (23h59 GMT) on 7-Jan-08, USD/JPY touches 112.07.

Bet is priced against USD/JPY of 114.07

The cost of this bet is USD 50.61

Your net profit is USD 49.39 (98% return)

Sorry, you may not purchase this bet - the markets are closed on the weekends. Please await Monday morning.

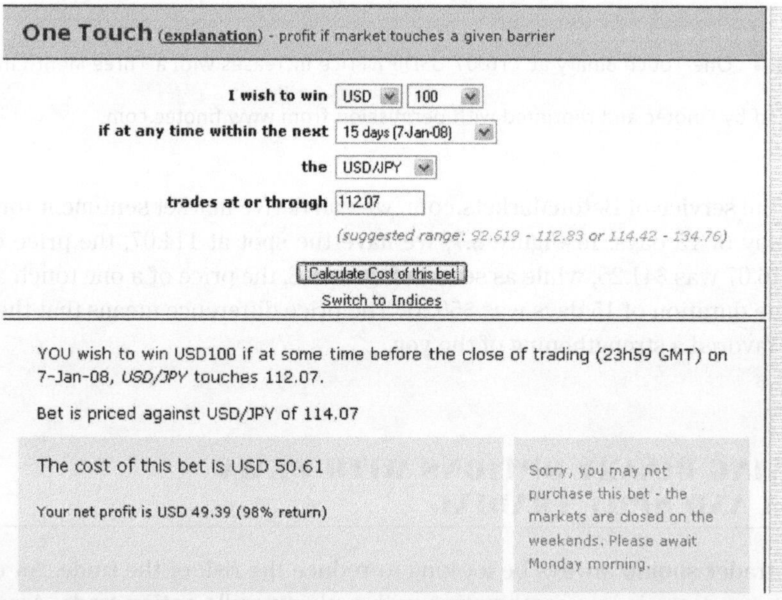

FIGURE 8.8   15-Day One-Touch Option on USDJPY Bearish Direction Probabilities
Source: Copyright BeTonMarkets

binary option acts as a rebate to the trader when the price is hit and therefore returns to the trader a sum of money. This rebate payment reduces the cost of the total trade. Here is how a binary option can be used as an additive protection to a regular option trade.

Another example is with a spot trade. A trader looking to take a long position in a currency will face increased volatility as time passes. To protect the account, the trader can use a regular option such as a call or put. This is called a married call or put. Let's look at an example in Figure 8.9.

At the end of 2007, the trader is looking to play a weakening in the British pound. This is based on the Bank of England's cutting rates and doing it unanimously in its December Monetary Policy Committee meetings. This trader is taking a short on the GBPUSD at 1.9837 right before Christmas. However, the upward channel shows a greater than 500-pip-wide potential move against him. The trader puts on a limit of 1. How can the trader protect his position with options?

One strategy is to buy a protective call. So he selects a February 15 call of 2.00, which is 200 pips out of the money. The trader puts on a close limit at 1.9109, which is the 50 percent Fib line. This is a long-term trade, then, with the trader hoping for a 700-pip

FIGURE 8.9 GBPUSD Weekly Chart
Source: © ProRealTime.com, web-based charting software

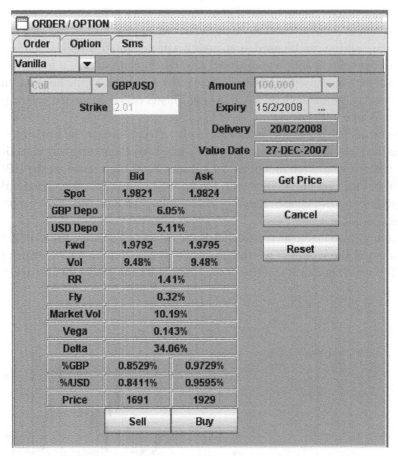

FIGURE 8.10 GBPUSD Call Option Quote at 2.01 Strike
Source: Priced by Finotec and reprinted with permission from www.finotec.com.

move. He considers an ATM option of February 15 at a 1.98 strike price. The cost is 2956 (see Figure 8.10).

If the trader is correct his move would be a 7000 move. Before he puts on a buy order he checks what can be done on a binary option. If he puts on the protective call, it will cost him a lot, nearly 3,000. And there is a risk that this would not even protect his position. The price can go beyond 1.98 and then come back. It's a major uncertainty. Consider the alternative of a one-touch option, which would be triggered at 2.01 as seen in Figure 8.11.

In this case, if the GBPUSD touches the trigger point even once, the trader will get his designated payout of 2000 pounds. The price need not stay there in the money as in a call option. Which alternative is better? A further strategy is once a touch event occurs to then place a break-even stop loss.

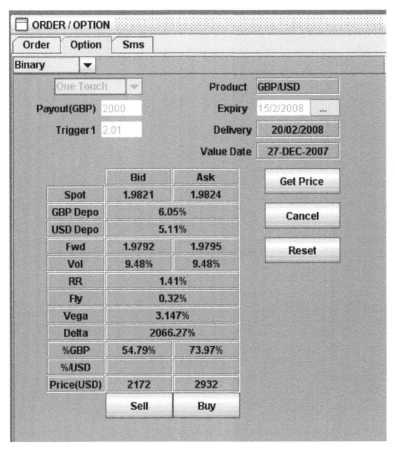

FIGURE 8.11 GBPUSD One-Touch Trigger at 2.01
Source: Priced by Finotec and reprinted with permission from www.finotec.com.

One-touch options are known as rebate options because they are used to rebate a trader when an event occurs that the trader wants to avoid.

SUMMARY

This chapter introduced the basic concepts and tactics relating to binary options. Binary options offer an alternative to standard options. They can be combined in different ways. But even if the binary options are not traded, they provide important insights on market direction. The forex option trader will greatly benefit by learning how to evaluate binary options whether they are trading them or not.

CHAPTER 9

Option Strategies for Extreme Outcomes and Scenarios

I n the coming years, extreme global events may occur and then present the forex trader with unique opportunities. Some of these events cannot be predicted, but many can and through scenario analysis forex option traders can be ready for future contingencies Armed with preparatory analysis of alternative option strategies for extreme events, the forex option trader will be ready to play those events out for potential profits.

RECESSION IN CHINA OR CONTINUED BOOM

The rise of China is a major theme for trading in the coming years. China is reported to consume 15 percent of the world's energy, 30 percent of the world's steel, and 54 percent of the world's cement. The recent economic growth of China at 11 percent cannot be sustained. "Current growth is too fast and at too high a cost," said Han Yongwen, the Chinese National Development and Reform Commission Secretary General. China's policy makers recognize the danger of an overheated economy and increased interest rates to control this. At the end of 2007, Chinese inflation rose to 6.9 percent (CNCPIYOY INDEX) (see Figure 9.1).

Contributing to Chinese inflation was an increase in food prices to levels such as 18.9 percent. While an overheated China is a concern to the Chinese, it presents opportunities for the forex option trader.

Another contributor to Chinese inflation is the rising value of the yuan. It rose 6.2 percent in 2007. The Chinese yuan has a managed float where it is allowed to move 0.5 percent on either side of a daily fixed reference point by the Bank of China. Furthermore, as Chinese exports increase, cash comes into the economy, pushing inflation up. The Chinese trade surplus extended to over 238 billion in 2007.

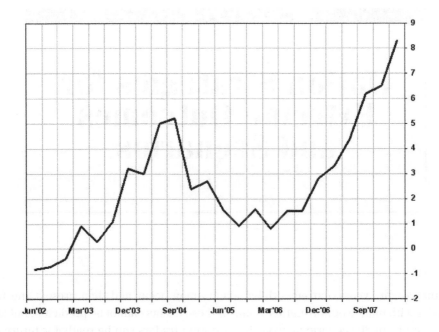

FIGURE 9.1   Chinese Inflation Levels
Data Source: Bloomberg Finance L.P.

Can the Chinese Stop the Powerful Forces Pushing Inflation?

How can the forex option trader detect and play a scenario of a Chinese collapse?

One of the key leading indicators for a forex trader to conduct an outlook on the Chinese situation is the CSI 300 Index. The CSI Index tracks 300 shares listed on the Shanghai and Shenzhen stock exchanges. The CSI 300 represents the powerful parabolic path the Chinese economy has experienced. But will it last? If the CSI starts to retrace and break down its support line, the Chinese economy will be perceived to be in a slowdown. The results will be a bear sentiment on currencies such as the AUD, which benefits from Chinese growth (see Figure 9.2).

Possible Strategy for Trading a Contraction in China: Buy Renminbi Puts

The Chicago Mercantile Exchange (CME) allows trading on the renminbi currency in its futures contract (see Figure 9.3).

The trader could consider shorting the renminbi futures contract and buying a protective call on the AUDUSD contract. This will allow a play on the weakening of the renminbi, but protect against a major move because a strong aussie is unlikely with a weakening renminbi.

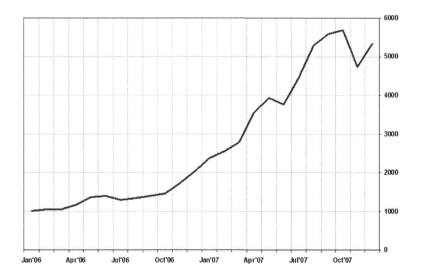

FIGURE 9.2 The CSI Index (SHSZ300)
Data Source: Bloomberg Finance L.P.

OPTION TRADING TO PLAY CARRY TRADES WITH HEDGE—PUTTING ON COLLARS

The carry trade will always be an attractive force in forex. As long as there are interest rate differentials, carry trades will occur. There are two major approaches for the forex trader. One is to play an unwinding of the carry trade, and the other is to play its return. Both strategies can occur throughout any year.

Exchange (CME) Chicago Mercantile Exchange		
Name	RENMINBI CUR FUT JUN 08	
Ticker	DOM8	DOM8
Contract Size	CNY 1,000,000	
Value of 1.0 pt	$ 1,000,000	
Tick Size	0.00001	
Tick Value	$ 10	
Current Price	0.14300	USD/CNY
Pt. Val x Price	$ 143,000	@ 23:04:46

FIGURE 9.3 Renminbi Currency Future Contract
Data Source: Bloomberg Finance L.P.

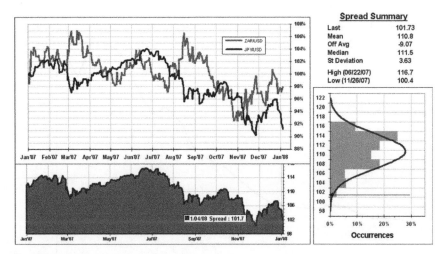

FIGURE 9.4 South African Rand and USDJPY
Data Source: Bloomberg Finance L.P.

There are several scenarios to pursue option trading involving a play on carry trades:

- *Trade a return of carry trade.* Buy options on the GBPJPY 6-month options.
- *Trade a decline and then a return of the carry trade.* Buy GBPJPY puts at the money (ATM) and then sell GBPJPY puts 3 months out ATM.
- *Trade a decline of the carry trade.* Trade ZAR versus JPY.

This can be done at the CME on the futures side. The idea of the trade is that an increase in market fear of carry trades would generate a scenario of a decline in the ZAR and a strengthening of the JPY. This would suggest a combination: a call on the futures contract of the yen and a call on the USDZAR. Buy a long-term call on the yen and a protective put on the USDZAR. If the yen gets weaker, the USDZAR pair will increase in value (see Figure 9.4).

$1000+ GOLD AND $200+ CRUDE OIL

At $100 oil (already achieved), the market had penetrated a psychological hurdle and is likely to enter into ranging behavior. Once crude oil nears $150 a $200 strike price may be on the horizon. Crude oil at $200 is a possible scenario that the trader may be facing or take advantage of market expectations in that direction.

The trader should carefully monitor oil market patterns for parabolic and channels. But the forex options scenario is to trade closely related markets. We know that there are close correlations between the commodities of gold, oil, copper, and the Canadian

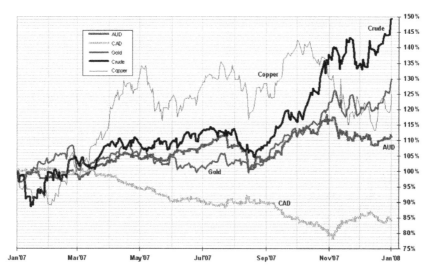

FIGURE 9.5 Copper, Gold, Oil, and the USDCAD and AUDUSD
Data Source: Bloomberg Finance L.P.

and Australian currencies. Look at Figure 9.5, which depicts their co-movements as of December 31, 2007.

Strategy: Play future surges in gold and oil, with calendar call spreads on these commodities. Buy aussie calls ATM when gold hits a new high, and sell aussie calls 200 pips higher. Or buy aussie calls ATM near term and sell aussie calls 3 months out. For those playing a retracement calendar, put spreads provide a good way to play a downward move in gold or oil.

TRADING $OIL SHOCK ($200) IN FOREX OPTIONS

While rising oil costs are often associated with the Canadian currency trading opportunities because Canada is a net exporter of oil, there are other currency plays. If energy prices move up however, Japan will be affected by an increase in its core inflation rates (see Figure 9.6). This affects everyday life like the prices of taxi rides in Tokyo, as well as business costs such as airfare. The effects of increased energy prices became evident when in December 2007 Japan reported the fastest growth in consumer inflation in nine years. A continued anticipation of high oil prices will be associated with pessimism among businesses. The trader should read the Tankan sentiment surveys that are released by the Bank of Japan. Continued increased oil prices could lead to expectations of a slowdown in the Japanese economy and therefore a weaker Yen.

Events leading to an oil shock may not be predictable but the forex option trader can, having missed the move up, play the diminuation of the shock by buying call options on dollar pairs or on the Dollar Index.

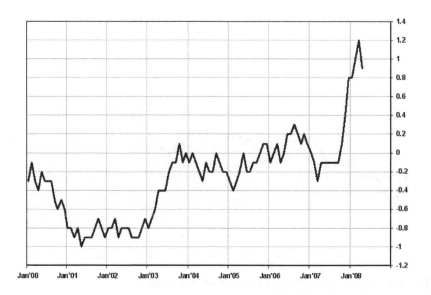

FIGURE 9.6 Rising Oil Costs
Data Source: Bloomberg Finance L.P.

PLAY A U.S. STAGFLATION AND INFLATION

A scenario of increased U.S. inflation with slower growth, also known as *stagflation*, is a forex option trading opportunity that can be extraordinary. In this situation, the central banks cannot cut rates too low for fear of stimulating inflation further, while they also can't raise rates.

The best way to play this is on the binary options on the Chicago Board of Trade (CBOT) as a 3-month calendar spread with buying call (playing a lowering of rates) and going out 3 months selling calls. This translates into anticipating that the Federal Open Market Committee (FOMC) will first lower rates and then stop lowering rates. Figure 9.7 shows how core U.S. inflation is threatening to increase.

PREEMPTIVE ATTACK ON IRAN

A geopolitical scenario of a preemptive attack on Iran by the United States or Israel can be played as a calendar spread where there is surge on oil nearing $200 and then a collapse. This scenario can be traded through the oil proxy currency of the Canadian dollar. A potential calendar option spread would be to buy oil at $50 above the spot, and then sell the same strike price 3 months out. In trading the Loonie, traders should keep in mind that oil prices are not the only factor contributing to Canadian dollar strength. The trader will need to assess economic conditions in Canada.

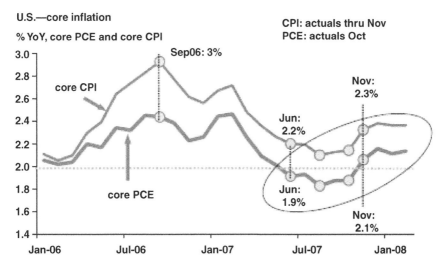

FIGURE 9.7   Core U.S. Inflation Threatening to Increase
Source: DBS Research

RECOVERY OF HOUSING

For those traders who missed the move down in housing that is associated with the weakening of the dollar, preparing for a recovery is an opportunity for option trading. How can this be done in forex? The first task is to spot a change in the trend in housing. A good way to do this is to use the Standard & Poor's (S&P)/Case-Shiller Composite Index, which tracks housing prices in 20 metropolitan areas. Additionally, if housing start data begins to show a bottoming out or improvement, it should be looked at as a leading indicator of a stronger currency.

SUMMARY

Putting on forex option trades is always about a speculation on the future. A good test for the trader is to hypothesize future extreme scenarios when prices in currency pairs or commodities would be surging or collapsing. Future extreme price action challenges can be anticipated, and longer-term calls, puts, or spread combinations offer ways where the trader can be ready for price action that tests the limits of predictability.

Putting It All Together

Entering the world of forex options can be a daunting experience. The best approach is an evolutionary one where the trader masters certain key skills and strategies and reaches a level of competence in those areas. Let's call this area "the trading fitness landscape." In this landscape the forex option trader will discover on a continuing basis in simulated and real trading what are his/her areas of strengths and weaknesses and what adaptations need to be made to survive toward profitabiity.

Having multiple skills becomes essential in forex option trading because the forex landscape changes frequently as the world goes through different economic cycles. For example, when the global economic environment is in a growth mode, trend continuation strategies will likely be more successful. When economic growth rates are slowing down, adapting to range trading is a strategy that the forex option trader needs to be able to accomplish. When uncertainty increases, volatility-based trades become advantageous.

ACHIEVING OPTIMAL FOREX OPTION TRADING FITNESS

There are three major forex option trading fitness categories. The goal of the forex option trader is to shape the best performance mix among these categories:

- Accuracy in choosing direction.
- Accuracy in choosing duration of the option.
- Strike price precision (accuracy in identifying the range potential).

The goal of the forex option trader is to shape the best performance mix among these categories. In order to achieve progress towards these goals, the trader should implement a forward testing of their performance. Let's look at how this can be accomplished.

FORWARD TESTING YOUR FOREX OPTION TRADING FITNESS

Some traders may discover that they have a high level of fitness in one or more of these three categories. Some traders may excel at anticipating direction. Other traders may have high-level skills timing the trade. Where to place the strike price is always very challenging. Finally, risk control needs to be mastered to preserve capital and avoid ruin through large drawdowns. The best way to identify your own fitness levels is not to back-test your strategies, but to forward-test them. Here are some initial exercises to test your skills. More challenges are available at www.learn4x.com/options.

1. Scan the currency pairs using the month candles, using a 3-month duration; choose a strike price that the option will not reach. Check the put/call ratios to help decide your direction.

2. Scan the currency pairs using the month candles and find a sideways channel pattern. Locate a strike price at support and resistance in 1 month that you believe it will not reach.

3. Find a parabolic pattern and select a strike price right above or below the tip (apex or zenith) that you believe the price will not be able to get to.

4. Find the 61.8 percent Fib line on weekly candles of a currency pair, and select the amount of time it would take for the candle to retrace to that level.

5. Locate on an economic calendar the date of the next central bank or Federal Open Market Committee (FOMC) interest rate decision. Select strike prices closest to support and resistance levels that you believe will be the range in place at the time of the decision.

6. Select two currency pairs that often move in high correlation with each other. Using the daily charts, find the time when the two pairs have reached a wide range between them. Put on a trade that plays a narrowing of that range.

7. Locate currency pairs that have their implied 3-month volatilities above their 1-month volatilities. Does it indicate a sell strategy?

8. Find a pair that has a volatility skew favoring a put and favoring a call. Decide whether to play a continuation of the skew or a reversal of the skew.

9. Test your skills in locating short-term momentum moves by placing a Sunday evening at-the-money (ATM) option put or call spread using two strike prices with 2-week maturity.

10. Find currency pairs in a week pattern in a classic sideways Bollinger bounce with a range of 200 pips or more. Put on a short strangle.

11. Find a currency pair that has the lowest implied volatility and put on an ATM call on that pair for 1-month duration.

WHERE TO TRADE FOREX OPTIONS

Forex option trades are accessible through a variety of sources. First, any futures commodity merchant (FCM) offers options on currency futures offered on the Chicago Mercantile Exchange (CME).

For the forex trader looking to place option trades on the underlying spot, there are several FCMs offering over-the-counter (OTC) options. Saxobank (saxobank.com), and IKON (ikongm.com) provide OTC options on a full range of currencies. Finotec (finotec.com), based in Cypress and Israel, in addition to OTC options on spot, offers binary options. If Finotec may be registered in the United States in the near future. Oanda (Oanda.com) offers a version of options called *box* options. In the third category of firms offering binary option trading is BetonMarkets.com and Hedgstreet.com, and Igmarkes.com. A fourth alternative is trading options on currency pairs through equity firms. Any equity firm offers the ability to trade forex options on the International Securities Exchange (ISE) and the Philadelphia Exchange (PHLX). A fifth alternative is trading options on exchange traded funds (ETFs).

In choosing a firm to trade forex options, the trader needs to evaluate several services. First is their ease of access to important option data such as the Greeks. Does the firm offer complete option tables called chains? The trader needs to look at the spreads typical in these options. There is great variation on the premiums charged for the same option strike price, and before a firm is chosen, a comparison of premium practices ought to be made. Another category that should concern the trader is access to expert opinion. Does the firm offer insights from their own option traders? Does the firm offer more sophisticated data such as volatility surface charts?

Selected *Futures* Columns

FOREX TRADER

The classic tools of trading are valuable as indicators in their own right, but also are important to study because they can spark ingenuity that can give you a unique edge.

Classic tools for trading forex

BY **ABE COFNAS**

When the word "classics" is mentioned, what comes to mind are the well-recognized works in fields that have endured the test of time: Plato's *Republic*, Shakespeare's *Macbeth*, Twain's *Huckleberry Finn*, Francis Ford Coppola's *The Godfather*, etc. Classics provide a reference point for all other works in a given field. They define the genre. As forex traders, we have our own classic tools and indicators, and study of them reinforces their value and, more important, provides a springboard from which we can evolve as analysts.

In technical analysis, with rapidly evolving technology, there is an expectation that the new is advanced over the old. For the emerging field of forex trading, time can only tell if new ideas of neural networks, chaos theory, fractals and computerized pattern recognition tools will become the classics for the conduct of future technical analysis. Before traders employ the latest technical indicator or signal generator, they should have a perspective on the classic technical analysis tools and techniques.

What is a classic is debatable. For simplicity's sake, our demarcation line between classic and modern will be the widespread adaptation of computers. Before computers, indicators were developed based on the acute observa-

TREND WITHIN THE TREND

When prices break through an inner, shorter-term trendline, you often can expect them to test a trendline drawn on an outer, or longer-term, time scale.

Outer trendline

A downward outer trendline starts with the highest high and connects to the next lowest highest high and so on.

Inner trendline

Inner

An inner trendline indicates a shift in sentiment and momentum intensity.

Source: www.xtick.com

tion of price action and accumulated wisdom of traders. They can be considered classics because they also are robust and have persisted beyond the ebb and flow of fads in technical analysis. Classic tools have been proven in direct experience, not computer simulations.

TREND ANALYSIS

At the core of classic analytical tools for forex trading are those that perform trend analysis, namely trendlines.

Understanding trendlines and how to use them generates a framework that a great deal of modern technical analysis relies upon. Trend analysis reveals the dominant direction of the currency. Common sense tells us that prices can be described essentially as moving up, down or sideways. Using trendlines we can develop an initial map of which direction has been dominant and what changes are projected onto the future horizon. Basic trendline analysis provides clues to a shift in momentum as the price breaks an inner trendline and moves toward an outer trendline drawn on a longer-term scale (see "Trend within the trend," left).

The important thing about classic trendline analysis is that once a major trend pattern has been identified, trading strategies can be synchronized with the trend itself.

A recent example was in the Australian dollar, which has experienced a long 26-week uptrend. Seeing such a trendline, a preferred strategy would be to look for buying opportunities on shorter-term pullbacks. However, patterns do not last indefinitely, and when the weekly trendline was broken in April, presumably due to a fear of a slowdown in Chinese demand for Australian exports, the alert trader would then reject buying opportunities and look to trade in the direction of the new prevailing shorter-term downtrend. Even without knowing the fundamental reasons behind the shift, a major trendline break alone is important enough traders should reassess their trading strategy (see "Turning point," right).

A simple trendline on a weekly chart can serve as a map of price direction. When prices get close to the peaks and troughs, the trader can prepare to shape a trade based on whether the price will fail or succeed in breaking the trendline.

THREE LINE BREAK

Once a trend is identified, a formidable challenge is detecting as early as possible trend reversals. This challenge applies to whether you are in a position with the trend or preparing an entry on a pullback or even with momentum. We can turn to another classic charting technique, three-line break, to provide some precise diagnostics for detecting trend reversals. Steve Nison in *Beyond Candles* is commonly credited for bringing this classic technique to light.

Three-line break charts evaluate price action in relationship to consecutive highs or lows created. A line or block is added when a new high is set. This is usually a white block or line. A black block or line is added if price moves to a

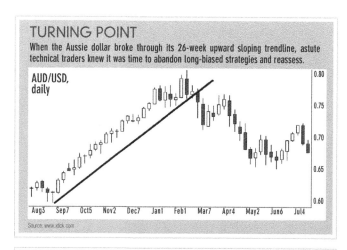

TURNING POINT
When the Aussie dollar broke through its 26-week upward sloping trendline, astute technical traders knew it was time to abandon long-biased strategies and reassess.

AUD/USD, daily

Source: www.xtick.com

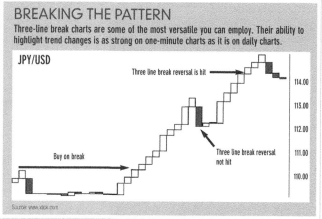

BREAKING THE PATTERN
Three-line break charts are some of the most versatile you can employ. Their ability to highlight trend changes is as strong on one-minute charts as it is on daily charts.

JPY/USD

Three line break reversal is hit

Buy on break

Three line break reversal not hit

Source: www.xtick.com

new low. The closing price is used as the reference point.

What the three-line break chart allows the trader to do is unambiguously determine if and where a trend reversal is taking place.

At any point in time, the trend reversal is found by counting back three lines or boxes. This means that for traders looking for a confirmation of an entry position, the three-line break chart will provide a location for the entry. For traders already in a position the break reversal point provides a location for a stop loss or trailing stop.

Reversals of trend patterns can be

detected even on a one-minute time-frame. In "Breaking the pattern" (above) what is striking is the clarity of a trend break signal that is followed by approximately a 50-pip move.

Three-line break charts distill market moves down to their most basic element. They reference price moves, not time. In this way, they simplify the trading process, something that can be appreciated by those of us who find trading agonizingly complex.

THE CHANNEL
A variation of the trendline is the channel pattern. The term itself borrows

Forex Trader continued

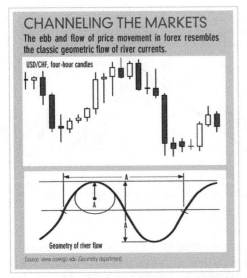

CHANNELING THE MARKETS
The ebb and flow of price movement in forex resembles the classic geometric flow of river currents.

USD/CHF, four-hour candles

Geometry of river flow

Source: www.oswego.edu (Geometry department)

from the geometry of how rivers flow. A channel is a formation that is formed when the energy of the water flow encounters a barrier, reverses and then encounters a barrier on the other side. This zig-zag pattern of resistance and support emerges in forex price movements because forex trading is a form of non-random energy dissipation.

The channel pattern observed in "Channeling the markets" (above)

depicts the geometry of a meandering river. Compare it to a four-hour USD/CHF pattern that emerged in recent trading. It is hard to tell the difference.

The forex trader seeing a channel pattern can project with confidence trading opportunities when the prices move from one side to the other and, in a sense, bounce off the channel banks.

POINT AND FIGURE
Another dimension of technical analysis of forex markets is measuring sentiment.

Particularly in forex trading, understanding market sentiment is more challenging because there is no volume data, as there is in futures. The question of who is in control, the buyers or sellers, still can be answered with the help of another classical tool, point and figure charts.

Point and figure was one of the earliest technical analysis tools used by

traders and really never has fallen out of use. It is seeing somewhat of a revival currently, as new charting software platforms for forex offer these charts.

Point and figure charts depict price as columns of Xs and Os. An additional "X" will be added on top of the preceding one if the price moves a defined amount, such as 10 pips or more. Similarly, if the price moves down by the defined amount, an O is added to the bottom. However, changing from a column of Xs to a column of Os isn't done until a larger move, described in terms of X times the pip size occurs. This is referred to the "box" size.

Using a configuration of 10 pips x 3 reversal, it will take a 30-pip price move in the opposite direction to generate a new column and indicate a shift of control between buyers and sellers.

Much like the three-line break, point and figure provides a clear view on the momentum of the price action. When price changes gain momentum, they will start forming long columns of Xs or Os on the point and figure chart. Traders using point and figure can spot resistance and support areas unambiguously and in advance.

For traders interested in confirming a larger trend direction, expanding the box size to 25 and even 50 pips provides a view of where the areas of outer resistance and support would be. From a tactical point of view looking at "Getting the point" (left), the price action is sideways but the most recent column of Os indicates that the sellers just took over with a break of support.

Seeing this action would prompt the trader to prepare for a sell entry order.

FIBONACCI ANALYSIS
The classic technical toolbox for the forex trader would not be complete without Fibonacci retracement levels. While they do not predict the price movement, they project future buying and selling zones. If you read professional analysis and bank reports of currency prices, you know that few comments leave out references to key upcoming Fibonacci areas.

Even if all Fibonacci Levels are self-

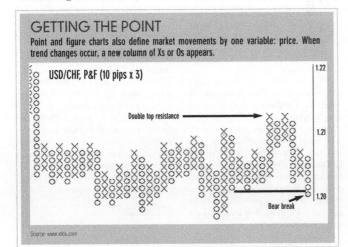

GETTING THE POINT
Point and figure charts also define market movements by one variable: price. When trend changes occur, a new column of Xs or Os appears.

USD/CHF, P&F (10 pips x 3)

1.22

Double top resistance

1.21

1.20

Bear break

Source: www.xtick.com

Forex Trader continued

fulfilling prophecies, being ignorant of them is not an option. For the Forex trader, a useful application of Fibonacci retracement levels is applying them to the weekly currency pair charts and observing whether the price action is close to the major levels.

For those unfamiliar with them, Fibonacci levels are based on ratios such as 61.8%, 50%, 38.2%, 161.8%, etc., drawn off key points on past price action, such as the low and high close of a recent strong uptrend. These levels are extended into the future and are considered key support or resistance levels for subsequent price action, as long as the recent high and low they were based off of hold (see "Fibonacci fever," left).

An advantage of Fibonacci analysis is that it can be applied in any direction and for any time frame as long as a significant move in price has occurred. As with any other set of technical analysis tools, Fibonacci levels become more effective when they converge with signals from other technical indicators.

VOLATILITY

We all know that prices vary and result in ranges between lows and highs. In technical analysis, ranges provide areas of resistance and support.

That range, however, does not give a clue as to the relative behavior of the prices. A price near its high or low in a range is not indicative that the location is unusually high or low. But finding a clue as to when the prices are really at an extreme is accomplished using a simple measure of statistics — the standard deviation.

Using principles of statistics that are more than a century old, we can objectively define the level of volatility in the market. This objective measure, called the standard deviation, is based on our understanding of the normal distribution of data around the mean, or average, value of that data.

Statistics tells us that in a normal distribution, approximately 68% of occurrences will be within one standard deviation from the mean. About 95% of all occurrences will be within two standard deviations and 99% of all occurrences will be within three standard deviations. You can find the formulas necessary for calculating the standard deviation of any collection of data in a multitude of statistics texts or statistics-based Web sites.

For forex traders, getting a measure of where a price is in relationship to its volatility is important if the trader

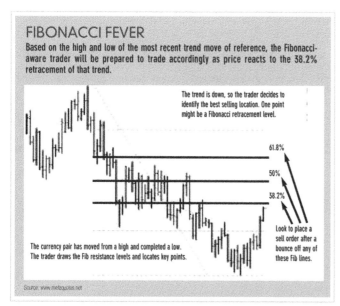

FIBONACCI FEVER

Based on the high and low of the most recent trend move of reference, the Fibonacci-aware trader will be prepared to trade accordingly as price reacts to the 38.2% retracement of that trend.

The trend is down, so the trader decides to identify the best selling location. One point might be a Fibonacci retracement level.

61.8%
50%
38.2%

Look to place a sell order after a bounce off any of these Fib lines.

The currency pair has moved from a high and completed a low. The trader draws the Fib resistance levels and locates key points.

Source: www.metaquotes.net

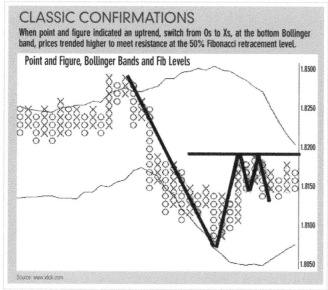

CLASSIC CONFIRMATIONS

When point and figure indicated an uptrend, switch from Os to Xs, at the bottom Bollinger band, prices trended higher to meet resistance at the 50% Fibonacci retracement level.

Point and Figure, Bollinger Bands and Fib Levels

1.8300
1.8250
1.8200
1.8150
1.8100
1.8050

Source: www.xtick.com

wants to be confident about price direction. When volatility is at its extremes, prices tend to meet key resistance.

While the concept of standard deviation has been around for decades, the most popular realization of this notion in the trading field, Bollinger bands, is more recent. Bollinger bands are simply a moving average line drawn with two additional lines — an upper band drawn at the moving average plus a standard deviation value and a lower band drawn at the moving average minus a standard deviation value.

The inputs used in the indicator affect its depiction significantly. Common values are 20 periods for the moving average and standard deviation calculation and drawing the upper and lower bands at two standard deviations from the moving average.

Applying Bollinger bands on a forex currency pair gives an instant picture of whether price action is at an extreme volatility. Gaining a view of volatility helps shape the entry or exit decision. For example, if the price action on a 30-minute chart is at the upper end of the Bollinger band, the trader needs to question whether price is topping out.

Bollinger bands can be varied by adjusting the number of standard deviations used as well as the moving average length. An exponential moving average can be substituted for the simple moving average. Some traders substitute a 2.618 standard deviation (a Fibonacci number) instead of the traditional two standard deviations.

COMBINING CLASSIC TOOLS

Individually, each classic technical analysis tool is useful, but when used together they are magnified in their effectiveness. For example, in "Classic confirmations" (left) when the trader seeks a convergence of Fibonacci levels and Bollinger bands, developing entry or exit tactics at the location of the convergence becomes justified.

Similarly, combining point and figure analysis with Bollinger bands can add confidence to locating areas of greater resistance or support. We can see in the chart that a double top in point and figure combined with a penetration of the upper Bollinger band, alerts the trader to a significant potential of a reversal.

It is instructive to remember the boast of Archimedes who claimed that if given a large enough lever — probably the most classic of physical tools — he could move the world. For aficionados of forex, the power to move the world may not be possible, but using a box of classic tools may help move the trader to more profits. |**FM**

Abe Cofnas is president of learn4x.com LLC. E-mail: learn4x@hotmail.com.

Forex Trader

BY ABE COFNAS

Trend principles, tactics and new tools

As 2005 gets underway. we are at extremes in the currency markets. More specifically, the U.S. dollar has been in a long-term downtrend. The phrase "the trend is your friend" has certainly shown itself to be a good mantra for those who have sold into the extended dip. And while many traders swear by it, we need to admit the obvious: The concept of trading with the trend is too vague as a tactical tool.

Beginning forex traders expectedly would follow-up that advice with a range of questions. How specifically do you trade with the trend? Where are the entry points? When do you get out? Are there principles to help the new trader trade with the trend? Can we build a strategic plan for trend trading in forex?

A prelude to shaping a trend trading strategy in forex is to first review inter-market conditions such as patterns in the U.S. dollar index (USDX) and gold. While each currency pair reflects specific trading of the dollar vs. that foreign currency, the USDX is a quick measure of global sentiment. Assessing gold trends also provides a leading indicator of global sentiment toward the dollar. When gold is breaking a previous sideways range or a downtrend, it offers a leading indicator of dollar sentient shifting.

The next step is selecting the time frame. Trends can be monthly, weekly, daily and even at the tick level. By scanning all of the time frames, you can quickly see the predominant trend direction. More important, countertrend waves can be identified. If the daily trend direction is diverging from the weekly or monthly, new trading opportunities can be shaped.

The next step is selecting a predominant trading direction. Finding a trade in either direction is always possible because forex prices are not linear and different laws of price action come into play across time frames. By pre-selecting a direction to trade, based on fundamentals or longer-term technical analysis, the focus becomes not what the trend is, but the best location for your next trade. For example, those expecting a major downtrend in the dollar in 2005 will focus on the best entry points for short trades until that major expectation changes.

Next, you need to focus on execution points. This is where the concept of "trading at the edge" comes into play. Trading at the edge is best understood as finding a probe of a key support or resistance level. This requires some contrarian thinking.

It is a natural tendency to try to buy when a price is going up or try to sell when it is going down, but there are retracements and waves. Thus, if the currency pair is in a downtrend but is retracing to its five-minute trendline, a trader looking to sell will watch for a probe of this trendline. Waiting for a retracement to support or resistance also reduces the risks of being wrong because stop losses can be placed rather tightly.

Selecting the exit is one of the most challenging problems. Getting out too early after initial profits feels good, but improving the average pip gain per trade is key to long-term success. After all, trading is hard work, and for the same level of effort, increasing the gains per trade is a legitimate goal. On the other side of the same coin is getting out to prevent a serious loss.

Fortunately, a time-proven charting method is accessible to help with every stage of the trend trading process: three-price or three-line break charts.

In a three-line break chart, only the highs and lows are shown. If a new high is reached in a selected time frame, a new rectangle is added above, and if a new low is reached a new rectangle is drawn below. We see that for the pound, there was a series of consecutive new highs with a few periods of reversals in the accompanying weekly chart. The trend is up, but where and when do you enter that trade? The intra-hour trend sequences helps us find a more precise location (see inset). Looking at the 30-minute three-line break patterns, we see that the trend aligns with the weekly trend direction with some reversals. This gives the trader the choice of entering into the trend by buying after a reversal occurs or entering at any point but with a stop three lines below.

In 2005 trend trading offers opportunities, and with three-line break charts the trend may become even more friendlier to profits.

Abe Cofnas is president of learn4x.com LLC. E-mail: learn4x@hotmail.com.

BREAKING DOWN PRICE
Three-line break charts can indicate trading opportunities on any time frame.

GBPUSD
WEEKLY 3 LINE
BREAK

1.9338

1.6764

BUY SIGNAL
ON 3 LINE
BREAK
REVERSAL

FEB 2

Get Out
at
1.9351

Get in at
1.9141

GBPUSD 30 MIN 3
LINE BREAK

Source: www.idick.com

Forex Trader

BY ABE COFNAS

Raising your forex intelligence quotient

Consider the following sequence of numbers: 1, 2, 3, 4, 5, 6. What's the next number? Of course, the answer is 7. The ability to predict the next number seems trivial, but it demonstrates a core factor in developing successful prediction in forex trading. To obtain a correct answer, you need to have a memory of numbers and you need to be able to retrieve that memory.

Let's look at another example: 1, 2, 3, 5, 8, 13, 21. Most will recognize that the next number is 34. The pattern is that each number is the sum of the previous two numbers. Traders should know this as the Fibonacci pattern that has applications in describing many different patterns and price movement.

These examples point to the greatest challenge for forex traders: predicting the market. How well you do that reflects, ultimately, your forex trading intelligence quotient, or FX I.Q.

A good place to begin to explore what constitutes your FX I.Q. is to consider an unpredictable string of events, such as the unprecedented sequence of four hurricanes in a short period of time in Florida. First, it is impossible to predict a hurricane in advance. Scientists can spot the hurricane but cannot say that next Friday at 1:30 p.m., for example, one will start. This is due to what is known as the Lorenz butterfly effect.

Named after M.I.T. Professor Edward Lorenz, who contributed to the founding of the field of chaos science, his research on hurricanes and how to predict them showed what Lorenz called the butterfly effect. The butterfly effect demonstrates a principle of the limitations of prediction when conditions are very complex. Lorenz demonstrated that the initial conditions that cause a hurricane are so numerous and complex that the flight of a butterfly could affect whether and where it forms and which way it goes. In other words, to predict a hurricane successfully, we would have to know every minute condition that affects its formation. Missing one small factor can cause predictions to be so far off they are useless.

That said, science has made great advances in predicting that, once a hurricane has formed, where it will go. They can do this because a hurricane, like anything, creates patterns and patterns, once they are formed, can be evaluated. The more data patterns that are collected for each hurricane improves the total knowledge base for creating future accurate models.

Predicting forex price movements is similar to hurricane forecasting. It is hard to predict the next move in a currency pair because all of the factors affecting the next move are not knowable. This is why any computer program, trading system or neural net has inherent limits on accuracy. These computer-based projections are unstable because they miss conditions that affect the market. They are vulnerable to the butterfly effect. If you leave out any one condition, it can and will affect the result. However, once a pattern or structure appears, confident projections of how the currency pair might behave, what path it will travel, is possible to predict with accuracy.

Because forex prediction requires a deep level of pattern recognition and analysis, few systems are consistently accurate in predicting forex prices. Most of us cannot expect to build such super models; however, we can use our inherent intelligence to predict prices. We can observe that successful trades are based on having a good memory of winning trading patterns. While each trade is a separate and unique combination of time and price, they all have in common patterns remembered by the trader. It is similar to being able to recognize a melody of a song, even when it is in a different key. The inner pattern and not the notes is remembered. Once a pattern is perceived by the trader, the trade itself emerges because the pattern predicts the sequence of future moves.

The recipe for raising your FX I.Q. is to add to your memory of patterns that correlate with previous successful trades. Forex prices and markets may seem chaotic but they are not random, although it can seem to be when you are trading due to the incompleteness of our knowledge. Forex prices reflect the reaction of nearly $2 trillion worth of sentiment daily that results in a diffusion of prices into a variety of repeated patterns.

For example, when a triangle pattern is spotted, showing a movement toward its vertex, the trader can predict a breakout is about to occur. When a head-and-shoulders pattern is identified, the forces of reversal are in play. A simple channel formation shows the trader that the market has a bouncing, zig-zag pattern. A forex trader cannot, however, obtain a great advantage by only having a knowledge base of patterns. The superior performance of the experienced trader occurs because he has a memory of successful trades.

By understanding the basis of intelligence in forex trading, the recipe for becoming smarter can be developed. Examining your own pattern of trading is a key aspect to improving your own FX I.Q. This is a first step. Logically, the next challenge would be the ability to achieve a series of wining trades. What is important to observe is not necessarily your actual trades, but the pattern of the trading. The ability to sustain a sequence of winning trades — say, five trades or eight trades in a row — is not a result of luck. The trader has mastered the ability to remember and identify set-ups and predict or project a resulting market direction.

With training and experience, sustaining large winning trade sequences is not theoretical. It is within the reach of anyone. All it requires is having or building your FX I.Q.

Abe Cofnas is president of learn4x.com LLC. E-mail: learn4x@hotmail.com.

■ TRADING TECHNIQUES

Visualizing price direction in forex

Running counter to the oft-purported theory of "random walk" price changes in forex, few would contend that inefficiencies don't exist in this widely fragmented, yet incredibly huge, market. For the trader, this means he can leave the neural nets locked up in their black box and rely on simpler methods for potential profit.

By Abe Cofnas

Every currency trade is the result of some prior process of self-inquiry directed at finding future direction. Each trader must ask, what is a good opportunity, which currency he should trade now and where it is going. While no one can know with certainty where a currency is likely to go, the forex market more than any other provides clues to its direction.

Unlike the equity markets where a "random walk" condition is considered the norm by many, most theoreticians argue that currency markets are not efficient. Forex is a market where perhaps 10,000 banks create an intermarket with negotiated bid and ask spreads. Here is where inefficiency is a benefit to the trader. As a result, those traders with better tools and analytical procedures may have an edge. Not being random means that trying to predict the next move of a currency is not futile and is a valid goal. To achieve this goal, traders can rely on technical analysis.

We do not need tea leaves to divine currency price direction. We may not even need extensive neural nets or systems software "black boxes." Certainly, reading the Web sites of the *Japan Times* (www.japantimes.com) and *The Financial Times* of London (www.ft.com) provides valuable on-going insights into the processes of globalization, the U.S. dollar and the political economy underlying currency flows. Easy access to information encourages searching for increasingly more prognostication tools. This leads to the tendency of accumulating a menu of indicators and then trying to apply them. It leads to chaos in analysis and not clarity of thinking.

A simpler, yet powerful way for a forex trader is to seek a more elegant framework for analysis. The way to do this is to return to basics by learning how to interpret charts and use their inherent visualization capabilities.

The 200-day horizon A fundamental tool in finding price direction is the 200-day moving average. While the excitement of the moment tends to divert attention to intraday and hourly price action, the 200-day moving average is an important horizon to steer your trading. Consider the euro vs. the dollar. The 200-day moving average provided an early clue that the curren-

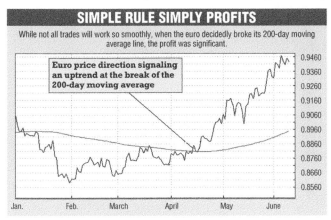

SIMPLE RULE SIMPLY PROFITS

While not all trades will work so smoothly, when the euro decidedly broke its 200-day moving average line, the profit was significant.

Euro price direction signaling an uptrend at the break of the 200-day moving average

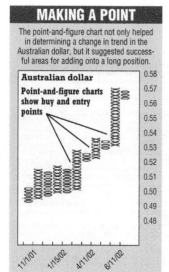

Australian dollar

Point-and-figure charts show buy and entry points

cy was moving into a test of its trend (see "Simple rule simply profits," left). When the euro broke the average and moved 100 pips away, the strategy to buy the euro should have been at the top of trading choices.

While moving averages often are viewed as a lagging indicator, the 200-day average shouldn't be seen as such, but as a tool that brings into focus the likelihood of a change in trend. In the case of the euro, this simple tool opened the door for capturing more than 500 pips of profit. The euro entered into a powerful trend up, brought to visual clarity by the 200-day moving average.

Useful rules for trading off the 200-day moving average are:

1. If price is 10% from the average, get ready to trade it.

2. If price breaks the average, put on half of your size.

3. When price breaks 10% above or below the average put on the rest of your size.

Point & figure A consistently reliable visualization of currency direction can be provided by breakouts on point-and-figure charts. Point-and-figure charts reveal the balance, or lack thereof, of buyers and sellers. They show where important breakouts would be before they happen.

Understanding the point-and-figure configuration is deceptively easy,

and yet it provides a key skill and discipline for trading. Point-and-figure analysis begins with knowing how to read the chart. There are two elements: Xs and Os. Xs mean buying is occurring, and Os mean selling is occurring. The size of the box, whether is an X or an O, can be directly adjusted. A good starting configuration is 25 pips. This means that if a price moves more than 25 pips, a new box in the form of an X or an O is added. As a result, the larger the box size, the fewer the number of columns.

Viewing a column of Xs or Os, it is easy to see buying and selling zones. A long column of Xs means that buyers are in control. A long column of Os means that sellers are in control. Point-and-figure charts show reversal of action and sentiment clearly. The charts can be drawn in real-time patterns moving at 10 pips or less. A set of three Os, or a selling column, will follow a buying column when the price reverses by three times the box value. It takes a 75-pip move to reverse a 25-pip point-and-figure column. The concept of a three-box reversal results in a simple visualization of the battle between buyers and sellers. A result is buying and selling signals that are robust and work across all time frames and currency markets.

The point-and-figure chart of the Australian dollar demonstrates an

easy visualization of a significant breakout, as well as places where there are multiple opportunities to buy into the uptrend (see "Making a point," left).

In applying point-and-figure analysis, here are some trading signals and rules:

1. When a breakout occurs using a 25-pip by three-box configuration and the breakout is in the direction of the trend, trade the breakout. Place your stop 75 pips below your trade or previous point-and-figure support.

2. If a new column appears with its minimum of three Xs or three Os, close your position or wait until one more box appears.

3. If a long column is in effect, expect a reversal and the appearance of a new column. Here, it is useful to use Fibonacci rules to determine if the new column is a reversal or a short-lived Fibonacci bounce.

Intermarket clues In developing an approach to visualizing what is going on in currencies, the novice trader usually spends all of his time looking at a particular currency and trying to ascertain what will happen next. The more experienced and effective trader will look at intermarket relationships or multiple markets.

It generally is accepted that currency price movements reflect a ▶

Dollar index (cash), daily

200-day moving average

TRADING TECHNIQUES

global flow of underlying economic factors, including, but not limited to, interest rates, differences in economic growth rates, current account deficits, etc. These factors contribute to the level of currency prices. If there is confidence in an economy, money flows from one region of the world to the economy that offers expectations of better returns. When more dollars flow to Europe than the United States, the euro will rise. These kind of economic data are hard to come by. A good way to visualize the political and economic factors that affect prices is by studying movements in the U.S. dollar index. The U.S. dollar index is a basket of six currencies. The New York Board of Trade, where futures on the index are traded, describes it as follows:

"The U.S. Dollar Index is computed using a trade-weighted geometric average of six currencies. The six currencies and their trade weights are: Euro (57.6%), Japanese yen (13.6%), pound (11.9%), Canadian dollar (9.1%), Swedish krona (4.2%), and Swiss franc (3.6%)."

When the dollar index broke through its 200-day moving average at 116, buying the dollar was rejected, even by the most ardent contrarians (see "Clear signal," page 33).

Here, again, a visualization of the future direction of the dollar and currencies paired with it is provided by a simple moving average. As a tool for forex trading, it is indispensable for a global perspective.

Multi-currency lineups In addition to observing dollar index movements, a technique that has a high payoff is a multi-currency lineup. Sequentially reviewing prices, currency by currency, takes time and loses immediacy in analysis. It is difficult for even skillful chart readers to discern multiple currency pairs. Today's forex charting programs do not make it easier.

Spread charting or graphic cascades that easily allow a scan of immediate intermarket conditions

> We don't have to wait for the industry to supply us better charts and new software. We need to work harder on using our insight and our eyesight.

generally are not available. However, a visual line-up of a point-and-figure setup provides an almost-instantaneous and accurate evaluation of which currencies are ready to break out or bounce off key support and which currencies are in buying or selling zones.

"Across the board" (below) groups the Swiss franc, British pound, euro and yen along a point-and-figure perspective. They are hourly charts. Scanning the last column provides an instant analysis of not only which currencies are near a breaking point but insight into the strength of price movement.

Ultimately the most forex trader-friendly charts are the ones that are the most comfortable for the trader, and no doubt for many the best charts will be complex groupings of multiple data compressions, advanced proprietary indicators, statistical inferences, etc. But for the busy trader, finding shortcuts to determining key trade factors always is an underlying motivation.

As forex trading platforms enter their next generation upgrades, we will expect to see charting that helps the trader visualize patterns and price direction. But we don't have to wait for the industry to supply us better charts and new software. We need to work harder on using our insight and our eyesight. Moving averages and point-and-figure charts already allow clear scans of the forex markets. They can take you further than you realize and closer to visualizing profits. **FM**

Abe Cofnas is president of Learn4x.com LLC, which provides education for forex traders. E-mail: learn4xtrading@aol.com.

ACROSS THE BOARD

Thanks to their simple representation of market action, point-and-figure charts are good methods for providing lucid depictions of multiple currencies on one screen.

Forex Trader

BY ABE COFNAS

The music of forex

I n *The Psychology of the Foreign Exchange Market,* author Thomas Oberlechner provides the results of research into how professional traders view the markets.

One approach he uses is to characterize these views with different metaphors. Oberlechner says the main metaphors used by forex traders are a bazaar, machine, living beast, gambling, sports, war and the ocean. Such uses are not accidental. Metaphors are an important way people organize information as well as form their own expectations of the market.

The major point behind the research is that the mindset used to understand and observe the forex markets is itself a factor in how you proceed to trade. The person who views the forex market as sports will look to winning trades as the main focus, but may become emotionally damaged when faced with a losing trade. In contrast, the person who views forex as an ocean may adopt longer-term views of market moves. Many view trading as a war and, as a result, formulate trading strategies that capture pip moves as if they were the enemy.

Forex traders also bring different perspectives based on their life experiences. Engineers often try to model the market and project direction based on equations. In contrast, doctors approach forex trading with the mindset of diagnosing the price action. Those traders who come from backgrounds such as the martial arts bring discipline and an ability to control emotions. Which is best? It turns out that forex trading is a great equalizer among all professions. In short, it depends on the individual.

That said, there is one vocation that tends to provide important insight into the forex markets. That field is music. The reason is there is harmony and rhythm in the markets.

The Webster Unabridged Dictionary of the English Language defines harmony as "a consistent, orderly or pleasing arrangement of parts; congruity." What is most interesting is that you don't need an in-depth knowledge of music to recognize a harmonic set of sounds or a cacophony of noise.

More experienced forex traders focus less on applying more indicators as they become familiar with the inherent rhythm of the market. Yet, those new to forex trading face the challenge of trying to find the inner harmony in all the noise and often turn to the large body of technical analysis to help them. Musical metaphors can help you deal with all that information.

Many traders have a favorite time interval. It could be a day chart or a one-hour chart. They pull up that chart and then apply a variety of analysis techniques to shape a trade. While this may be a rationale set of procedures to evaluate the market, another effective technique to consider is to let the time interval choose you. Consider the experience of driving your car and trying to find a radio station. Selecting the scan button allows you to listen for a few moments to each station until the right tune comes along. You do not need to know in advance all of the songs being played at every station. Similarly, the forex market is constantly streaming a variety of patterns. There are many potential trades. By scanning through the price action that is playing, a tradable pattern will be perceived.

For example, you might see a sideways pattern (as shown in the chart) in almost any time interval. The engineer would recognize this pattern as a simple harmonic motion, sinusoidal in time with a single resonant frequency. He might even try to write an equation to project its path. Yet, someone versed in music would not need equations to sense the pattern as being clearly melodic with a repetition of the tones. Whether the source was the vibration of a string on a violin or a result of the energy released by the clash of buyers and sellers, it is an unmistakable non-random cycle of self-similarity.

In further understanding forex prices and how they move harmonically, we cannot ignore Fibonacci ratios. Currency pairs often move between support and resistance in tune to a Fibonacci syncopation. The application of Fibonacci patterns as a universal phenomenon is further underscored as musicologists have discovered them in the works of many composers including Debussy, Bartok, etc. The next time you listen to the second half of Scott Joplin's Maple Leaf Rag you will notice the pattern of 13 stressed and 8 unstressed notes.

By understanding that currency prices are not linear movements, but expressions of emotions and human behavior, the forex trader begins to move beyond a linear approach to trading. By expanding your perspective on the underlying tones of the market, you will likely see nested patterns that are recursive. The ability to obtain the much sought trading edge may well depend on how you look for it. It would be wise to look for patterns and listen to the market.

Abe Cofnas is president of learn4x.com LLC. E-mail: learn4x@hotmail.com.

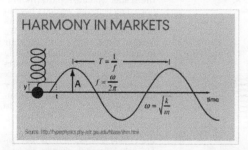

HARMONY IN MARKETS

$$T = \frac{1}{f}$$

$$f = \frac{\omega}{2\pi}$$

$$\omega = \sqrt{\frac{k}{m}}$$

Source: http://hyperphysics.phy-astr.gsu.edu/hbase/shm.html

Forex Trader

BY ABE COFNAS

Evolution of the forex trader

New forex traders too often mistakenly try to master technical analysis as a first step in preparing to trade. A ritual practice for novice traders is to use as many technical indicators as possible. As a result, a great deal of time is spent trying to absorb a vast amount of information. This leads to frustration because the list of available technical indicators is extensive. New traders frequently ignore fundamentals relating to forex, perhaps because such information cannot be neatly packaged. But technical trading does not exclude fundamentals, it merely acts as though fundamentals are worked into the price, so an understanding of fundamentals is still necessary.

What do forex traders need to know to get started? The path for evolving into a capable trader must involve a test of knowledge in the context of experience. To get immediate experience, many individuals choose to open demo accounts, start trading and then assess the results. A demo account can provide effective training, but without guidance the results of a demo account cannot be reliably transferred to real trading. Still other individuals start trading forex with mini-accounts offering huge leverage of up to 400 to 1. The appeal of a small account is understandable since it allows someone to start trading forex with as little as $500, but does not automatically provide a realistic transferable experience, and new traders should use less leverage.

Most new accounts end in failure. Is this pattern inevitable? Successful trading in forex exists, but the path requires a process of learning that has distinct central features, phases and a central logic of action.

By success we mean the ability to struggle and yet survive through losses and surprises. Long-term success takes skills in adapting to changing market conditions. Without those special skills the market will remove the trader as unfit. There are a lot of variations in successful trading a trader can employ to avoid extinction. Some traders may have enormous skills in identifying direction and find comfort in longer term trading objectives. Other traders may be better suited for short-term trading. Every person needs to discover what special skills give their trading a natural advantage.

One of the most common experiences for new traders is being wiped out quickly. Avoiding deep losses is equivalent to a tree avoiding its central branch from being cut. The tree will survive — even thrive — when minor branches are cut. In fact, through small disasters growth in nature occurs. Loss control and the ability to keep the account intact is the paramount skill that has to be learned by traders. Losses provide opportunities to learn new tactics. New traders who focus on achieving big and quick gains expose themselves to losses that kill.

A third component that graduates a beginning trader to higher levels of success is intelligence. Intelligence in trading is not about predicting market moves. Currency markets reflect a complex interaction of global economics, geopolitics and psychology, making it nearly beyond prediction. Many trading systems that offer a novice trader tools to trade have an appeal because they represent a short cut to success. These systems use a variety of algorithms to process market data and then generate an alert or even a trade signal. Trading systems fail to improve trading because they fail to model how the market works. Systems work, some of the time; but they all share the dangerous effect of limiting the learning ability of the new trader. Why improve your own skills when all you need is a system that does it for you?

Yet the new trader has a more powerful alternative for acquiring and improving intelligence — the experience of other successful traders. Successful traders know how to recognize high probable patterns that provide trading opportunities. Rather than trying to predict market moves they know how to react to market moves. They learn how and when to join the crowd. The wisdom of the crowd has been a reliable source of survival throughout nature, whether it is a flock of birds, a swarm of bees or a price wave. New forex traders can learn more from other successful traders than from manuals and programs.

Is there a single preferred learning path that leads to forex success? Probably not. There is an evolutionary path with stages where trading survival skills emerge. As more firms offer "education" in an attempt to generate new customers, many beginners will be lured by training and tools that offer a short cut, but it will be those education programs that enable a person to acquire trading skills, test their knowledge in real trading challenges and share the successful experience of others that will contribute to the evolution of a successful forex trader.

Abe Cofnas is president of learn4x.com LLC. E-mail: learn4x@earthlink.net.

Forex Trader

BY ABE COFNAS

Balancing fears

One of the enduring characteristics of the forex market is that it is embedded within the global economy. The exchange of one currency for another reflects at the same time economic transactions between nations, companies and individuals. With approximately $2 trillion per day being exchanged through the interbank system, when current trends shift, the resulting levels of resistance and support must be respected. They are in fact contour maps of consensus. Resistance and support levels provide a technical map of the range of prices. But observing the charts for technical levels of support and resistance is only one dimension of analysis. Underlying every support and resistance level are expectations and fears about the performance of the underlying economies. A good place to begin to understand what moves prices beyond the intraday swings is to inventory forex fears. Gaining an understanding of what central banks "fear" can provide valuable knowledge to shape forex trading strategies.

Foremost among forex fears is **fear of inflation**. Every central bank in the world's major raison d'etre is to manage a nation's money flow to minimize and stabilize inflation. The prescription for inflation is interest rate increases. The United States has raised interest rates 14 times since June 30, 2004. The European Central Bank has raised its rate to a 3-year high of 2.5% and has signaled a policy to be ready to raise its rate again until the threat of inflation is past. The strength of the Canadian economy has resulted in a renewed fear of inflation and has led the Bank of Canada to raise rates. Raising interest rates is not enough to combat inflation. Central banks also provide signals through statements when they raise rates regarding their expectations for continued rate increases

Fear of deflation is a factor taken into account by the forex market. When a nation faces deflation, such as Japan, its central banks will try to add liquidity to its economy to encourage a weaker currency. Japan's fight against deflation by having a 0% interest rate regime is close to being done, and the Bank of Japan is signaling the fear of deflation also is almost done. The expectation that the 0% interest rate policies will change will provide new support to a strengthening yen.

Fear of recession and an economic slow down acts as a powerful driver of a change in currency values. The rate of housing starts and employment levels in all nations are closely watched and a decline in these numbers can accentuate negative sentiment and cause the currency of that nation to lose value. A critical variable to watch are survey results of consumer sentiment that may signal a lack of confidence in economic health.

Fear of oil price surges. Industry runs on energy and can't quit just because of a price spike. Higher oil prices fuel fears of increased inflation and fears of an economic slowdown because most of the economies of the developing world depend on hydrocarbon fuels. Additionally, the rise in oil prices has caused oil exporting countries, mainly the Organization of the Petroleum Exporting Countries (OPEC) nations, to be in the position of net lenders of capital to the United States, thereby increasing our fear of being financially dependent on OPEC for financing our debt.

Fear of China must be added to our inventory of fears. China's explosive growth, more than 10% annually, provides increased anxiety about the ability to sustain this level of growth. Chinese economic growth results in the importing of global resources to fuel its manufacturing base. It is a major importer of agricultural commodities and if a slowdown in China occurs, its negative impact on Australia, Japan and Canada would be huge, causing fear of a slowdown in those and the world's economy. Also, world markets like stability and China has been unpredictable, creating fear that a major change in policy could leave many trading partners holding the bag.

Fear of an economic slowdown in the United States pervades the market. The United States is the major developed economy in the world and any signs of weakness can cause a flight of capital to non-U.S. currencies.

Fear of the current account deficit in the United States can be considered a separate fear worthy of attention. The United States' external deficit is at about 5.5% of GDP. Simply put, the U.S. imports far exceed its exports.

Federal Reserve Chairman Ben Bernanke in a recent speech related that deficit to U.S. citizens, businesses and governments having to raise $635 billion on international capital markets. This heavy borrowing raises fears that non-U.S. buyers of U.S. assets and debt will someday decline causing a major increase in U.S. interest rates and a resulting disruption in the U.S. economy.

These fundamental fears are enduring fundamental pivot points that shape the forex market. At this time in the world economy when economic growth is strong worldwide, when interest rates are increasing globally and when commodity sectors such as energy and resources are setting new highs, the forex trader would be wise to notice any change in the current balance of fears.

Abe Cofnas is president of learn4x.com LLC and author of *Understanding Forex: Trading to Win*. E-mail him at learn4x@earthlink.net.

Forex Trader

BY ABE COFNAS

The gift of the break-even trade

Understanding your experience in forex trading depends on what measures are used. A straightforward approach often applied is quantifying our results in terms of profit vs. losses. Being profitable is where all of us desire to be. Yet, this measure cannot be, by itself, sufficient to sustain our motivation. All traders have periods of losses en route to profits. As a result, a single-minded desire for profits may itself be a factor in furthering losses and actually reduce the potential for success.

Once a person desires profits, resulting losses turn into disappointments. The experience of disappointment may then unleash a host of destructive emotions. The problem becomes how we handle the losses and not the fact that they occur. How can a trader overcome becoming obsessed with profits and being emotionally unprepared for the realities of losses?

The solution is to step outside the conventional profit and loss paradigm that dominates us and realize that between the realm of profits and losses is a neutral zone that allows the trader to pause. From a mathematical perspective the neutral zone is represented by the number 0. Obviously one moves from the negative numbers of losing trades to the positive column of winning trades. But having trades that are break-even, or 0 on the profit and loss register or reasonably near that range, is actually a very good outcome. Foremost among its benefits is it allows one to keep intact the capital at risk for another and perhaps better trade. Breaking even may not elicit the praise of others but it is a sustaining event. How you get to break even is also important.

If the 0 entry on the trading log is the result of a profitable trade turning into a loss, it may represent an astute observation by the trader that conditions have changed and getting out is preferable to seeing negative numbers. On the other hand, a break-even trade may be the outcome of a quick exit by the trader fearing a loss. A frequent number of these break-even trades in one's account may reveal the trader is becoming overwhelmed by the setting in of destructive emotions such as anxiety, guilt, fear or greed. We all know that this is not an uncommon experience.

However, the break-even trade also can become a huge opportunity to evolve into a mature trader by going beyond an obsession for profits. Many of us approach each trade in an arrogant fashion, as the chance to grab profits, to scalp or take pips from the market. This concept reflects a common held view that trading is a zero-sum battle between the trader and the market, where the trader wins or loses against the market. But some of the best trading programs produce a win ratio just above 50% (see "Waiting on a winner"). The majority of trades are roughly break-even. Every flat or small losing trade keep us in the game. Traders get in trouble when they stubbornly hold onto a trade refusing to believe their hunch, system or simply their timing, is wrong.

Yet, there is a better and ultimately more effective approach. What if we humbly reconfigure our mindset and view the forex market as a magnificently complex place full of opportunity, that when properly understood provides valuable trades? We would experience a shift in our entire mental and emotional focus. The market then becomes not our enemy, but a field of opportunities that when understood can produce profits. Those who take this approach do not demand nor expect pips to be handed over as if they belong to us. Instead we aspire to obtain a great trade by recognizing a winning pattern. Pips become what we earn by applying our knowledge. The market becomes our partner, it is a reciprocal relationship. The ability to trade each day by emptying ourselves first of ego satisfaction may not be easy, but it is the distinguishing characteristic of traders in the process of transforming and evolving themselves from frenetic beginnings to a level of competence. If your next trade is neither a profit nor a loss, pause and relax, because in the case of forex trading, the result of 0 is a positive number.

Abe Cofnas is president of learn4x.com LLC. E-mail: learn4x@earthlink.net.

WAITING ON A WINNER

The top technical currency programs throughout the last three years.

	Manager	% Winning Months	Avg. Winning ROR	% Losing Months	Avg. Losing ROR	Up Dev / Down Dev	Compound Annual Return
1	Monarch Capital Mgmt.	58.82	8.74	41.18	-3.12	3.62	50.06
2	Spot Forex Mgmt. (Zurich)	61.76	7.02	38.24	-3.76	2.61	37.49
3	MIGFX Inc. (Managed)	76.47	5.47	23.53	-2.73	2.31	26.2
4	Pacific Asset Mgmt. (Alpha)	41.18	17.16	58.82	-7.12	2.34	25.14
5	Alterama Inc. (Trendoscil FX)	50	10.93	50	-6.06	2.19	24.12
6	Grossman Asset Mgmt. (IPS Currency)	55.88	4.61	44.12	-2.33	2	19
7	Wallwood Consultants (Forex)	64.71	5.23	35.29	-4.97	1.4	18.73
8	Spot Forex Mgmt. (Geneva)	61.76	3.06	38.24	-1.31	2.9	17.51
9	DKR Capital (DKR Strat. Currency)	70.59	3.35	29.41	-3.17	1.9	17.44
10	EChange Capital	58.82	5.05	41.18	-3.87	1.4	15.64

Note: Top 10 programs based on compound annual return. Most have a 2/1 upside/downside standard deviation.

Source: Barclay Map

Forex Trader

BY ABE COFNAS

Patterns of losses in forex

osing trades are part of the total trading experience. While losing trades can't be avoided (don't believe the hype from firms that claim 50 winning trades in a row), traders should look to benefit from an analysis of their losing trades and perhaps find errors that we can avoid repeating.

Let's begin with the notion that not all losses are equal. The difference between an experienced trader and a beginner is an awareness of the distribution and causes of losing trades. There are types of losses that are unavoidable and consistent with a solid trading strategy. Once we identify the root cause of losses we can minimize them.

Order entry glitches are avoidable. Traders should master entering orders on a platform before trading real money.

Being stopped out quickly, or frequently, is a sign your model needs tweaking. Setting wider stops is too simplistic and increases risk. A useful technique in setting stops is to use the ATR (average true range) as a guide. Developed for commodities, ATR gives a quick indication of whether the range around a candlestick on a chart is getting greater. If the ATR is eight pips, a five-pip stop is within the recent range and could easily be stopped out. It's a good idea to be sure that a stop is set to twice the ATR to keep a trader away from the vibration of the candle (see "Breathing room").

Counter-trend signals are more complex and result in larger losses when wrong. New traders should avoid picking tops and bottoms and concentrate on trends. Keep an eye on the four-hour chart. If upon a trade entry, the five-minute price action is moving against the trend, the trader should wait for both the four-hour and five-minute patterns to align.

Wrong analysis of technical conditions causes losses. Beginning traders often don't recognize signs of indicator divergence and enter a position when key indicators such as a stochastic crossover or the MACD histogram are pointing the other way. Before one puts on the trade, the trader should have a setup of indicators that will be applied. This setup will vary between traders; but whatever it is, it should be applied consistently. Changing entry rules results in inconsistent trading and prevents the trader from learning how to improve.

Perhaps more difficult than learning from losses is learning from winners. It is nice when fate steps in and turns a mistake

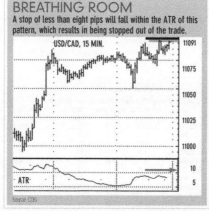

BREATHING ROOM

A stop of less than eight pips will fall within the ATR of this pattern, which results in being stopped out of the trade.

USD/CAD, 15 MIN.

Source: COG

into a winning trade but you need to correct inconsistent trading patterns even if it results in the odd winner. You will not always profit from good trades or get punished for poor decisions, so it is important to stay disciplined and stay consistent.

The most common and most difficult types of losses to minimize relate to the trader trying to predict a directional move. Instead of using personal sentiment, you can reduce risk by substituting market sentiment for your own. There is wisdom in the behavior of crowds. Chances are that market sentiment reflects all the economic data available, some of which you may have missed. Ignorance of economic data releases contributes to potentially large losses. A trade put on before a major economic report is a mistake because the market could move right through stops with large slippage.

Another category of losses relate to exiting a position. Most common is when a profitable trades turns into a loss of 20 pips or more. In this case, the trader's hope that he is correct masks the realities. This can occur after a trader experiences a streak of winning trades and thinks he's invincible. The emotional disposition of the trader can set up future losses. Many traders have a sudden series of losses following a series of wins. This may not be a turn of bad luck, but instead be reflective of temporary patterns or a trader believing his signals are all of a sudden fool proof. Experience is the most powerful teacher for this type of error. It is far easier to recoup a small loss. Getting out of a position that is turning against you liberates you to get ready for the next trade.

One of the most significant and avoidable kinds of losses is one that exceeds a defined risk parameter. Any losses that exceed 5% of equity in an account are on the critical path to catastrophic results. The next time you review your forex trading performance, focus on the pattern of your losses and ask yourself which ones could have been avoided, prevented or reduced. The simple fact is while there are many ways to lose in forex, becoming a better loser is the right path to become a better trader. Losing professionally is the best kind of loss.

Abe Cofnas is president of learn4x.com LLC and author of *Understanding Forex: Trading to Win*. E-mail him at learn4x@earthlink.net.

Forex Trader

BY ABE COFNAS

The DJIA-currency connection

The Dow Jones Industrial Average Index's recent historic highs have brought great fanfare. We need to ask: Are there deeper intermarket implications in this milestone, particularly for forex traders? Let's lift this milestone and look what lies underneath.

The first question is: how did this occur while the U.S. dollar declined? A major contributing factor for a dollar decline has been the end of interest rate increases by the Federal Reserve Bank last August after 17 consecutive increases. The Dow closed on this date at 11,173.8 and the U.S. Dollar Index (USDX) closed at 8466. We can see that the pace of decline of the dollar increased as the Dow rallied.

WRONG DIRECTION?
Forex traders need to pay attention to the current inverse relationship between the Dow and the U.S. Dollar Index.

Today, market sentiment consensus is forming that there is little probability for a rate increase, and if a slow-down in U.S. consumer spending occurs, the potential for a decrease in rates will help lower the dollar value further. There is also a global dynamic behind the U.S. dollar decline as the Euro zone's economic growth increases expectation for an interest rate increase in Europe. So we have the scenario where U.S. rates may go down and European rates may go up. This would put further pressure on the dollar.

Looking at the Dow against the USDX, we can say that generally a declining dollar has been good for the Dow. The benefit of this inverse relationship is the impact on earnings of U.S. based global corporations. A weak dollar lowers the cost of exports. Foreign purchasers of U.S. products have greater buying power.

But there are other underlying impacts. All of the Dow component corporations have significant foreign assets. Those assets are priced in foreign currencies which must be converted into U.S. dollars at key accounting intervals. In times of dollar declines, these assets gain in accounting valuation. For example, Caterpillar Corp. issues loans in a foreign currency to its customers to finance equipment purchasing and leasing. These loans are at a level where they have a material impact on their earnings. Caterpillar states in its 2006 10K report: Because "we make a significant amount of loans in currencies other than the U.S. dollar, fluctuations in foreign currency exchange rates could also reduce our earning and cash flow. During times of dollar declines, collecting loans in foreign currencies is a favorable event." Conversely, if the dollar went into a period of strengthening, Caterpillar's earnings would be adversely affected.

Another example is one of the world's best known multinationals, Coca-Cola. They report that 72% of their net operating revenue comes from outside of the United States. This makes Coca-Cola very sensitive to currency fluctuations. Wal-Mart is another example of the intimate connection between the U.S. dollar and a company's operating health. They are on a major international acquisition path and have reported that more than 20% of their net sales are now generated by non-U.S. based operations. Wal-Mart also is very sensitive to fluctuations in the value of the Chinese renminbi because China is a significant manufacturing source for Wal-Mart's products. No Dow component company is exempt from currency impacts.

There are several messages here. The first is globalization. By investing in the components of the Dow, investors are really playing global economic and currency events. Traders can no longer make investment decisions with regard to only U.S. market conditions. Also, the Dow's historical highs occurred as the global economy has expanded. World economic growth is at 5% and the International Monetary Fund team expects that to continue in 2007 and 2008. And second, currency valuations will continue to affect the current and future operating profits of these multi-nationals. By understanding the currency dynamics behind the Dow move, we can be better prepared for the ultimate retracement.

The final message is that of currency and economic vigilance. Equity traders need to watch for a global growth slowdown, commodity price inflation , a yen strengthening and for the euro's strength to cut into euro exports. If these scenarios can combine, it could spell the end in the Dow's run. It is more important than ever to follow the fundamental and currency forces that move the charts.

Abe Cofnas is president of learn4x.com LLC and author of *Understanding Forex: Trading to Win*. E-mail: learn4x@earthlink.net.

FOREX STRATEGIES

Trading the short-term fluctuations in forex is an alluring undertaking, but one that many traders embark upon with little preparation and often too much leverage. Here are some guidelines for day-trading forex.

Putting sunlight on day-trading forex

BY **ABE COFNAS**

Until recent years, the opportunity to put on a trade was governed by the cycle of day and night. But a unique characteristic of forex trading is its 'round-the-clock sequence of trading. Starting Sunday when the sun rises in Asia until Friday late afternoon when the New York markets close, forex is available and liquid.

While some condemn such short-term market fluctuations as random noise that can't be traded or tracked systematically, there are techniques you can employ that give you the best chance to profit over shorter periods. We'll look at a few of those techniques here.

For so-called day-traders, however, which in futures markets typically means traders who are flat at the end of every trading day, the practical question arises: What is a day trade in forex if forex is a continuous week of trading? To answer, we do not need to delve into the nature of human circadian biorhythms; we just have to be arbitrary. Let's effectively define a forex day trade as a trade that is completed

during the waking hours of a trader. A day trade might also be considered a trade initiated and completed within the trading hours of either the Asian, European or U.S. equity markets.

One caveat: At the start of scanning the markets, the forex trader should check if any major economic reports are scheduled for that day. The release of these reports significantly affects currency pair moves. Unless you know specific techniques for trading this kind of news, stay away and let the market

digest the news and resume technical trading patterns.

FINDING THE TEST ZONE
In the mind of the beginning forex day-trader is the simple thought: What should I trade today? What will give me my 10 pips on the day? In contrast, the more experienced forex trader is looking to answer a different set of questions, questions that will indicate which currency pairs are in a "test zone." In other words, the beginning trader perceives the day-trade as a reprieve from analysis, whereas the more experienced trader knows that the trade itself is a result of analysis.

The search for currencies that are in this test zone starts by looking backward in time. We start by looking for the location where the price is probing or testing a pattern — a key Fibonacci resistance or support area, trendline or moving average. In a real sense, the day trade takes shape days and sometimes weeks before the decision to trade. Using this analysis, the currency pair approaching a key

61.8% Fibonacci level, while another currency pair is simply moving between Fib levels, is the preferred pair to trade. The price action at these locations is more likely to result in a real change in sentiment and trend patterns.

Finding your initial day trade requires applying some key decision rules as to which direction the next trade will be and approximately where it will be located. The actual trigger conditions for the trade will wait for the right confirming moment. "Branching out" (above) outlines a decision tree for a day trade.

Let's look at an example of how in real time these decision rules help shape a trade. After a large surprise dollar sell-off on Aug. 5 following news on employment numbers in the United States, the currency markets went into a consolidation period (see "Break, hesitation & break," right).

Turning to a four-hour chart, we can see that the USD/JPY shows resistance forming at 111.00. Notice the candle tested resistance at 111.00 a second time, after six four-hour candles. A day-trader would also notice that this 111.00 location is a 61.8% Fibonacci resistance level. It looks like a sideways range and a lot of waiting are ahead of us. The four-hour chart provides the horizon, however, for the next trade.

Because the price action is probing the 61.8% Fibonacci level, a trade in either direction can be taken. Either buy the currency pair on a break

BRANCHING OUT
When seeking short-term trading opportunities, consider following this basic decision tree as a basis of your trading plan.

Evaluate trend directions

Select the direction of your next trade

Buy → Sell

Select location of your trade → Select location of your trade

Buy on break of resistance
Or
Buy on bounce off support

Sell on break of support
Or
Sell on bounce off resistance

above the 61.8% line, or sell it on a failure to break that area. The trader can wait for the price to break the line and then enter a market order to buy or you could place a standing stop order to be filled on the break. The fill might be higher than desired on a stop order, but the trader would be in the action.

As it turned out, the FOMC announcement on Aug. 10 of an increase in interest rates by another 25

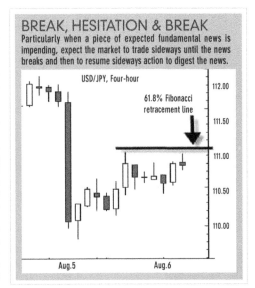

BREAK, HESITATION & BREAK
Particularly when a piece of expected fundamental news is impending, expect the market to trade sideways until the news breaks and then to resume sideways action to digest the news.

USD/JPY, Four-hour

61.8% Fibonacci retracement line

112.00
111.50
111.00
110.50
110.00

Aug.5   Aug.6

basis points moved the market through the 61.8% point and moved it 50 pips (see "Action & reaction," page 26). A breakout trade would have worked well. Waiting for a bounce of resistance would not have worked in this case.

Even more instructive is the price action of the next few hours. After the FOMC announcement, the USD/JPY made its move to a new high and then stopped going higher and followed in a sideways action. What we are seeing is the cycle of surge and hesitation starting over again. A new opportunity to enter a trade is shaping up. The allure of forex day-trading comes from the ability to miss a trading opportunity and just move ahead to the next one.

DAILY OPPORTUNITY
It's hard to quantify how many good opportunities the forex day-trader has in one trading session. However, a sensitivity analysis would show that we have six big currency pairs (the EUR/USD, GBP/USD, USD/CHF, USD/JPY, USD/CAD and AUD/USD) and at least two commonly traded crosses (EUR/GBP and EUR/JPY). This gives us eight pairs to provide day trade set-ups.

A day trade in forex often can provide more well-founded opportunities to trade than available capital in an average account. The trader doesn't have to rush or force a trade, but choose among competing opportunities.

Filtering through the field of potential trades can be done by looking for patterns and selecting a key time

Forex Strategies continued

interval. Pay close attention to trend-lines and channel patterns at any timeframe. "Trading the channel" (below) depicts currency prices moving along a meandering channel, offering highly repetitive buying and selling points.

A good rule of thumb for the beginning day trader is to use the four-hour time interval referenced in our earlier USD/JPY example. It represents a long enough amount of time for prices to evolve wider ranges that are tradeable. During a four-hour period the currency price often exhibits ranges that provide enough pip distance between resistance and support to allow for reasonable day-trading goals.

A common occurrence is a cluster effect where the action in one currency pair cascades across all major pairs and there are numerous simultaneous opportunities to trade. The distribution of trading opportunities, however, is not random, and patience in waiting for the right opportunity is a valuable skill to acquire.

Putting on the trade, after all is what the analysis leads to, but it should not be a spontaneous event. While there is no single rule of action on what a price trigger is, we can narrow conditions to be sure that the trade is reasonable and can be supported by a combination of technical factors. For example, in "Timing critical" (right) the price is bouncing off the lower channel line and a buy would coincide with a confirmation that the position is oversold based on the relative strength index (RSI) breaking its own trendline.

During any given session in forex trading, patterns emerge inviting a trade. The skilled trader waits for a high probability trade where confidence is high that the trade will work. Contributing to confidence may well be the trader's own psychological mind set and optimism. Ultimately, the profit and loss tally will demonstrate whether you're engaged in wishful thinking or a winning game.

SCALPING OR SURFING?
In entering a trade, the differences between a scalper and a surfer would be evident by the differences in profit limits. A scalper would either put on a very small limit of 15 pips as soon as the trade is entered, or watch the trade enter into profits and then take it out. The tendency to take early exits and leave profits on the table is a major result of scalping attempts.

Also important to realize is the noise introduced by the spread. A 3-5 pip spread means that there is increased risk of trying to grab a quick 10 pips with a market move and having the profits turn into negative territory.

ACTION & REACTION
After the Fed announced the rate increase, the market jumped and then settled in for more sideways movement.

USD/JPY, Four-hour

61.8% Fibonacci level breaks

111.50
111.40
111.30
111.20
111.10
111.00
110.90
110.80
110.70

Aug.9   Aug.10

TRADING THE CHANNEL
If you can identify a channel pattern before it runs its course, it can provide you with multiple low-risk trading opportunities.

Channel patterns provide repetitive trade signals

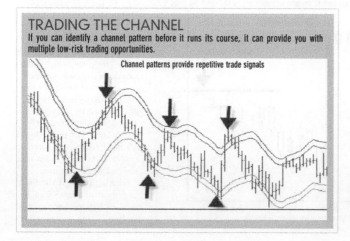

In contrast, a surfer would want to ride the move to the technical limits. This would require managing the position with trailing stops or having a longer target at the next level of resistance. The surfer requires a greater tolerance of risk to allow the currency pair to move along its path to profits.

The challenges to both approaches are real. Whether you look for a quick grab of profits that will pay for a dinner date or for a trade that makes the month's mortgage payment, day trading forex has embedded in its market patterns the potential for achieving a variety of trading goals. Forex day trading offers a range of opportunities and with it a concomitant range of risks — but there is an entrance requirement — a due process of analysis. |**FM**

Abe Cofnas is president of learn4x.com LLC. E-mail: learn4x@earthlink.net.

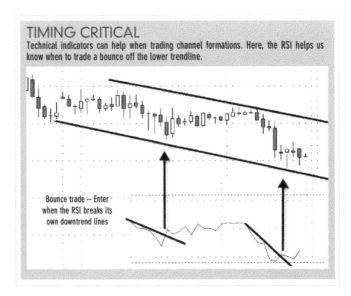

TIMING CRITICAL
Technical indicators can help when trading channel formations. Here, the RSI helps us know when to trade a bounce off the lower trendline.

Bounce trade – Enter when the RSI breaks its own downtrend lines

Forex Trader

BY ABE COFNAS

The forex flu

It was clear that the yen patterns, influenced by the titanic volume of the carry trade (estimated to be above $1 trillion), were getting ready to breakdown this summer. The monthly chart of the key GBP/JPY pair showed an ominous parabolic pattern, which was an early sign of unsustainable buying. We know now that the subprime market worries were the catalyst for a shift in market tastes away from high yield/high leveraged instruments. The bloated carry trade currencies broke their patterns, the flow of cash hurried back to their debt based origins to buy back overextended investments, and a great deal of the carry trade still continues.

The resulting enormous moves of the last week of August was also a signature of mass emotional contagion. What can the forex trader learn from this that will improve his analytical and trading skills when currencies and markets break with feverish patterns the next time?

The first lesson is that knowledge of big picture price patterns and fundamentals gives you an edge in forex. Aug. 10 was a key milestone. The yen found support at 117 and had been in sideways action for several days. But notice on the four-hour chart that we had six four-hour candles crowded around the 117 area. There was plenty of time to be ready for a breakout (see "Saw it coming?"). The pre-breakout period is best indicated by a sideways channel. The four-hour sideways channel is among the most reliable because it enables an instant view of where the "smart" large money flow has been able to push the price.

The second lesson is that there are embedded patterns even in the midst of the chaos of the moment. When a sudden breakout comes, many traders are caught off guard. But it is very useful to know that even in the apparent fury of the move there is an ebb and flow that is tradeable. In fact, the entire pattern has three phases, a pre-breakout period of susceptibility, a period of contagion and then a period of diffusion. These phases replicate themselves in multiple time frames.

A third lesson is the contagious nature of forex price movements. Contagion is an apt phrase because the forex patterns that arose in the wake of the subprime market emotional fever are quite similar to the patterns exhibited when influenza epidemics and pandemics arise. Both share the classic paths generated by parabolic equations. When a parabolic curve emerges, in any time frame, it is a predictor of a topping pattern. This is true in markets as well as in nature.

A third lesson, perhaps paramount for the future, is that more than ever there are inter-market connections between forex and equities. During the subprime market crisis we could see that the USD/JPY pair had become a very accurate predictor of market moves as the USD/JPY and the DJIA moved with a high degree of synchronicity (see "In sync").

In the coming months, the markets will continue to be intertwined and the seemingly unpredictable black swan events will occur. Armed with pattern recognition skills and tools, the forex trader can be ready. These events should not be feared because they can be traded.

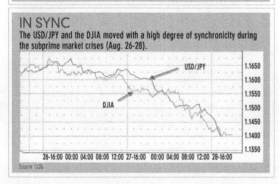

SAW IT COMING?
There was plenty of time to prepare for a breakout.

JPY, four-hour

Pre-Breakdown Yen Patterns

Source: ProRealTime.com

IN SYNC
The USD/JPY and the DJIA moved with a high degree of synchronicity during the subprime market crises (Aug. 26-28).

USD/JPY

DJIA

Source: CQG

Abe Cofnas is president of Learn4x.com and author of the forthcoming book *The Forex Trading Course: A Self-Study Guide to Becoming a Successful Currency Trader* (Wiley Trading). E-mail: Learn4x@earthlink.net.

Index